OXFORD TEXTBOOKS IN LINGUISTICS

Series editors

Keith Brown, Eve V. Clark, April McMahon, Jim Miller, and Lesley Milroy

The Grammar of Words

OXFORD TEXTBOOKS IN LINGUISTICS

General editors: **Keith Brown**, University of Cambridge; **Eve V. Clark**, Stanford University; **April McMahon**, University of Sheffield; **Jim Miller**, University of Auckland; **Lesley Milroy**, University of Michigan

This series provides lively and authoritative introductions to the approaches, methods, and theories associated with the main subfields of linguistics.

PUBLISHED

The Grammar of Words
An Introduction to Linguistic Morphology
by Geert Booij

A Practical Introduction to Phonetics
Second edition
by J. C. Catford

Meaning in Language
An Introduction to Semantics and Pragmatics
Second edition
by Alan Cruse

Principles and Parameters
An Introduction to Syntactic Theory
by Peter W. Culicover

Semantic Analysis
A Practical Introduction
by Cliff Goddard

Cognitive Grammar
An Introduction
by John R. Taylor

Linguistic Categorization
Third edition
by John R. Taylor

IN PREPARATION
Pragmatics
by Yan Huang

The Grammar of Words

An Introduction to Linguistic Morphology

Geert Booij

OXFORD
UNIVERSITY PRESS

OXFORD
UNIVERSITY PRESS

Great Clarendon Street, Oxford OX2 6DP

Oxford University Press is a department of the University of Oxford.
It furthers the University's objective of excellence in research, scholarship,
and education by publishing worldwide in

Oxford New York

Auckland Cape Town Dar es Salaam Hong Kong Karachi Kuala Lumpur
Madrid Melbourne Mexico City Nairobi New Delhi Shanghai Taipei Toronto

With offices in

Argentina Austria Brazil Chile Czech Republic France Greece
Guatemala Hungary Italy Japan South Korea Poland Portugal
Singapore Switzerland Thailand Turkey Ukraine Vietnam

Oxford is a registered trade mark of Oxford University Press
in the UK and in certain other countries

Published in the United States
by Oxford University Press Inc. New York

© Geert Booij 2005

The moral rights of the author have been asserted

Database right Oxford University Press (maker)

First published 2005

British Library Cataloguing in Publication Data

Data applied for

Library of Congress Cataloging in Publication Data

Booij, G. E.
The grammar of words : an introduction to linguistic morphology /
by Geert Booij.
p. cm.—(Oxford textbooks in linguistics)
Summary: "This is a basic introduction to how words are formed.
It shows how the component parts of words affects their grammatical
function, meaning, and sound."—Provided by publisher.
Includes bibliographical references and index.
ISBN 0-19-925847-3 (alk. paper)—ISBN 0-19-928042-8 (alk. paper)
1. Grammar, Comparative and general—Morphology. I. Title. II. Series.
P241.B66 2005
415'.9—dc22   2004023696
ISBN 0-19-925847 3 (pbk)
ISBN 0-19-928042 8 (hbk)

1 3 5 7 9 10 8 6 4 2

Typeset in Times and Stone Sans by
RefineCatch Limited, Bungay, Suffolk

Printed in Great Britain by
Ashford Colour Press Limited, Gosport, Hampshire

Contents

Preface

Each textbook provides a specific perspective on the discipline that it aims to introduce. Therefore, writing this book has not only been a challenge for me because of the didactic demands that each textbook imposes on its writer. It also forced me to rethink my own ideas on morphology in confrontation with those of others, and to come up with a consistent picture of what morphology is about. This perspective is summarized by the title of this book, *The Grammar of Words*, which gives the linguistic entity of the word a pivotal role in understanding morphology.

It is with much pleasure that I would like to thank a number of colleagues for their constructive comments on an earlier draft of this book. Andrew Carstairs-McCarthy (University of Canterbury at Christchurch, New Zealand), Ingo Plag (University of Siegen), Sergio Scalise (University of Bologna), Caro Struijke (Vrije Universiteit Amsterdam), and Greg Stump (University of Kentucky at Lexington) read the whole manuscript, and gave extremely valuable advice. Maarten Mous and Marian Klamer (both University of Leiden) provided useful feedback for a number of chapters, and Mirjam Ernestus (Max Planck Institute for Psycholinguistics, Nijmegen) had a critical look at Chapter 10. Jenny Audring and Lourens de Vries (Vrije Universiteit Amsterdam), Maarten Kossman (University of Leiden), and Jaap van Marle (Open Universiteit Heerlen) also commented on a number of points. None of them should be held responsible for what I wrote in this book.

Another form of support for this project came from my colleagues at the University of Wisconsin at Madison, in particular Mark Louden, Monica Macaulay, and Joe Salmons. They made it possible for me to spend a very pleasant month in Madison, in which I could work on parts of this book.

It is my sincere hope that this textbook will prove to be useful for a new generation of students of language, and that they will enjoy reading and thinking about the many wonderful intricacies of human language.

Amsterdam   G.B.

Typographic Conventions

Small capitals	For lexemes, semantic components, and morphosyntactic categories
Bold type	For technical terms first introduced
Italics	For citation forms when not set on different lines
Single quotation marks	For quotations from other authors
Double quotation marks	For glosses
Questions marks	For formal or semantic oddness
Asterisks	For ungrammaticality
//	For underlying phonological representations
[ ]	For phonetic representations

Abbreviations and Symbols

A	Adjective, transitive subject
ABL	Ablative
ABS	Absolutive
ACC	Accusative
AFF,aff	Affix
ALL	Allative
ANTIPASS	Antipassive
AP	Adjective Phrase
APPL	Applicative
AUX	Auxiliary
CAUS	Causative
COM	Comitative
COMP	Completive aspect
COORD	Coordination
CVB	Converb
DAT	Dative
DO	Direct Object
DS	Different Subject
DIM	Diminutive
ERG	Ergative
EVID	Evidential
F	Foot
FEM	Feminine
FUT	Future
GEN	Genitive
H	High Tone
IMP	Imperative
IMPF	Imperfective
INCOMP	Incompletive aspect
IND	Indicative
INF	Infinitive
INSTR	Instrumental
INTR	Intransitive

IO	Indirect Object
L	Low Tone
LCS	Lexical Conceptual Structure
LOC	Locative
M	Mid Tone
MASC	Masculine
N	Noun, Number of tokens
n_1	number of hapaxes
NEG	Negation
NEUT	Neuter
NF	Non-future
NOM	Nominative
NOM1	Nominalized Verb Stem 1
NONFUT	Non-future
NP	Noun Phrase
O	Transitive object
OBJ	Object
P	Preposition, Productivity
P*	Global productivity
PART	Partitive
PAS	Predicate Argument Structure
PASS	Passive
PERF	Perfect(ive)
PERS	Person
PL	Plural
PP	Prepositional Phrase
PRES	Present
PRET	Preterite
PROG	Progressive
PTCP	Participle
Q	Qualifying
R	Relation, Relational
REL	Relative case
RHR	Right-hand Head Rule
S	Sentence, intransitive subject
s	strong
SC	Subject Concord
SG	Singular

SUBJ	Subject
SUPERL	Superlative
t	trace
TMA	Tense–Mood–Aspect
V	Verb, Vowel, number of types
VP	Verb Phrase
w	weak
WFR	Word Formation Rule
X, Y, x, y	variables
σ	syllable
ω	phonological word
<	derives from
>	results in, changes to
·	syllable boundary
-	morpheme boundary
´	primary stress, high tone, long vowel
`	secondary stress, low tone
⇒	is transformed into
→	is realized as, is changed to
⇔	linked to
>>	ranked higher than
[ ]	phonetic form
//	phonological form, underlying form

List of Figures

List of Tables

Part I

What is Linguistic Morphology?

1

Morphology: basic notions

1.1 Relations between words

When you use an English dictionary to look up the different meanings of the verb *walk*, you will not be surprised that there are no separate entries for *walk, walks*, and *walked*. You will also not feel disappointed if your dictionary does not contain a separate entry for *walking*. If you come across the sentence *My staff walked out yesterday*, and you want to find out what *walked out* means ("go on strike") you will not look for an entry *walked out*, but rather for an entry *walk out*. In many dictionaries, *walks, walked*, and *walking* are not even mentioned in the entry for *walk*. It is simply assumed that the language user does not need this information. The reason for the absence of this information is that these different English words are felt to be instantiations of the same word, for which *walk* is the citation form. So we have to make a distinction between the notion 'word' in an abstract sense (**lexeme**) and the notion 'word' in the sense of 'concrete word as used in a sentence'. The concrete words *walk, walks, walked*, and *walking* can be qualified as **word forms** of the lexeme WALK. Small capitals are used to denote lexemes when necessary to avoid confusion between these two notions 'word'. English dictionaries assume that the language user will be able to construct these different forms of the lexeme WALK by applying the relevant rules. These rules for computing the different forms of lexemes are called rules of **inflection**.

This example shows that dictionaries presuppose knowledge of relations between words. It is the task of linguists to characterize the kind of knowledge on which the awareness of the relation between the word forms *walk, walks, walked*, and *walking* is based. Knowledge of a language includes knowledge of the systematicity in the relationship between the form and meaning of words. The words *walk, walks, walked*, and *walking* show a relationship in form and meaning of a systematic nature, since similar patterns occur for thousands of other verbs of English. The subdiscipline of linguistics that deals with such patterns is called **morphology**. The existence of such patterns also implies that word may have an internal constituent structure. For instance, *walking* can be divided into the constituents *walk* and *-ing*. Therefore, morphology deals with the internal constituent structure of words as well.

Dictionary makers assume that these forms of the lexeme WALK are formed according to rules, and therefore need not be specified individually in the dictionary. The same assumption plays a role in the case of nouns and adjectives. For English nouns, the plural form does not need to be specified in the dictionary if it is regular, and neither does the adverbial *-ly* form in the case of adjectives. For example, my English–Dutch dictionary (Martin and Tops 1984) does not mention the adverbs *correctly* and *economically* in addition to *correct* and *economical*. On the other hand, it does specify the adverb *hardly*. Why is that so? Is it due to inconsistency or sloppiness on behalf of the dictionary makers, or is there a principled reason behind this choice? There is indeed a reason: the meaning of *hardly* cannot be predicted from that of *hard* and *-ly*.

This kind of knowledge is also relevant when searching for information on the internet and in other digital data resources such as corpora of actual language use and electronic dictionaries. Suppose you want to collect information on tax. You might find it helpful if the search engine is programmed in such a way that it will not only recognize documents with the word *tax*, but also documents with the words *taxation, taxable*, and *taxability* as relevant. In fact, for many search engines this is not the case. The words *taxation* and *taxable* are both derived from the verb *to tax* which is related to the noun *tax*. The word *taxability* in its turn is derived from *taxable*. Hence, we may qualify this set of related words as a **word family**.

On the other hand, when searching for information on tax issues, you would not like your search engine to retrieve documents with the words *taxi, taxis, taxon*, or *taxonomy* that also begin with the letter sequence *tax*. This example shows that analysis of the systematicity in the relations between words is essential for the computational handling of language data. What we need for this purpose is a morphological **parser**, a computer program that decomposes words into relevant constituents: *tax-ation, tax-able*, and *tax-abil-ity*.

There is an intuitive difference between the members of the word family of TAX mentioned above and the set of word forms *walk, walks, walked, walking*. The different words related to the verb *to tax* are not felt as forms of the same word, but as different though related words that each have their own entry in the dictionary, that is, are different lexemes. We speak here of **lexeme formation** (or **word-formation**): TAXABILITY has been formed on the basis of TAXABLE through the addition of *-ity*, and TAXABLE in its turn has been formed on the basis of the verb TAX, just like TAXATION. The verb TAX itself has been formed by turning the noun TAX into a verb.

So far we have taken for granted that we can distinguish words from other linguistic units such as phrases, and we are no doubt influenced by the orthographical convention of using spaces to indicate word boundaries. Determining if a particular linguistic unit is a word is not always that easy, however, and certainly not for languages without a written tradition. Even for English we might not be certain. Why is *income tax* to be considered as a word rather than a phrase? After all, its constituents are separated by a space in its spelt form. The issue of word demarcation is taken up a number of times in this book.

Word-formation is traditionally divided into two kinds: **derivation** and **compounding**. Whereas in compounding the constituents of a word are themselves lexemes, this is not the case in derivation. For instance, *-ity* is not a lexeme, and hence TAXABILITY is a case of derivation. The word INCOME TAX, on the other hand, is a compound since both INCOME and TAX are lexemes. Changing the word class of a word, as happened in the creation of the verb *to tax* from the noun *tax*, is called **conversion**, and may be subsumed under derivation.

Another dimension of this kind of knowledge about words assumed by dictionary makers of English manifests itself in the fact that words that are quite common in English might not be covered by a dictionary. For instance, my English–Dutch dictionary does not mention *bottle factory*, although it does mention *bottle baby, bottle bank, bottleneck*, and a number of other words beginning with *bottle*. Yet, I have no problem in understanding the title of the novel *The Bottle Factory Outing* written by Beryl Bainbridge. What the dictionary presupposes is that the user of English knows the words *bottle* and *factory*, and that the compound *bottle factory* refers to a particular kind of factory, not to a particular kind of bottle: it is the rightmost of the two word constituents that determines what kind of thing the compound denotes. This is a systematic fact of English. Therefore, one can understand the meaning of *bottle factory* without having ever come across that word before. That also applies to the even more complex word *bottle factory outing*. This example illustrates the creative aspect of morphological knowledge: it enables us to understand or coin new words. Morphological knowledge may thus lead to **rule-governed creativity** in the use of language. If we want to be understood, our new linguistic expressions must comply with the rules of the language. It is these rules that enable every language user to produce and understand linguistic expressions that she has never come across before.

The examples of morphological knowledge discussed so far come from English. The reason for this choice in an introductory chapter is a practical one: English is the language that all readers of this book are assumed to understand. English is not the obvious choice when one wants to discuss the nature of morphological systems in general, certainly not in the realm of inflection. After all, English has a relatively poor inflectional system, in which only a few grammatical distinctions are expressed. For instance, whereas English has only four different forms for regular verbs such as WALK, Romance languages such as French, Italian, and Spanish have tens of different forms for verbs. We should be aware of these considerable differences in morphological richness between languages. Therefore, it is important to look at a wide variety of languages in order to get a good idea of the morphological possibilities of natural language.

1.2 Paradigmatic and syntactic morphology

The term 'morphology' has been taken over from biology where it is used to denote the study of the forms of plants and animals. Its first recorded use is in writings by the German poet and writer Goethe in 1796. It was first used for linguistic purposes in 1859 by the German linguist August Schleicher

(Salmon 2000), to refer to the study of the form of words. In present-day linguistics, the term 'morphology' refers to the study of the internal structure of words, and of the systematic form–meaning correspondences between words. Consider the following sets of English words:

(1) a. buy   b. buyer
     eat   eater
     paint   painter
     sell   seller
     send   sender

In these sets of words we observe a systematic form–meaning correspondence. The words in (1b) differ from the words in (1a) in that they have an additional part -er, and a corresponding meaning difference: each word in (1b) has the meaning "one who Vs", where V stands for the meaning of the corresponding verb in (1a). This is the basis for assigning a word such as *buyer* an internal morphological constituency: *buy-er*. The form differences between these two sets of words concern two properties: the words in (1b) have the additional sound sequence [ər] (or [ə] in standard British pronunciation) compared to the words in (1a), and they are nouns, whereas the words in (1a) are verbs. The form differences thus have a phonological and a syntactic dimension. The meaning difference is quite clear: the nouns in (1b) subsume the meaning of the corresponding verbs, and have some extra meaning due to the presence of -er. Since the nouns are formally and semantically more complex than the corresponding verbs, we will say that the nouns have been derived from the verbs. That is, there is a **direction** in the relationship between these two sets of words. The word *buyer* is a **complex word** since it can be decomposed into the constituents *buy* and -er. The word *buy*, on the other hand, is a **simplex word**, because it cannot be decomposed any further into smaller meaningful units, only into sound segments.

The notion 'systematic' in the definition of morphology given above is important. For instance, we might observe a form difference and a corresponding meaning difference between the English noun *ear* and the verb *hear*. However, this pattern is not systematic: there are no similar word pairs, and we cannot form new English verbs by adding h- to a noun. There is no possible verb *to heye* with the meaning "to see" derived from the noun *eye*. Therefore, such pairs of words are of no relevance to morphology. Similarly, we do not assign morphological constituency to German *fressen* "eating by animals" although it forms a pair with *essen* "to eat", since there is no morphological constituent *fr-* that occurs in other word pairs as well. The words *fressen* and *essen* are in fact related historically (*fr-* derives from the early Germanic word *fra*), but *fressen* is no longer a complex word. So words can lose their status of complex word.

The existence of related words with a systematic form–meaning difference is crucial in assigning morphological structure to a word. The following Dutch words for different kinds of fish all end in *-ing*:

(2)   bokking "bloater", haring "herring", paling "eel", wijting "whiting"

Yet, we do not consider this *-ing* a morphological constituent with the meaning "fish" because there are no corresponding Dutch words *bok, haar, paal,* and *wijt* with a meaning related to the corresponding words ending in *-ing* (these words do exist, but with a completely unrelated meaning).

The two sets of words given in (1) form **paradigms**. The term 'paradigm' is used here in a general sense to denote a set of linguistic elements with a common property. All words in (1a) are verbs, and thus form a paradigm. The same applies to the words in (1b) which are all nouns ending in *-er*. In our definition of morphology as given above we see two different perspectives. When we speak about morphology as the study of the systematic form–meaning correspondences between the words of a language, we take a paradigmatic perspective, since we take properties of classes of words as the starting point of morphological analysis. When morphology is defined as the study of the internal constituent structure of words, we take a syntagmatic perspective.

We distinguish these two different perspectives on language because language units exhibit **syntagmatic** and **paradigmatic relationships**. They have a syntagmatic relationship when they are combined into a larger linguistic unit. For instance, the words *the* and *book* have a syntagmatic relationship in the phrase *the book*. In contrast, the determiners *a* and *the* are paradigmatically related: they belong to the set of determiners of English, and can both occur at the beginning of a noun phrase, but never together: **the a book*. Hence, they belong to the paradigm of determiners of English.

A clear instantiation of a primarily syntagmatic approach to morphology is **morpheme-based morphology**. In this approach, focus is on the analysis of words into their constituent morphemes. That is, morphology is conceived of as the syntax of morphemes, as the set of principles for combining morphemes into words. **Morphemes**, the morphological building blocks of words, are defined as the minimal linguistic units with a lexical or

a grammatical meaning. For instance, the noun *buyer* consists of two morphemes, *buy* and *-er*. The verbal morpheme *buy* is called a **free** or **lexical
morpheme**, because it can occur as a word by itself, whereas *-er* is an **affix**
(hence a **bound morpheme** that cannot function as a word on its own). This
is indicated by the hyphen preceding this morpheme: it requires another
morpheme to appear before it in a word. Each of these morphemes is listed
in the morpheme list of English: *eat* as a morpheme of the category Verb
(V), and *-er* as an affixal morpheme of the category Noun (N) that is
specified as occurring after verbs: [V —]. This specification of the affix *-er*
assigns it to the subcategory of affixes that combine with verbs, and hence
we call it a **subcategorization** property of this affix. The morphological
structure of *eater* might be represented as follows:

(3)   [[eat]$_V$ [er]$_{N\text{-aff}}$]$_N$

This complex word can be created by the general mechanism of **concatenation**, the combination of elements into a linear sequence. This word is well
formed because the requirement that *-er* occur after a verb is met. The fact
that this combination of morphemes is a noun, and not a verb, follows from
the generalization that English suffixes determine the category of the complex words that they create: since *-er* is an affixal noun, the whole word is a
noun.

Thus, the language user is able to coin new **polymorphemic** words (words
consisting of more than one morpheme) through the concatenation of
morphemes, and of morphemes with words that are themselves polymorphemic. An example of the latter is the formation of the verb *tranquillize*,
itself derived from *tranquil* through the addition of *-ize*. The formation of
tranquillizer is not a matter of concatenating three morphemes. Instead, it is
a two-steps operation. First, the bound morpheme *-ize* has been added to
the simplex adjective *tranquil*, resulting in the verb *tranquillize*. Subsequently, the bound morpheme *-er* has been added to this verb. The morphological structure of this word is therefore a layered one, and can be
represented in the form of a string with labelled bracketing, or as a tree
(Figure 1.1). In short, morphology might be seen as morpheme syntax,
as the set of principles that tell you how to combine free and bound
morphemes into well-formed words.

This syntagmatic approach can be contrasted to a primarily paradigmatic approach to morphology. In the latter one, the creation of new
complex words is seen first and foremost as the extension of a systematic

[[[*tranquill*]_A[*ize*]_{Vaff}]_V [*er*]_{Naff}]_N

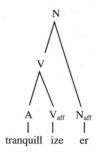

Fig. 1.1 The morphological structure of *tranquillizer*

pattern of form–meaning relationships in a set of established words to new cases, resulting in new words. Once we have discovered the abstract systematic pattern behind the words in (1), we will be able to extend this pattern to, for instance, the verb *swim*, resulting in the word *swimmer*:

(4)   Pattern [x]_V : [x-*er*]_N "one who Vs"; *swim : swimm-er*

(the variable *x* stands for the string of sound segments of the verb). In the gloss "one who Vs", the symbol V stands for the meaning of the verb. The gloss indicates that nouns ending in -*er* have a meaning that encompasses the meaning of the corresponding verb.

In this approach, it is not denied that the word *swimmer* consists of two constituent morphemes, but they are not the basic building blocks. Instead, words and relationships between words form the point of departure of the morphological analysis, and morphemes have a secondary status in that they figure as units of morphological analysis. Bound morphemes such as -*er* do not have lexical entries of their own, and only exist as part of complex words and of abstract morphological patterns such as (4).

From the point of view of language acquisition the paradigmatic perspective on complex words is the starting point of morphological analysis. When acquiring one's mother tongue, one has to discover the existence of morphological patterns on the basis of the individual words encountered in the input data. Only when language users have acquired a sufficient number of words of the relevant type, can they conclude to a systematic abstract pattern in sets of related words that might be used for the coinage of new words.

This paradigmatic pattern can receive a syntagmatic interpretation as well: the pattern can be interpreted as a **morphological rule** for the attachment of bound morphemes to words. That is, paradigmatic relationships can be projected onto the syntagmatic axis of language structure. The pattern in (4) can thus be interpreted as the following morphological rule:

(5) $[x]_V \rightarrow [[x]_V\ er]_N$ "one who Vs"

This rule states that nouns with a particular meaning ("agent nouns") can be derived from verbal lexemes by adding the affix -er to the stem form of the verb. On the left side of the arrow, the requirements on the properties of the input words are specified, on the right side the formal and semantic properties of the output words. The arrow indicates the direction of the operation (input left, output right). The assumption of such affix-specific morphological rules means that bound morphemes do not exist as lexical items of their own, but only as part of morphological rules. Consequently, we get a slightly different representation of the morphological structure of the word *tranquillizer* given in Figure 1.2 (compare Figure 1.1).

Fig. 1.2 The morphological structure of *tranquillizer* without affix labels

Instead of assuming a rule for this word-formation pattern, one might also express this regularity in the form of a **template** for the coining of new nouns in -er of the following form that is formally equivalent to the morphological rule (5):

(6) $[[x]_V\ er]_N$ "one who Vs"

The morpheme concatenation approach and the **lexeme-based** rule approach may in fact lead to similar analyses of word structure. In both approaches, the polymorphemic noun *swimmer* will have the internal structure $[[swim]_V\ er]_N$. The (minor) difference is that in the rule approach, the bound morpheme -er has no lexical category label of its own, since it is not a lexical entry. Yet, we should realize that rule (5), the rule interpretation of an extendable word pattern, has a paradigmatic flavour: it is not a rule about morpheme concatenation, but it specifies a formal and semantic operation (affix attachment and change of meaning) on lexemes. Similarly, template (6) is an abstract scheme that specifies the common properties of a set of words, but can also be used as a 'recipe' to create new words.

It is essential that morphological rules can take **established** words as their inputs. If an established polymorphemic word has idiosyncratic properties, these properties will recur in words derived from it. For example, the complex noun *transformation* has a specific conventionalized meaning in generative syntax (the change of a syntactic structure). Hence, the same idiosyncratic meaning will recur in the adjective *transformational* derived from this noun *transformation*. Similarly, the adjective *edible* not only means that something can be eaten, but also that it can be eaten safely. This idiosyncratic meaning aspect of *edible* recurs in the derived noun *edibility*. Therefore, we must allow for established polymorphemic lexemes to function as the bases of word-formation. That is why morphological rules must be lexeme-based.

A particular challenge for the morpheme-based approach to morphology is the existence of morphological operations that do not consist of the concatenations of morphemes, so called **non-concatenative morphology**. The past tense forms of English irregular verbs, for instance, are not made through addition of a morpheme to a stem, but by replacement of vowels, as in *sing-sang*, and *grow-grew*. Another example (taken from Kutsch Lojenga 1994: 135) is that Ngiti, a Central-Sudanic language of Congo makes use of tones to distinguish morphologically related words. The plural form of a number of nouns is made by replacing the tones of the last two syllables (a sequence of a Mid tone and a Low tone) of the singular noun by a High tone. (The grave and acute accents indicate Low and High tones respectively; the absence of an accent indicates Mid tone.)

(7) SINGULAR   PLURAL
     màlimò   malímó   "teacher(s)"
     kamà   kámá   "chief(s)"
     màlàyikà   màlàyíká   "angel(s)"

This process of forming plural nouns cannot be stated straightforwardly in a syntagmatic approach to morphology since there is no addition of a (tonal) morpheme. This pattern can be expressed straightforwardly in paradigmatic terms, as a systematic difference in form (tone pattern) correlating with the semantic distinction between singular and plural. Such a paradigmatic account of this regularity may look as in (8) where the templates for singular and plural nouns of Ngiti are given:

(8) $[\ldots V^M.V^L.]_{Nsg}, [\ldots V^H.V^H.]_{Npl}$

The superscripts L, M, and H indicate the tone assigned to the vowel (V), and the Vs stand for the last two vowels of the words.

There are also cases of **paradigmatic word-formation**, in which a new word is formed by replacing one constituent with another. For instance, the Dutch compound *boeman* "lit. boo-man" has a particular idiosyncratic meaning "ogre, bugbear". Its female counterpart *boevrouw* has obviously been coined by replacing the constituent *man* "man" with *vrouw* "woman" rather than by directly combining *boe* and *vrouw* into a compound, given the fact that the two compounds share this idiosyncratic meaning. Such a case of word-formation cannot be accounted for in a purely syntagmatic approach to morphology, neither a morpheme-based nor a rule-based one. It is based on specific words, and therefore a typical case of **analogy**:

(9) man : vrouw = boeman : *boevrouw* "female bugbear"

The paradigmatically oriented definition of morphology given above expresses directly that morphology is lexeme-based. Lexemes form the point of departure of morphological processes. In lexeme formation (or word-formation) we create new lexemes on the basis of other lexemes, whereas in inflection, specific forms of lexemes are computed (instead of lexeme formation we will speak of word-formation when there is no risk of misunderstanding). The processes of word-formation and inflection together form the morphological part of a grammar.

Morphology deals with both the form and the meaning of linguistic expressions. Hence, one might qualify morphology as **word grammar**, that part of the grammar that accounts for the systematic form–meaning relations betweeen words. In other words, it is a set of **correspondence rules** between forms and meanings of words. The notion 'word grammar' stands in opposition to 'sentence grammar', the grammar which describes the systematic relations between form and meaning at the sentence level.

1.3 The functions of morphology

The two basic functions of morphological operations are (i) the creation of new words (i.e. new lexemes), and (ii) spelling out the appropriate form of a lexeme in a particular syntactic context.

An example of the first function, lexeme formation, is given in section

1.1: the coining of the word *bottle factory* from the existing lexemes *bottle* and *factory*. Morphology thus provides means for extending the set of words of a language in a systematic way. The coinage of *bottle factory* is a case of compounding, in which two lexemes are combined into a new one. In the other type of word-formation, derivation, exemplified by the word *swimmer*, use is made of morphological operations on lexemes, whereas in compounding, two or more lexemes are combined into a new word.

Why do we need new words? One obvious reason is that language users need new expressions for new objects, or for new concepts. Once there is an entity or concept "factory for the production of bottles", it is quite easy to be able to refer to such a concept with one word, *bottle factory* instead of using a circumscription. Thus, word-formation has a **labelling function**. Creating a word label for a new kind of entity, event, or property may have the additional pragmatic advantage that it draws attention to the new concept involved. For instance, the word *construction grammar* has been created to denote a particular school of linguistic thought in which the linguistic notion 'construction' plays a central role. By coining this label, a new linguistic school has been established, and thus its ideas will draw attention more easily. New verbs have been created to express new types of events or actions, such as the English verbs in *-ize: legal-ize* "to make legal", *tranquill-ize* "to make tranquil", that express the causation of an event or property.

However, this is not the only function of word-formation. Another important function is that of syntactic **recategorization**: by using morpho- logically related words of different syntactic categories, we achieve stylistic variation and text cohesion, as the following examples (from Kastovsky 1986: 595) show:

(10)   He made *fists* . . . He *defisted* to gesture.
       If that's not *civil, civilize* it, and tell me.
       [. . .] and whether our own conversation doesn't sound a little *potty*. It's the *pottiness*, you know, that is so awful.

A pragmatic reason for coining new words is found in the domain of **evaluative morphology**. In many languages **diminutive** forms of words are not used primarily for indicating the small size of the object denoted, but for giving a positive or negative evaluation. For instance, the Portuguese diminutive noun *avôzinho* (from *avô* "uncle") means "dear uncle" rather than "small uncle", and in Dutch the diminutive noun *baantje* "job" derived from *baan* "job" is used to refer to a job without prestige. A related phenomenon is that of the use of **attenuative** forms. The English morpheme *-ish* is often used to express the notion "sort of, not exactly": when we use *nine-ish* instead of *nine* as the time for an appointment, we mean that we do not expect people to be there at nine sharp. Thus, we might use morphology to express our subjective feelings towards something or to weaken or relativize a notion.

The function of inflection is primarily that of making forms of lexemes, including the correct forms of a lexeme appropriate for particular contexts. For instance, in an English clause, the verb has to agree with the subject with respect to number (singular or plural) and person (third or non-third), and this determines the choice between *walk* and *walks*: in a clause with present tense, *walks* has to be chosen if the subject is third person singular, and *walk* otherwise. In many languages, the form of a noun is determined by its syntactic context, and each noun has a number of **cases**. For instance, the Polish noun KOT "cat" has the case forms shown in (11). We call this structured set of word forms the **inflectional paradigm** of this lexeme (note that this is a more specific use of the notion 'paradigm' as introduced above in section 1.2). The term 'inflectional paradigm' may also be used to denote the abstract inflectional pattern, the set of labelled cells that these word forms occupy. As can be read off this paradigm of case forms, when the lexeme KOT occurs in direct object position and therefore has accusative case, the word form *kota* has to be used if the word has a singular meaning, and the form *koty* if it has a plural meaning. That is, one of the accusative forms has to be chosen for this syntactic position.

(11)		SINGULAR	PLURAL	
NOMINATIVE		kot	kot-y	"cat, subject"
GENITIVE		kot-a	kot-ów	"of the cat"
DATIVE		kot-u	kot-om	"to the cat"
ACCUSATIVE		kot-a	kot-y	"cat, object"
INSTRUMENTAL		kot-em	kot-ami	"with the cat"
LOCATIVE		koci-e	kot-ach	"on the cat"
VOCATIVE		koci-e	kot-y	"o, cat"

Another function of morphology is that the relation between sentences in a text can be established by using morphological markers of **coreferentiality**. In Wambon, a language of New Guinea (examples from de Vries

1989: 62), verbal forms have Same Subject (SS) forms and Different Subject (DS) forms (1SG = first person singular, 3SG = third person singular, NF = non-future):

(12) Nukhe   oye   khetak-mbel-o   topkeka-lepo
     I   pig   see-SS-COORD   flee-1SG.PAST
     "I saw a pig and I fled"
(13) Nukhe   oye   khetakha-lev-o   topkeka-tmbo
     I   pig   see-1SG.NF.DS-COORD   flee-3SG.PAST
     "I saw a pig and it fled"

Both examples consist of two clauses, with the coordinating element *-o* linking these two clauses. This coordinative morpheme is attached to the verb of the first clause. The word *khetakmbelo* in (12) has the Same Subject form, which indicates that in both clauses we have the same subject "I". In (13), on the other hand, the word *khetakhalevo* is a Different Subject form, which indicates that the subject of the next clause is a different one. It is not "I", but the pig that fled. This kind of subject marking is called **switch reference**.

1.4 Morphology and the lexicon

The set of lexemes of a language comprises two subsets: simplex lexemes and complex lexemes. These lexemes are listed in the **lexicon** to the extent that they are established, conventionalized units. A complex lexeme like NINISH is a well-formed lexeme of English, but need not be listed in the lexicon since it is completely regular, and there is no conventionalization involved.

The lexicon specifies the properties of each word, its phonological form, its morphological and syntactic properties, and its meaning. The basic structure of lexical entries for the lexemes *swim* and *swimmer* may look as follows:

(14) /swɪm/   /swɪmər/
     $[x]_V$ $[[x]_V\ er]_N$
     SWIM$_{ACTIVITY}$ PERSON PERFORMING SWIM$_{ACTIVITY}$

The first line in these lexical entries specifies the phonological form of these lexemes: a sequence of sound segments between slashes. On the second line, categorial information, and internal morphological structure of a word are specified. On the third line, the meaning of the lexeme is specified, here indicated by the use of small capital letters. The subscript ACTIVITY specifies the type of event expressed by this verb. A lexical entry thus expresses a correspondence between phonological, syntactic, and semantic pieces of information, just like morphological rules or templates, which do the same at a more abstract level, in a generalized fashion, with variables taking the place of the individual properties of lexemes.

Most complex words have been derived by one of the available word-formation processes of a language. Indeed, as we saw above, one of the main functions of morphology is to expand the set of available words. Once a complex word has been formed, it may get established as a word of the language. This means that it is used by more than one native speaker, and on different occasions, and that language users will recognize it as a word they have come across before. The set of established words of a language functions as the **lexical norm** or **lexical convention** of that language. For instance, in British English the machine that is used for drawing money from one's bank account is called a *cash dispenser*, and in American English it is called an *automatic teller machine (ATM)*. In fact, it would also have been possible to use the compound *money machine* for this device, but the established words function as a lexical norm, and hence they can block the creation of the compound *money machine*. That is, the lexicon as the set of established lexical units of a language may have a **blocking** effect on the creation of new words. It does not mean that *money machine* is an ill-formed word, only that its use might not be appropriate.

When a possible word has become an established word, we say that it has lexicalized. An important effect of **lexicalization** of complex words is that one of its constituent words may get lost, whereas the complex word survives. For instance, the Dutch verb *vergeet* "to forget" no longer has a simplex counterpart *geet*, unlike its English counterpart *forget* for which the corresponding word *get* does exist. We therefore consider *vergeet* a **formally complex word**. It still behaves as a complex verb since it selects a past participle without the prefix *ge-*, just like other prefixed verbs of Dutch. For example, the past participle of the prefixed verb *ver-wacht* "to expect" (derived from the verb *wacht* "to wait") is *verwacht*. Similarly, the past participle of the verb *vergeet* is *vergeten*, not **gevergeten*. This may be contrasted with the verb *verbaliseer* "to fine" in which the part *ver-* has no prefix status. The past participle of this verb is *ge-verbaliseer-d*, with the prefix *ge-* present.

The term 'lexicalization' is also used for a related phenomenon, namely that established words may have idiosyncratic, unpredictable, properties. The meaning of *honeymoon*, for example, is not predictable on the basis of the meanings of its constituent lexemes *honey* and *moon*, and this requires this compound to be listed in the lexicon. Having idiosyncratic properties thus implies for a word that it has to be listed, but the inverse is not necessarily true: a complex word that is listed may have fully predictable properties, and may be listed only because it is an established word, that is, belongs to the lexical norm.

The notion 'lexicon' refers to the repository of all information concerning the established words and other established expressions of a language. It is an abstract linguistic entity, to be distinguished from the notion **dictionary**, which refers to practical sources of lexical information for the language user in some material (paper or electronic) form. A dictionary will never provide a full coverage of the lexicon due to practical limitations of size and requirements of user-friendliness, and because the lexicon is expanding and changing daily. The third related notion of relevance here is that of the **mental lexicon**, the mental representation of lexical knowledge in the brain of the individual language user. The mental lexicon of an individual is always smaller than the lexicon in the linguistic sense: nobody knows all the established words of a language. Moreover, the mental lexicon exhibits an asymmetry between production and perception: we understand probably about five times more words of our mother tongue than we actually use in language production.

In many languages, morphology is extremely important for the size of the lexicon. In all European languages, the number of established complex words is much higher than the number of simplex words. Consequently, the morphological rules of a language have two functions: they indicate how new lexemes and word forms can be made, and they function as **redundancy rules** with respect to the established complex words of a language. For instance, the lexical information that LOVER is a noun, and that the meaning of this word comprises that of the verb LOVE is redundant information. These properties are specified in rule (5). On the other hand, the information that this noun is an established word of English, with a particular idiosyncratic meaning "male sweetheart, suitor" is unpredictable, non-redundant lexical information.

Morphological patterns that can be systematically extended are called **productive**. The derivation of nouns ending in *-er* from verbs is productive in English, but the derivation of nouns in *-th* from adjectives is not: it is hard to expand the set of words of this type such as *depth, health, length, strength*, and *wealth*. Marchand (1969: 349) has observed some occasional coinings like *coolth* (after *warmth*), but notes that such word coinings are often jocular, and hence do not represent a productive pattern. If we want to coin a new English noun on the basis of an adjective, we have to use *-ness* or *-ity* instead. In the case of unproductive patterns, the morphological rule involved functions as a redundancy rule only, and not as a rule for the creation of new words.

Lexical storage of complex morphological forms is also relevant in the realm of inflection. For example, Dutch has two plural endings for nouns, *-s* and *-en*. The second one is normally used for words consisting of one syllable. In the case of the monosyllabic noun *boon* "bean", the regular plural is *bon-en*, as expected. However, for *zoon* "son" both the irregular *zoon-s* and the regular *zon-en* can be used. Hence, the plural form *zoon-s* has to be specified in the lexicon.

The morphological system of a language is not its only source of complex words. There are at least three other sources: borrowing, phrases becoming words, and word creation.

As to **borrowing**, European languages have borrowed many words from Greek and Latin, often with French as the intermediary language. Consider the following list of Dutch verbs and their English glosses:

(**15**) deduceer   "deduce"
        induceer   "induce"
        produceer   "produce"
        reduceer   "reduce"
        reproduceer "reproduce"

A verb like *produceer* can be analysed into three parts: *pro-duc-eer*, that is, it is a polymorphemic word. The constituent *-eer* is a recurrent part of all these words, and so is *-duc-*. The sequences *de-, in-, pro-*, and *re-* are also recognizable elements in this set of verbs. Yet, we cannot say that these verbs have been created by a rule of Dutch or English morphology since there is no lexeme DUC from which these words could have been derived. Instead, a word such as *produceer* has been created by borrowing the French version *producer* of the originally Latin verb *producere*, and by adapting its form by turning the French ending *-er* into *-eer*. The polymorphemic nature of such words remains recognizable in the borrowing languages. These borrowing patterns have led to a **pan-European lexicon**, a large stock of cognate complex words in the major languages of Europe.

A second non-morphological source of complex words is the **univerbation** ("becoming a word") of phrases. Phrases may lexicalize into words, and thus lead to complex words. Examples from English are *jack-in-the-box, forget-me-not* (nouns), and *dyed-in-the-wool, down-at-heel, over-the-top* (adjectives). The following Dutch words all begin with *te-*, originally a preposition, the etymological cognate of English *to*:

(16)   te-gelijker-tijd "lit. at same time, simultaneously"
       te-rug "lit. to back, back"
       te-vreden "lit. at peace, satisfied"
       te-zamen "together"

In the first example, *tegelijkertijd*, the three constituents are clearly recognizable, and their meanings are relevant. The words *gelijk* "identical, same", and *tijd* "time" are current words of Dutch (the form of *gelijk* used here is *gelijker*, with an old inflectional ending *-er*). Therefore, *tegelijkertijd* is a complex, polymorphemic word. So the fact that a word is polymorphemic does not imply that it has been created by morphological rule. The second example, the word *terug*, is also interesting because it serves to illustrate a recurring problem of analysis for the linguist: when do we consider a word complex? Although *rug* "back" is a word of Dutch, it remains to be seen if we should consider *terug* a simplex or a complex word. In fact, many native speakers do not recognize the word *rug* in *terug* because of the more abstract meaning of *terug*, which no longer refers to a part of the human body.

Language users may also make new words by means of **word creation** (or **word manufacturing**). The following types can be distinguished:

(17)   **blends:** combinations of the first part of one word with the second part of another: *brunch* < *breakfast* + *lunch*; *stagflation* < *stagnation* + *inflation*;
       acronyms: combination of initial letters of a word sequence: *NATO* < *North Atlantic Treaty Organization*; *yup* < *young urban professional*;
       alphabetisms: combination of the first letters of words, pronounced with the phonetic value of these letters in the alphabet: French *SVP* < *S'il vous plaît* "please"; Dutch *KLM* < *Koninklijke Luchtvaart Maatschappij* "royal airline company"; English *CD* "compact disc", *SMS* "Short Message Service";
       clippings: one or more syllables of a word: *mike* < *microphone, demo* < *demonstration*, French *labo* < *laboratoire* "laboratory", German *Uni* < *Universität* "university".

In the case of compounds, only one of them may be shortened, as in German *U-Bahn* < *Untergrund-bahn* "metro", English *e-mail* "electronic mail", and *FAQ-list* "frequently asked questions list". In **ellipsis**, the first constituent is taken to represent the whole as in Dutch *VU* < *VU-Ziekenhuis* "Free University Hospital" (*VU* is itself an acronym for *Vrije Universiteit* "Free University"). The difference between the hospital and the university meaning of the acronym can still be expressed, because these words differ in gender, and hence select different definite articles: *het VU* (hospital) versus *de VU* (university).

Instead of the term clipping, linguists also use the term **truncation**, especially in relation to the formation of personal names which have an affective load and function as **hypocoristics** (names of endearment). In many cases, the stressed syllable of the full form is the core of the truncated name, which consists of one or two syllables (the acute accent indicates word stress):

(**18**) English   Dave < Dávid, Liz < Elízabeth, Kate < Kátherine, Sue < Súsan
Dutch   Hans < Johánnes, Henk < Héndrik, Sanne < Suzánne
French   Dom < Dominíque, Val < Valeríe, Fab < Fabríce
Spanish   Dina < Alexandrína, Marga < Margaríta, Neto < Ernésto

Truncation may operate in connection with the addition of an ending. In English the endings -*y* or -*ie* can be added to the truncated form, in German these truncated names may end in -*i*, -*e*, or -*o*:

(**19**) English   Becky < Rebecca, Suzy < Suzanne, commie < communist
German   Andi < Andréas, Daggi < Dágmar, Fundi < Fundamentalist,
Wolle < Wolfgang, Realo < Realist

A characteristic of word creation is that it makes use of reduction for the creation of new words, unlike normal morphology. Consequently, the meaning of the new word cannot be derived from its form straightforwardly, and it therefore lacks semantic transparency. In blending, for instance, the constituent parts that determine the meaning are not fully present in the word, and hence the meaning is not recoverable from these constituents. In *stagflation*, the parts *stag-* and -*flation* do not have themselves the meanings "stagnation" and "inflation" respectively. Thus, the English language user cannot know what the word *stagflation* means when hearing or reading it for the first time, unlike what is the case when one encounters *bottle factory* for the first time. This also applies to acronyms: if you do not know a certain acronym, there is no way to find out about its meaning on the basis of your knowledge of the language. In the case of clipping, its full form is not recoverable on the basis of the clipping, and so its meaning is also unpredictable, although it is sometimes possible to guess.

Word creation is thus different from word-formation in the strictly morpho-logical sense, where the meaning of the newly created word is recoverable from that of its constituents, and it is typically an intentional form of language use. The lack of transparency of these words serves to create incrowd groups who understand these shortened words, and so they have an important sociolinguistic value. They may also establish intimacy (as is the case for truncated personal names), or informality (German *Uni* is more informal than *Universität* "university").

This overview of word creation does not exhaust the set of special form–meaning correspondences in words. There is also **echo-word-formation**, a kind of reduplication, as in English *zigzag, chitchat*, French *fou-fou* "some-what mad" or with rhyming words (Dutch *ietsiepietsie* "a little bit", *ukkepuk* "small child"), and **sound symbolism** in words beginning with the same sound sequence. For instance, words with initial *sw-* typically denote swinging movements (*sweep, swing, swingle*, etc.), and the following Dutch words with *kr-* all refer to unpleasant, twisted notions: *krijs* "to shout", *kramp* "cramp", *krank* "ill", *krimp* "shrink".

The similarity at a more abstract level between morphology proper and word creation is that both are based on patterns of paradigmatic relation-ships between sets of words.

So far, we have seen that the set of established words of a language can be expanded in a number of ways. The lexicon, however, is not just a set of words, but also comprises word combinations. English (like most Germanic languages) has many verb–particle combinations, also called **phrasal verbs** of the type *to look up* which clearly consist of two words which are even separable:

(20)   a. The student looked up the information
       b. The student looked the information up

The verb *look up* cannot be one word since its two parts can be separated, as in sentence (20b). A basic assumption in morphology is the hypothesis of **Lexical Integrity**: the constituents of a complex word cannot be operated upon by syntactic rules. Put differently: words behave as atoms with respect to syntactic rules, which cannot look inside the word and see its internal morphological structure. Hence, the movement of *up* to the end of the sentence in (20b) can only be accounted for if *look up* is a combination of two words. That is, phrasal verbs such as *look up* are certainly lexical units, but not words. Words are just a subset of the lexical units of a language.

Another way of putting this is to say that *look up* is a **listeme** but not a lexeme of English (DiSciullo and Williams 1987).

Other examples of lexical multi-word units are adjective noun combinations such as *red tape, big toe, atomic bomb*, and *industrial output*. Such phrases are established terms for referring to certain kinds of entities, and hence they must be listed in the lexicon. Some languages tend to prefer such multi-word units to morphologically complex words as denoting expressions. This is for instance the case for the Papuan languages of New Guinea.

In sum, morphology is only one of the means for expanding the lexicon of a language: there are other ways of creating lexical units, and the set of complex words can be enlarged by other means than regular word-formation.

1.5 The goals of morphology

The word *morphology* can be used in two ways: it refers to a subdiscipline of linguistics, but it may also be used to refer to that part of the grammar of a language that contains the rules for inflection and word-formation, that is, the word grammar. This kind of ambiguity also applies to words like *phonology, syntax*, and *semantics*. When we talk about the goals of morphology, it is obviously the first meaning of the word that is relevant here.

Why do linguists want to do morphology? The first reason is that it is the linguists' task to describe and analyse the languages of the world as accurately and as insightfully as possible. Hence, they have to deal with the morphological phenomena of a language, and therefore need a set of tools for description. Morphology provides such tools, a set of analytic notions, which are discussed in greater detail in Chapter 2. A related, second goal of linguists is developing a typology of languages: what are the dimensions along which languages differ, and how are these dimensions of variation related and restricted? Do all languages have morphology, and of all possible kinds? Are there explanations for the morphological similarities and differences between languages? The kinds of morphology that we come across in the languages of the world are discussed in greater detail in Part II (word-formation) and Part III (inflection).

Thirdly, morphology is a probe into the nature of linguistic systems, and hence into human, natural language. For example, morphology quite clearly shows that linguistic structure has two axes, a syntagmatic axis and a paradigmatic one. Morphology also serves to get a better understanding of the nature of linguistic rules and the internal organization of the grammar of natural languages. Thus we may get to know more about the architecture of the human language faculty and about the nature of rule-governed creativity in the domain of language (Part IV).

Finally, morphology can be used to get a better insight as to how linguistic rules function in language perception and production, and how linguistic knowledge is mentally represented. Both psychological and historical evidence throw light on this issue. Thus, morphology contributes to the wider goals of cognitive science that explores the cognitive abilities of human beings (Part V).

Summary

Morphology, the study of the internal structure of words, deals with the forms of lexemes (inflection), and with the ways in which lexemes are formed (word-formation). New words are made on the basis of patterns of form-meaning correspondence between existing words. Paradigmatic relationships between words are therefore essential, and morphology cannot be conceived of as 'the syntax of morphemes' or 'syntax below the word level'. Morphology serves to expand the lexicon, the set of established words of a language, but is not the only source of lexical units, and not even that of all complex words, which also arise through borrowing, univerbation, and word creation.

The established (simplex and complex) words of a language are listed in the lexicon, an abstract linguistic notion, to be distinguished from the notions 'dictionary' and 'mental lexicon'. Morphological rules have two functions: they specify the predictable properties of the complex words listed in the lexicon, and indicate how new words and word forms can be made.

Morphology as a subdiscipline of linguistics aims at adequate language description, at the development of a proper language typology, and at contributing to debates on the organization of grammars and the mental representation of linguistic competence.

Questions

1. My English–Dutch dictionary does not mention all English adverbs in *-ly*. However, it does mention the adverb *supposedly*. Why do you think this exception is made?

2. Why should we consider *taxable* a case of derivation rather than compounding although *able* is a lexeme of English?

3. Give the morphological structure (labelled bracketing) of the following English words: *unhappiness, contrastive, disconnecting, contradiction, blue-eyed, connectivity*.

4. Try to determine the morphological constituency (if any) of the following English words: *colleague, cordial, correlate, electrometer, elongation, evaporate, eternity, euphemism, habitual, happy, music, negotiable, performance, theology*. To what extent do these words raise problems for morphological analysis?

5. Here is a set of pairs of singular and plural nouns in Oromo, a language spoken in Ethiopia and Kenya (Stroomer 1987: 76–7).

raadda	raaddoollee	"young cow(s)"
uwaa	uwoollee	"woman/women"
eela	eeloota	"well(s)"
kobee	kobeellee	"shoe(s)"
kobee	koboota	"shoe(s)"
harree	harreellee	"donkey(s)"
sangaa	sangoollee	"ox/oxen"

   Which plural endings are found in these data, and what are the stem forms of these nouns?

6. Consider the following English verbs: *forbid, forget, forgive, forgo, forswear*. What evidence can you adduce for these verbs being complex?

7. What kind of sound symbolism may be involved in the following English verbs: *spew, spit, spout, spatter, sprout, sprawl*?

8. A bilingual child with parents who have different native languages may be said to have a *mother tongue* and a *father tongue*. How can we account for the coining of *father tongue*?

9. Blending is quite popular as a means of creating new English words. Try to come up with some meaning for the following recent blends: *falloween, giraffiti, metrosexual, nicotini, pedlock*. Why can't you be sure about their meanings if you happen not to know them? (You can find the meanings of these words on the website www.wordspy.com.)

10. Bacronyms are words that are reinterpreted as acronyms, for instance *George* as a name for an organization with the acronymic interpretation *Georgetown Environmentalists Organized against Rats, Garbage, and Emissions*.

a.   Which kind of word creation is the word *bacronym* itself an instantiation of?

b.   Do you know bacronyms in your native language?

Resources for morphology

The internet is a very useful resource of information about languages and linguistics. Important websites for morphologists are Linguist List (www.linguistlist.org), the website of the Summer Institute of Linguistics (www.sil.org), with many links to other relevant websites, and www.yourdictionary.com where one can find morphological subgrammars and morphological parsers for a number of languages. A survey of the languages of the world is found in Grimes (2003): www.ethnologue.com. A website devoted to recent English neologisms is www.wordspy.com.

Two recent handbooks of morphology are Spencer and Zwicky (1998), and Booij *et al.* (2000–4 = *BLM* in the references; in vol. i you will find a number of articles on the history of morphological research). The classical handbook of English morphology is Marchand (1969). Spencer (1991) and Carstairs-McCarthy (1992) are textbooks on morphology, with a lot of attention to current theoretical debates in morphology. A number of important articles on morphology have been reprinted in Katamba (2003).

Further reading

Morpheme-based morphology is defended in Lieber (1980), Selkirk (1982), and DiSciullo and Williams (1987). Morphology as 'syntax below the word level' is argued for in Lieber (1992).

The notion word-based (= lexeme-based) morphology is defended in Aronoff (1976) and in Anderson (1992). The importance of paradigmatic relationships for morphology is highlighted in van Marle (1985) and Becker (1990*a*).

The relation between morphology and the lexicon is discussed in detail in a number of publications by Jackendoff (1975, 1997, 2002). The principle of Lexical Integrity is defended in Bresnan and Mchombo (1995).

The functions of word creation are clarified in Ronneberger-Sibold (2000). Word creation and sound symbolism in English are dealt with extensively in Marchand (1969).

2

Morphological analysis

2.1 The atoms of words

Words can be chopped into smaller pieces. At the phonological level, words can be divided into syllables or segments, and segments into their constituent phonological features. At the morphological level, words may consist of more than one unit as well, which we may call the morphological atoms of a word: pieces that are no further divisible into morphological subparts. Just as there are different kinds of atom in chemistry, there are different kinds of atom in morphology, and it is quite useful for morphological analysis to be acquainted with their classification. A good classification is an important analytic instrument, developed in order to get a better understanding of the structure and formation of words.

As we saw in Chapter 1, the Polish lexeme KOT "cat" has a paradigm of case forms; compare this to the case forms of the noun KOBIETA "woman" in (1). Each cell of the paradigm of Polish nouns is occupied by a **grammatical**

(1)

	SINGULAR		PLURAL	
NOMINATIVE	kot	kobiet-a	kot-y	kobiet-y
GENITIVE	kot-a	kobiet-y	kot-ów	kobiet
DATIVE	kot-u	kobieci-e	kot-om	kobiet-om
ACCUSATIVE	kot-a	kobiet-ę	kot-y	kobiet-y
INSTRUMENTAL	kot-em	kobiet-ą	kot-ami	kobiet-ami
LOCATIVE	koci-e	kobieci-e	kot-ach	kobiet-ach
VOCATIVE	koci-e	kobiet-o	kot-y	kobiet-y

word, i.e. a form of a lexeme with a particular property for the grammatical categories number and case. Grammatical words may share the same word form. For instance, both the GEN.SG and the ACC.SG form of KOT have the form *kot-a*. The phenomenon that two or more grammatical words have the same word form is called **syncretism**. The distinction between lexeme, grammatical word, and word form shows that the general notion 'word' subsumes a number of different notions. In most cases it is clear which interpretation of 'word' is intended, but sometimes it will be necessary to use the more specific notions.

Each of the word forms of KOT consists of a stem and an **inflectional ending** (or **desinence**). The **stem** of a word is the word form minus its inflectional affixes, in this example *kot-*. It is the stem that forms the basis for word-formation, not the whole word form. This might not be so clear for the Polish noun KOT, because the NOM.SG word form *kot* of this word happens to have no overt ending. However, the noun KOBIETA does have an overt ending. For that reason, one may speak of a **zero-ending** for the NOM.SG. form of KOT, and likewise for the GEN.PL form of KOBIETA. The following example from Italian also illustrates the role of the stem. The singular form of *macchina* "machine" has the inflectional ending *-a*, and the plural ending is *-e*:

(2) macchin-a "machine"   macchin-e "machines"   macchin-ista "machinist"

It is the stem *macchin-* that is used as the basis for word-formation, as shown by *macchinista*. In English, the form of the stem is identical to that of the SG word form, and this is why English morphology is sometimes qualified as word-based morphology, in contrast to the stem-based morphology of, for instance, most Romance and Slavic languages. This is a superficial difference: these languages all have lexeme-based morphology, they only differ in that the stem-forms of lexemes do not always correspond to word forms.

Stems can be either simplex or complex. If they are simplex they are called **roots**. Roots may be turned into stems by the addition of a morpheme, as the following examples from Polish (Szymanek 1989: 87) illustrate:

(3) a. butelk-a "bottle"   b. butelk-owa-ć "to bottle"
         filtr "filter"   filtr-owa-ć "to filter"
         bial-y "white"   biel-i-ć "to whiten"
         głuch-y "deaf"   głuch-ną-ć "to become deaf"

The verbs in (3b) are given here in their citation form, the infinitive. The **citation form** is the form in which a word is mentioned when we talk about it, and the form in which it is listed in a dictionary. In many languages, the infinitive is the citation form of a verb. In languages with case, the NOM.SG form is the citation form of nouns. Each of these Polish infinitives consists of a root, followed by a verbalizing morpheme that turns the root into a stem, and is followed by the infinitival ending -ć. It is the stem-forms that are used when new words are derived from these verbs.

Stem-forming suffixes play an important role in many Indo-European languages. Italian verbs, for instance, have a **thematic vowel** after the root morpheme, and this thematic vowel recurs in words derived from these verbs:

(4) larg-o "wide"   al-larg-a-re "to widen"
     profond-o "deep"   ap-profond-i-re "to deepen"
     al-larg-a-ment-o "widening"
     ap-profond-i-ment-o "deepening"

The thematic vowel is not a part of the root, as it does not occur in the roots *larg-* and *profond-*. On the other hand, it cannot be seen as part of the infinitival suffix, because we do not want to miss the generalization that all infinitives end in *-re*. Hence, the vowels preceding the ending *-re* must be assigned a morphological status of their own. Consequently, the noun *allargamento* contains five morphemes: a prefix *al-*, a root *larg*, a thematic vowel *-a-*, the derivational morpheme *-ment*, and the inflectional ending *-o*. So this word has five morphological atoms, which cannot be decomposed further into smaller morphological constituents. Each of these five atoms has a different name because they have different functions in the make-up of this word.

The general term for bound morphemes that are added to roots and stems is affix. If an affix appears before the root/stem, it is a **prefix**, if it appears after the root/stem, it is a **suffix**. So *al-* and *ap-* are prefixes, whereas *-a*, *-ment*, and *-o* are suffixes. Two other types of affixation are illustrated in (5):

(5) **infix** (within a root): Khmu (Laos) *s-m-ka:t* "roughen" < *ska:t* "rough"; Alabama (Stump 2001: 131) *ho-chi-fna* "smell, 2SG" < *hofna* "to smell", *chifip-as-ka* "poke, 2PL" < *chifipka* "to poke";
     circumfix (combination of prefix and suffix): Dutch *ge-fiets-t* "cycled, PAST PARTICIPLE" < *fiets* "to cycle"; German *Ge-sing-e* "singing" < *sing* "to sing"

Infixation and circumfixation are much rarer than prefixation and suffixation.

Affixes are bound morphemes, but not all bound morphemes are affixes. There are many roots from Greek and Latin that are used in so called **neo-classical compounds** but do not occur as words by themselves. These compounds are called 'neo-classical' because they consist of constituents from the classical languages Greek and Latin that were combined into compounds long after these languages ceased to be 'living languages'. In such compounds either one or both constituents are not lexemes:

(6)   micro-: micro-scope, micro-phone; micro-gram, micro-wave
      tele-: tele-phone, tele-vision, tele-communication
      -graph: di-graph, sono-graph, photo-graph, tele-graph
      -scope: micro-scope, tele-scope, cine-scope, spectro-scope

Neo-classical roots such as *scope* and *graph* can also be used nowadays as words, but in that case they have a more specific meaning than in these compounds. Such non-lexical roots are called **combining forms** since they only occur in combination with other morphemes. These bound roots cannot be considered affixes since that would imply that words such as *necrology* would consist of affixes only. This goes against the idea that each word has at least one stem. Thus, we might adapt our definition of what compounds are, and define them as combinations of lexemes and/or non-affixal roots.

The bound morphemes in neo-classical compounds have an identifiable meaning, but there are also morphemes that have no clear meaning. In the word *cranberry* the part *berry* is identifiable, and this makes us interpret the word *cranberry* as denoting a particular kind of berry. Yet, *cran-* has no particular meaning. Similarly, the Dutch compound *stiefvader* "stepfather" denotes a particular kind of father, and hence can be parsed into *stief* and *vader*. However, the morpheme *stief* does not occur as a word. This phenomenon of **cranberry morphemes** is widespread, and is to be expected since complex words can lexicalize and thus survive, even though one of their constituent morphemes has disappeared from the lexicon. The following examples from Dutch illustrate the same phenomenon for derived words with suffixes that are still used for coining new words (the constituent before the suffix does not occur as a lexeme):

(7)   arge-loos "naive", beslommer-ing "chore", dier-baar "dear, precious", le-lijk "ugly", moei-zaam "difficult", sprook-je "fairy tale", veil-ig "safe"

These recognizable suffixes determine the syntactic category of the word of which they form a constituent. For example, *-baar* is a suffix that creates adjectives, and hence *dierbaar* is predictably an adjective. This implies that when we have to decompose words into morphemes, not all morphemes have an identifiable lexical or grammatical meaning. Cranberry morphemes like English *cran-* and Dutch *dier-* thus form a problem for an exclusively meaning-based definition of the notion morpheme. This also applies to another kind of non-affixal bound roots, the recurrent constituents of words borrowed from Latin such as the following English verbs:

(8) conceive, deceive, perceive, receive
     adduce, deduce, induce, produce, reduce
     admit, permit, remit, transmit

It makes sense to consider these words complex, because of recurrent elements such as *ad-*, *con-*, *de-*, *in-*, *per-*, *pro-*, *re-*, and *trans-* which are prefixes, and bound roots like *-ceive*, *-duce*, and *-mit*. Although these bound roots have no identifiable meaning, they should be recognized as morphemes since they determine the form of corresponding noun: all verbs in *-ceive* have a corresponding noun in *-ception*, those ending in *-duce* one in *-duction*, and verbs in *-mit* one in *-mission*. There is a wealth of such bound morphemes in the non-native part of the English lexicon, as the following examples illustrate:

(9) arct-ic, cred-ible, in-del-ible, gradu-al, mor-al, mus-ic, negoti-ate, per-for-ate, per-nic-ious

In lexeme-based morphology these bound roots do not have a lexical entry of their own, they only occur as part of established (listed) complex lexemes. In morpheme-based morphology, on the other hand, they will have to be represented as bound lexical morphemes with their own lexical entry. The advantage of the lexeme-based approach is that it correctly predicts that new combinations of a prefix and a bound root such as *demit* or *perduce* are not to be expected, because we cannot assign a meaning to such new combinations.

Boundness of morphemes is also created through allomorphy. **Allomorphy** is the phenomenon that a morpheme may have more than one shape, corresponds with more than one morph. A **morph** is a particular phonological form of a morpheme. Allomorphy is found in both affixes and root morphemes. In the Italian examples in (4) we saw the prefixes *al-* and *ap-*. In fact, these are two allomorphs of the prefix *ad-*, in which the final consonant /d/ has assimilated to the first consonant of the root morpheme. This kind of allomorphy can be accounted for by assuming one common **underlying form** /ad/ for the different allomorphs of this prefix, and a rule of assimilation that derives its different surface forms.

Allomorphy is also found in root morphemes. In languages such as Dutch, German, and Polish, **obstruents** (that is, stops and fricative consonants, which are articulated with a high degree of obstruction in the mouth) are voiceless at the end of a word. Hence we get alternations of the following kind in pairs of singular and plural nouns:

(10)	Dutch	hoed [hut] "hat"	hoed-en [hudən]
	German	Tag [ta:k] "day"	Tag-e [ta:gə]
	Polish	chleb [xlɛp] "bread"	chleb-y [xlɛbɪ]

The symbols between brackets represent the phonetic forms of these word forms; the phonetic symbols are taken from the International Phonetic Alphabet (IPA). This is the alphabet used in dictionaries and grammars to indicate the phonetic forms of words in an unambiguous way. This is necessary because orthographical conventions differ from language to language. For instance, the vowel [u] is represented as *u* in German, but as *oe* in Dutch, as illustrated by the first example in (10).

Some linguists prefer to restrict the term 'allomorphy' to those cases in which the variation in phonetic shape of a morpheme does not follow from the automatic phonological rules of the language. The alternation between voiced and voiceless stops exemplified in (10) is determined by a phonological constraint that excludes voiced obstruents in syllable-final (Dutch and German) or word-final (Polish) position. Hence, the variation in shape of these morphemes is an automatic effect of the phonology of the language. This is usually accounted for by assuming a common underling form for the different realizations of the morpheme involved, with a morpheme-final voiced obstruent. In the singular forms that lack an overt ending, a process of syllable-final or word-final devoicing then applies. The plural forms will not undergo this process because in these forms the relevant segments do not occur in final position.

This type of alternation can be contrasted to the alternation between voiceless and voiced obstruents in English, as in the singular–plural word pair *wife–wives*. This alternation applies to a small and closed set of English words only. That is, there are alternations that are restricted to a specific set of words. Another example is that the Dutch diminutive suffix has five different shapes (*-tje*, *-je*, *-etje*, *-pje*, and *-kje*); the choice of one of these depends on the phonological composition of the stem. For instance, the allomorph *-je* has to be selected after stems ending in an obstruent. The alternations involved are unique to diminutive words, and do not follow from general phonological constraints of Dutch. Therefore, a distinction is made between phonology proper (the variation of the kind mentioned in (10) that is the effect of automatic phonological rules) and **morphophonology**, the domain of phonology in which alternations are restricted to a specific subset of words. The term 'allomorphy' might therefore be reserved for such non-automatic alternations, which can be accounted for in two ways. One option is to assume a common underlying form for the allomorphs, and derive the surface forms by means of one or more morphophonological rules, that is, rules whose application depends on non-phonological properties such as the feature DIMINUTIVE. Alternatively, the allomorphs can be listed individually in their surface form, with a specification of the phonological context in which they occur.

In some cases the non-automatic alternation is unique for one or a few words. For instance, the English adjective *platonic*, related to the noun *Plato*, has the morphological structure *platon-ic*, with the root *platon-* and the suffix *-ic*. The morpheme *platon-*, an allomorph of *Plato*, is a bound morpheme since it does not occur as a word of its own. This kind of allomorphy, a heritage from Greek (in the case of *Plato*) and Latin, increases the set of bound non-affixal morphemes enormously. An example from the Latinate substratum of English is *act*, *act-or* vs *ag-ent* with the bound root *ag-*. Although it has to be listed, the allomorph *platon-* does not require its own entry in the lexicon: it can be specified in the lexical entry for *Plato* as the allomorph to be used for the derivation of words from *Plato* by means of non-native suffixes. The same applies to the bound root *ag-*.

Another, more radical form of formal variation in paradigms is the phenomenon of **suppletion**, where there is no phonological similarity between the different forms of a lexeme. In the English word pair *good–better* we observe the suppletive root *bet* for *good*, followed by the comparative suffix *-er*. Thus, we might say that the lexeme GOOD comprises two different stems, *good* and *bet*. In the pair *bad–worse* the suppletive simplex form *worse* even expressses both the meaning of the stem *bad* and the comparative meaning. Some linguists also use the notion 'suppletion' in the domain of word-formation. In the following examples of inhabitative names in Italian you can observe a formally regular case of derivation, a case of allomorphy, and a case of suppletion respectively:

(11)   Milano–Milan-ese, Forlì–Forliv-ese, Chieti–Teat-ino

Although alternations in the phonological shape of a morpheme may not be the effect of the phonology of a language, the choice of a particular allomorph or suppletive root can still be phonologically conditioned (Carstairs 1988; Kiparsky 1994). For instance, the Dutch agentive suffix -*aar* is selected after stems ending in the vowel [ə] + *l, r, n* (that is, in a phonologically defined environment), and the allomorph -*er* elsewhere. The Italian verb *andare* "go" has two suppletive roots: *and-* when the root is not stressed, and *vad-* when the root is stressed in the verbal paradigm; see (12). This example illustrates that the choice between suppletive roots may be phonologically governed as well.

(12)

	SINGULAR	PLURAL
1.PERS	vádo	andiámo
2.PERS	vái	andáte
3.PERS	vá	vánno

2.2 Morphological operations

Morphology not only deals with the analysis of existing words into their constituent pieces. The language user is able to make new words or forms of words, and it is this form of creativity that is the focus of morphology. The key notion involved is that of 'morphological operation'. This term denotes a particular kind of linguistic activity, and invokes a dynamic perspective on morphology. Two types of morphological operations have been discussed so far: compounding and affixation. They are the proto-typical cases of **concatenative morphology**, in which morphological constituents are concatenated in a linear fashion. Compounding and affixation are the most widespread types of morphology since they create words with a high degree of **transparency**, that is, words of which the formal morphological structure correlates systematically with their semantic interpretation.

The formal operations available in morphology have several functions. Affixation is used both in word-formation and in inflection, and this applies to a number of other morphological operations discussed in this section as well.

For each morphological operation, we have to define the set of **base words** to which it applies. Often, the operation is restricted to base words of a particular syntactic category. This is the input category of the operation. The outputs of an operation also belong to a specific syntactic category. The input category of the English suffix *-able* is V, and the output category is A. Hence, verbs are the base words of the suffix *-able*. Thus, in the case of derivation, the morphological operation may result in words of another syntactic category or subcategory than that of the input words. In that case, we speak of a **category-changing** or **class-changing** operation.

If compounding and affixation were the only kinds of morphological operation, morphology could be said to consist of just one operation—concatenation. In such a view, the elements to be concatenated are lexemes and affixes. Affixes are provided with a subcategorization feature that specifies with which kind of morphological elements it has to combine. For instance, the suffix *-able* will be specified as $[V—]_A$, which means that it takes verbs to form adjectives.

The reason why the term 'morphological operation' is more adequate than the term 'concatenation' is that there are also morphological processes that do not consist exclusively of the attachment of affixes to words. In this section I present a short survey of these operations, which are dealt with in more detail in subsequent chapters on derivation and inflection.

A special kind of affixation is the attachment of a complete or partial copy of the base as a prefix or a suffix. This is called **reduplication**, illustrated by the following examples (Uhlenbeck 1978: 90) from Javanese:

(13) a. **full reduplication:**
       baita "ship"   baita-baita "various ships"
       səsupe "ring"   səsupe-səsupe "various rings"
       omaha "house"   omaha-omaha "various houses"

      b. **partial reduplication:**
       gəni "fire"   gəgəni "to warm oneself by the fire"
       jawah "rain"   jəjawah "to play in the rain"
       tamu "guest"   tətamu "to visit"

In the examples of partial reduplication, the prefix consists of a copy of the first consonant of the base followed by the vowel schwa [ə]. The doubling effect of full reduplication is often reflected by its meaning contribution: for nouns it may express plurality or distributivity (as in 13a), for verbs a high intensity of the action expressed, and for adjectives a higher degree of the property mentioned by the adjective.

Reduplication is a kind of affixation (or compounding, in the case of full reduplication), and hence to a certain extent a case of concatenative morphology. Yet, it is clear that we cannot list reduplicative affixes with their phonological content in the lexicon since this content depends on the phonological composition of the stem. The obvious analysis is the assumption of an abstract affix RED(UPLICATION) that triggers a phonological operation of copying. The copy is then attached to the copied stem.

A second type of morphological operation is the use of tone patterns. Tone patterns belong to the **suprasegmental** properties of languages. In Ngiti, the plural form of kinship terms is expressed systematically by the tone pattern Mid–High on the stem, whatever the tone pattern of the singular (Kutsch Lojenga 1994: 135):

(**14**)   SINGULAR   PLURAL
    àba-du   abá-du "my father(s)"
    adhà-du   adhá-du "my co-wife(s)"
    andà-du   andá-du "my uncle(s)"

Thus, we may speak of a **tonal morpheme** Mid–High which is superimposed on the segmental material of the stem of these nouns. This is why such a tonal morpheme is sometimes called a **suprafix**. This is a case of non-concatenative morphology since this kind of affix is not linearly ordered with respect to its base.

Many languages make use of **internal modification**. Standard examples are the patterns of vowel alternation in the roots of the so-called strong verbs in Germanic languages, called **ablaut, vowel gradation**, or **apophony**. Such vowel alternations are used in a number of Indo-European languages for different forms of the verb:

(15)   Classical Greek: leip-o "I leave"; le-loip-a "I have left", e-lipon "I left"

The *e* in the first root form alternates with *o* in the second, and zero in the third (the second form also exhibits partial reduplication). This pattern of vowel alternation is reflected in Germanic languages, as the following examples from Dutch illustrate:

(16)   geef [ɣeːf] "to give"   gaf [ɣɑf] "gave"   gegeven [ɣəɣeːvən] "given"
    help [hɛlp] "to help"   hielp [hilp] "helped"   geholpen [ɣəhɔlpən] "helped"
    schiet [sxit] "to shoot"   schoot [sxoːt] "shot"   geschoten [ɣəsxoːtən] "shot"

Vowel alternations also play a role in the derivation of deverbal nouns of such verbs, as shown by the related Dutch deverbal nouns *hulp* "help" and *schot* "shot". They only differ from their verbal bases *help* and *schiet* with respect to the root vowel.

Ablaut is not the only kind of vowel alternation with a morphological function. German exhibits an alternation between back vowels and front vowels in singular–plural noun pairs:

(17) Apfel [ɑpfəl] Äpfel [ɛpfəl] "apple(s)"
      Bach [bɑx] Bäche [bɛçə] "brook(s)"
      Buch [bu:x] Bücher [by:çər] "book(s)"

This kind of alternation is called **umlaut** (also called **vowel mutation** or **metaphony**). Historically it is a case of assimilation: back vowels of roots are fronted before a high front vowel in the following syllable (the plural suffix contained a high vowel originally).

If we only take the first example of (17) into consideration, we might conclude that plural formation in German is a case of non-concatenative morphology: the plural is created by the replacement of the back root vowel by its front counterpart. However, an alternative analysis in terms of affixation is also possible. Given the three examples in (17), we might conclude that there are at least three different plural suffixes in German: ø (zero), *-e*, and *-er*. In addition, the plural nouns may exhibit stem allomorphy, a vowel alternation triggered by the attachment of the plural suffix. Such morphologically conditioned alternations may also affect consonants (Lieber 1987, 2000). English has cases of consonant modification as well, for instance *defend–defence, offend–offence, belief–believe*, and *proof–prove*.

An interesting kind of non-concatenative morphology is found in, among others, Semitic languages: **root-and-pattern morphology**. The basis of each lexeme is a skeleton of consonants, in most cases three, which functions as the root of the lexeme. The abstract pattern of consonants is combined with one or more vowels which are intertwined with the sequence of consonants. In addition, the lexeme may contain a prefix and a suffix. In the words of Modern Hebrew in (18) (Clark and Berman 1984: 545) the roots *g-d-l* "grow" and *k-t-b* "write" have been used (the *k* and *b* may surface as *x* [x] and *v* respectively). The vowel patterns that are intercalated with the consonantal skeletons are called **transfixes** since they are spread across the consonantal sequence.

(18)	*Pattern*	*Root* g-d-l	*Root* k-t-b
	CaCaC	gadal "grow, get bigger"	katav "write"
	hiCCiC	higdil "enlarge"	hixtiv "dictate"
	CCiCa	gdila "growth"	ktiva "writing"
	miCCaC	migdal "tower"	mixtav "letter, missive"
	haCCaCa	hagdala "enlargement"	haxtava "dictation"

The morphological structure of the words in (18) can be represented as the linking between three different morphemes. Each of these morphemes forms a phonological tier of its own: (i) the skeletal tier that consists of a pattern of consonantal and vocalic slots that is characteristic of a particular morphological category, (ii) the sequence of consonants that represents the lexeme, and (iii) the vowels that fill the vocalic slots of the skeletal tier. The words *gadal* and *gdila* in (18) can be represented as in Figure 2.1. The consonants of the lexical root, and the vowel pattern (*a-a* for the base verb and *i-a* for the nominalization) are both linked to the central skeletal CV tier. These three tiers are then conflated into one sequence of sounds at the phonetic level of the grammar, where the phonetic forms of words are specified.

Fig. 2.1 Three-tiered representations of words

The morphological operations discussed so far all have the effect that the phonological form of the input word is changed somehow. Conversion, on the other hand, consists of a change in syntactic (sub)category only. The conversion of nouns to verbs is quite common in European languages; see (19). The verbs are given here in their citation form, the infinitive. The conversion from noun to verb is not indicated directly by means of an affix, and is therefore also called **implicit transposition**, as opposed to **explicit transposition**, which denotes cases of category-changing word-formation in which the change is marked through the addition of an affix. Note that conversion does have indirect morphological effects: the verbs in (19) are recognized as such by their verbal inflectional endings, the infinitival suffixes (except the English verb since there is no overt infinitival ending in English). The category change may also have an effect on the stress pattern, as in the English pair *convért* (V)—*cónvert* (N), where the noun is derived from the verb, with concomitant stress shift from the last to the first syllable.

(19)	Noun	Verb
Dutch	fiets "cycle"	fiets-en "cycle"
English	chain	(to) chain
French	guide "guide"	guid-er "guide"
Latin	corona "crown"	coron-a-re "crown"

If one wants to treat conversion as a kind of affixation, one is forced to assume a **zero-morpheme** that is added to the input word. However, there is no independent evidence for such a zero-affix, and we do not even know if the zero-morpheme should be taken to be a prefix or a suffix. Therefore, conversion as exemplified in (19) is better analysed in terms of the following morphological rule:

(20) $[x]_N \rightarrow [[x]_N]_V$

The verbs in (19) therefore have the structure $[[x]_N]_V$.

A defining property of the notion 'conversion' is that it has a direction: in the examples above, the verb has been derived from the noun. This phenomenon must therefore be distinguished from **multifunctionality**, the situation in which words can be used for different syntactic categories without a particular direction in the relation between these different uses of words. In Maori, for example, the word *waiata* can be used as a verb "to sing", as a noun "song", and as a participle "singing" (Bauer 1993: 510). In Sranan, a creole language of Surinam, the word *hebi* functions as an adjective "heavy", a noun "weight", an intransitive verb "to be heavy", and a transitive verb "to make heavy" (Voorhoeve 1979: 43).

Change of category without overt morphological marking is also found in the case of **middle verbs**, which are intransitive and denote a property, whereas the corresponding activity verb denotes an activity (examples from Dutch):

(21) Deze aardappelen schillen gemakkelijk
      These potatoes peel easily
      "These potatoes are easy to peel"

Mars hapt zo heerlijk weg
Mars eats so nicely away
"Mars is so pleasant to eat"

(Mars is a kind of candy bar.) This kind of change from one subcategory of verbs to another subcategory may be subsumed under conversion because there is a clear direction in the relation between the verbs involved: the middle verb is derived from the activity verb.

In Chapter 1 you were introduced to the notion of paradigmatic word-formation, in which a morphological constituent of a word is replaced with another one. A typical case of this kind of word-formation is **affix sub-stitution**, the replacement of one affix with another. In Dutch, female counterparts of agent nouns can be formed by replacing -er with -ster (Booij 2002a: 6):

(22)   aanvoerd-er "captain"   aanvoerd-ster
        betwet-er "lit. better knower, pedant"   betweet-ster
        rederijk-er "rhetorician"   rederijk-ster
        reizig-er "traveller"   reizig-ster
        oproerkraai-er "ring leader"   oproerkraai-ster

The operation of substitution as a viable way of making new words has developed from systematic relationships between words derived from the same base. In this case, both -er and -ster can be added to Dutch verbs to form agent nouns. Thus a pattern $[x\text{-}er]_N$: $[x\text{-}ster]_N$ could be observed, which was then extended to other nouns in -er without a straighforward verbal base. For instance, there is no Dutch verb *reizig* "to travel", and yet, the agent noun *reiziger* has a female counterpart in -ster. The presence of the /d/ in *aanvoerdster* also betrays that this word is derived from *aanvoer-der*. The /d/ does not belong to the verbal stem *aanvoer* "to lead", but is part of the allomorph -der that is used after stems ending in /r/. Since it is -er that is replaced, the /d/ shows up in the female agent noun as well.

A prototypical case of paradigmatic word-formation is **back formation** in which the direction of derivation is inverted: the less complex word is derived from the more complex word by omitting something. Well-known examples from English are *to sculpt* from *sculptor*, and *to babysit* from *babysitter*. The noun *sculptor* is a borrowing from Latin. Because English has word pairs of the type $V–[V+or]_N$, (*terminate–terminator*, etc.), the verb *sculpt* could be reconstructed from the noun *sculptor* by reinterpreting this word as having the structure $[[sculpt]_V or]_N$. The paradigmatic dimension involved here is that a word ending in -or is assigned an internal morphological structure with a verbal base on the basis of existing verb–noun pairs such as *terminate–terminator*.

The emergence of the verb *to babysit* can be reconstructed as follows. The word *babysitter* is a regular compound consisting of two nouns, *baby* and the deverbal noun *sitter*. However, there is no general process of N + V compounding in English. The exceptional NV compound *babysit* could therefore only arise through back formation. In the same way, the Dutch NV compound *stofzuig* "to vacuum-clean" arose through back formation from the regular NN compound *stofzuiger* "lit. dust sucker, vacuum cleaner". In the cases of *to babysit* and *stofzuig*, the structure $[[N] [V \text{ } -er]_N]_N$ has been reinterpreted as $[[N \text{ } V]_V \text{ } -er]_N$, and subsequent back formation led to the rise of these N + V compounds.

2.3 Morphological typology

The catalogue of morphological operations presented in section 2.2 raises the question to what extent the languages of the world make use of these possibilities. First, we can locate each language on a scale of degree of **synthesis**, the average number of morphemes in a word. On one end of the scale we find **isolating languages** that do not make use of morphology at all. A classical example of such a language is Vietnamese (which, however, is said to have compounds). At the other end of the scale we find **polysynthetic languages** such as Greenlandic and Alaskan Yup'ik, languages in which words may contain a considerable number of suffixes after the root.

Before we have a look at some relevant examples, I will first give a short clarification of the notational conventions used in **interlinear morphemic translation**. These conventions are of considerable importance for our understanding of the structure of sentences and words. A space marks the boundary between two words, and a hyphen represents a boundary between two morphemes within one word. Lexical morphemes are represented by lower case letters, and grammatical categories by small capitals. If one morpheme on the first line represents more than one piece of lexical or grammatical information in the morphemic gloss, the categories are separated by a dot, as in the following Latin example (Lehmann 1982: 205):

(23) Manu-s   manu-m   lava-t
      hand-NOM.SG   hand-ACC.SG   wash-3SG
      "One hand washes the other"

The only exception to this use of the dot is its absence in combinations of the category PERSON and the category NUMBER, as in 3SG.

Let us now have a look at some examples of polysynthetic words in which the conventions just discussed are also exemplified—first Greenlandic (Fortescue 1984: 273) and then Alaska Yup'ik (Mithun 1999: 28):

(24) tuqu-riikatap-puq
      die-long.ago–3SG.INDIC
      "He died long ago"

      anglani-tu-llru-u-nga   caknek
      enjoy-customarily-PAST-IND.INTR-1SG   very.much
      "I used to enjoy myself very much"

The first example is a sentence of one word only, the second one contains two words. When we compare this with the number of words in the English glosses (four and seven respectively), we get some idea of what it means for a language to be polysynthetic.

The second scale on which we may rank languages as to their morphological properties is that of **fusion**. In some languages, a word is easily segmentable into its constituent morphemes. An example is Turkish, a language that is therefore characterized as **agglutinative:** the stem of a word is followed by one or more suffixes, each with their own meaning:

(25) çocuk-lar-nız-dan
      child-PL-your.PL-ABL "from your children"

Most Indo-European languages are **fusional** in their inflectional system since different inflectional properties are often expressed by one and the same morpheme. In the Polish word form *koty* "cat, NOM.PL" the ending -*y* expresses simultaneously the properties NOMINATIVE and PLURAL. In the English word *walks*, the ending -*s* expresses three properties: PRESENT TENSE, SINGULAR, and 3.PERSON. Such morphemes that serve to express more than one morphological property are called **portmanteau morphemes**.

When a language tends to be more agglutinative, it will tend to have more morphemes per word than a fusional language, and hence it will be higher on the scale of synthesis as well. The average number of morphemes per word in Turkish is estimated to be four times higher than that in English (Csató and Johanson 1998: 208).

The kind of typological classification discussed so far mainly has a descriptive and orientational function: by locating a language on a number of scales, we know roughly what kind of morphological system we may expect. But it does not provide fine-grained classifications. Germanic languages are fusional in their inflectional systems, but agglutinative in their system of derivational word-formation. Moreover, for an adequate descriptive classification other parameters are also relevant, for instance the parameter of reduplication: languages of the Austronesian family make wide use of reduplication patterns, whereas this does not apply to most Indo-European languages of Europe. Languages may also differ in the extent to which they make use of prefixation or suffixation.

Morphological typology becomes theoretically interesting if it enables us to predict certain properties of a language on the basis of other properties. For instance, the following **morphological universal** has been proposed by Greenberg (1963: 95):

(26)   If a language has the category of Gender, it always has the category of Number.

This universal has the form of an implication, and hence it predicts that of the four following logically possible languages only the first three exist:

(27)   a. Languages with Gender and Number
       b. Languages with Number only
       c. Languages without Gender or Number
       d. Languages with Gender only

Thus, an **implicational universal** is a restriction on the class of possible natural languages, and hence contributes to the definition of the notion 'possible natural language'.

Some implicational universals pertain to markedness phenomena. **Markedness** is the asymmetrical distributions of properties. An example of a **markedness universal** is that there are many languages in which the singular is not expressed by a morpheme, but only the plural, whereas there are no languages where only the singular is expressed by a morpheme. For example, the asymmetric distributional pattern of singular and plural morphemes given in Table 2.1 has been found. This table shows that

Table 2.1. *Distribution of Number morphemes*

	Absence of SG *morpheme*	*Presence of* SG *morpheme*
Presence of PL *morpheme*	English, Dutch	Latvian, Italian
Absence of PL *morpheme*	Chinese, Maori	

Source: Croft 1990: 69.

languages with a singular morpheme only must be excluded in order to restrict the degree of variation in natural language. Hence, we might formulate the following implication universal for this markedness pattern: 'if singular number is expressed by a morpheme, then plural number as well'.

This generalization concerning the expression of number has to be amended slightly, however. There are languages where, for those entities that always occur in pairs or in groups, the plural form of the noun has no overt suffix, and the singular form ends in a **singulative** suffix. This is the case for Turkana (Dimmendaal 1983: 224–8), a language of Kenya with the singulative suffixes -*a* and -*it* (the prefixes are gender markers):

(29)   *singulative*   *plural*
       ɛ-sɪkɪn-a "breast"   ŋ-sɪkɪn "breasts"
       e-turkàna-ɪt "Turkana person"   ŋ-tùrkanà "Turkana people"

This reversal of the markedness pattern concerning singular–plural in a special domain is called **local markedness** (Tiersma 1982).

The use of **hierarchies** in morphological typology is illustrated by the following hierarchy for the different values for the category number:

(30)   singular > plural > dual

This hierarchy ranks singular above plural, and plural above dual. It expresses that singular forms are less marked than plurals, and plurals are less marked than duals. This means that if a language has a **dual** (that is, a word form with 2 as the value for the category number), it has also a plural, and if a language has a plural, it also has a singular. Hence, this hierarchy restricts the variation space of natural language: certain types of logically possible languages are excluded, such as a language with singular and dual only.

Not all the typological universals are absolute ones; some are statistical tendencies only. For instance, there are many more languages that only use suffixes (Turkish is an example) than there are languages that only use prefixes. Hence, there is a suffixing preference in natural languages. Yet, there are languages that are exclusively prefixing, so there is no absolute universal involved here. Many of the universals discussed in Greenberg (1963) are of this statistical nature.

Summary

Words can be divided into different kinds of morphemes such as roots and affixes, the morphological atoms of language. These morphemes may vary in shape (allomorphy), a variation that does not always follow from the phonological system of the language. In the case of suppletion, different stems co-occur in the paradigm of one lexeme.

The set of morphological operations available to human languages comprises more than concatenation: conversion, reduplication (concatenation plus copying), different types of phonetic modification, root-and-pattern morphology, and paradigmatic word-formation also play a role.

Languages do not all make the same use of the available morphological operations, and can be classified according to the indices of synthesis and fusion. In addition to this purely classificatory typology, morphologists make cross-linguistic comparisons of morphological systems in order to find constraints on the degree of morphological variation of natural language.

Questions

1. Identify the bound constituents of the following English words: *disagreeable, acceptability, ungrammaticality, discriminatory, permafrost, fascination, protolanguage, versification, intolerance, productivity, unidirectionality.*

2. Consider the sets of morphologically related words in French in the table that exhibit variation in the underlined vowel of their base word (Dell and Selkirk 1978).

Base word	Derived words	
[œ]	[œ]	[ɔ]
fleur "flower"	fleurette "small flower"	floral "floral"
seul "alone"	seulement "only"	solitude "solitude"
peuple "people"	peuplade "tribe"	populaire "popular"
[ɛ]	[ɛ]	[a]
vain "idle"	vainement "in vain"	vanité "vanity"
clair "clear"	éclairer "to light"	clarifier "to clarify"
mer "sea"	amerrir "to land on the sea"	marin "sailor"
africain "African"		Africaniste "Africanist"
humain "human"		humanité "humanity"
similaire "similar"		similarité "similarity"

a. Formulate the rule that accounts for these vowel alternations.
b. Is this rule an automatic phonological rule or a morphophonological rule?

3. In the following past tense forms of English verbs, the past tense suffix has three different phonetic shapes: *kept, walked, kissed, hugged, lived, added, fitted, coded.*

a. Which are the three phonetic forms of this suffix?
b. Formulate the rules (or rule) that account for this phonetic variation.

4. Make a morphological analysis of the following words of the Amerindian language Cree, and give the interlinear morphemic glossing of the last word (Cowan and Rakušan 1985: 111):

niwa:pahte:n "I see (it)"
kiwa:pahte:n "you see (it)"
niwa:pahte:na:n "we see (it)"
kiwa:pahte:na:wa:w "you (plural) see (it)"
nima:čiše:n "I cut (it)"
kima:čiše:n "you cut (it)"
nima:čiše:na:n "we cut (it)"
kima:čiše:wa:w "you (plural) cut (it)"
nitapin "I sit"
kitapin "you sit"
nitapina:n "we sit"
kitapina:wa:w "you (plural) sit"

5. Consider the following past tense forms of English: *kept, wept, slept.* Which kinds of operation have been used for making these verbal forms?

6. In written Arabic, verbs can be derived from nouns, as the following examples (Becker 1990*b*: 14) show:

zayt "oil"   zayyata "to oil"
bukla "buckle"   bakkala "to buckle"
turki: "Turk"   tarraka "to Turkify"
tilifu:n "telephone"   talfana "to telephone"
tilifiziu:n "televison" talfaza "to televise"

a. Give a three-tiered representation of the verbs *bakkala* and *talfana*.
b. Give the consonantal template and the vowel template for the morphological category of denominal verbs.

7. The following are singular and plural nouns in Bulgarian (Cowan and Rakušan 1985: 99):

teátər   teátri   "theater(s)"
bóbər   bobri   "beaver(s)"
pésen   pesni   "song(s)"
psalóm   psalmi   "psalm(s)"
báncik   báncigi   "band saw(s)"
ízverk   ízvergi   "monster(s)"

Give the (morphological and phonological) rules for plural noun formation for this set of word forms.

8. Which types of morphological processes are involved forms in the table (Melčuk 2000: 578) of the Tagalog verbs *patáy* "to kill" and *sulat* "to write"?

	PAST	PRESENT
ACTIVE	pumatáy	pumápatáy
	sumulat	sumusulat
PASSIVE	pinatáy	pinápatáy
	sinulat	suinusulat

9. Consider the following pairs of singular and plural nouns of Agta (Wiltshire and Marantz 2000: 558):

takki   taktakki   "leg(s)"
labáng   lablabáng   "patch(es)"
uffu   ufuffu   "thigh(s)"

Formulate the morphological rule that accounts for the formation of the plural nouns.

10. In Italian, adjectives can be derived from nouns and adjectives through the addition of the suffix *-oso* or *-astro*, as illustrated by the following examples (source Scalise 1984: 59):

fama "fame"   famoso "famous"
virtú "virtue"   virtuoso "virtuous"
giallo "yellow"   giallastro "yellowish"
blu "blue"   bluastro "bluish"

Give the stem-forms of the four base words listed here.

Further reading

A survey of the different types of morphological operations can be found in chapter 8 of *BLM*, and in Payne (1997). A detailed analysis of vowel and consonant mutation is given in Lieber (1987). The multi-tier interpretation of root-and-pattern morphology has been proposed by McCarthy (1981). This kind of morphology is also found in a number of non-Semitic languages (Broselow 2000).

Formal theories of morphology as a set of operations on lexemes (processual morphology) have been developed in Anderson (1992) and Stump (2001).

Morphological typology is discussed in Comrie (1981) and Croft (1990). The suffixing preference is dealt with in Cutler *et al.* (1985). The verbs of the Athapaskan language Slave are famous for their morphological complexity (Rice 1989, 2000), and Amerindian languages in general for their polysynthetic nature (Mithun 1999). Polysynthesis is discussed from a theoretical point of view in Baker (1988, 1996,

2001). Possible explanations for the suffixing preference are discussed in Hawkins and Cutler (1988), and in Hall (1988).

Information on the World Atlas of Language Structures that also includes morphological typology can be found at http://linguistics.buffalo.edu/people/faculty/dryer/dryer/atlas. The Universals Archive of the University of Konstanz may be consulted at http://ling.uni-konstanz.de/pages/proj/sprachbau.htm. The website of the Surrey Morphology Group provides typological information on agreement and syncretism: http://www.surrey.ac.uk/LIS/SMG.

A standard for interlinear morphemic glossing is presented in Lehmann (1982). More recent versions are the set of glossing rules proposed by the Leipzig typologist group, based on Lehmann (1982), which can be found at www.eva.mpg.de/lingua/index.html, and Lehman (2004).

Part II

Word-Formation

3

Derivation

3.1 Lexeme formation

The basic function of derivational processes is to enable the language user to make new lexemes. Lexemes belong to lexical categories such as N, V, and A and the derived lexemes may belong to a different category than their bases. The examples in (1) from Dutch illustrate the possible categorial shifts, and also cases in which the lexical category does not change (Booij 2002*a*: 87). Words are divided into two kinds of lexical classes: open and closed classes. In most languages, nouns, adjectives, and verbs form open classes. As illustrated in (1), these classes can be extended by means of word-formation. Function words such as determiners, conjunctions, pronouns, and adpositions (pre- and postpositions) form closed sets of words that cannot be extended by regular word-formation patterns. The base words that form inputs to word-formation are normally also words of these open classes, but there are exceptions. For instance, the Dutch diminutive suffix -*je* can be attached to the demonstratives *dit* "this" and *dat* "that", as in *dit-je-s en dat-je-s* "odds and ends", and to phrases such as the PP *onder ons* "between us", with the corresponding diminutive *onderons-je* "private chat". This extension of the input domain to function words and phrases is typical for highly productive word-formation processes.

(1) *Derivation of nouns*

A → N suffixation	schoon "beautiful"	schoon-heid "beauty"
V → N suffixation	spreek "to speak"	sprek-er "speaker"
prefixation	praat "to talk"	ge-praat "talking"
N → N suffixation	moeder "mother"	moeder-schap "motherhood"
prefixation	zin "sense"	on-zin "nonsense"

Derivation of adjectives

N → A suffixation	meester "master"	meester-lijk "masterly"
V → A suffixation	lees "to read"	lees-baar "readable"
A → A suffixation	blauw "blue"	blauw-ig "blueish"
prefixation	gewoon "common"	on-gewoon "uncommon"

Derivation of verbs

N → V suffixation	analyse "analysis"	analys-eer "to analyse"
prefixation	slaaf "slave"	ver-slaaf "to enslave"
A → V suffixation	kalm "calm"	kalm-eer "to calm down"
prefixation	bleek "pale"	ver-bleek "to turn pale"
V → V suffixation	krab "to scratch"	krabb-el "to scratch lightly"
prefixation	rijd "to ride"	be-rijd "to ride on"

Many languages have a fourth open lexical class, that of adverbs. This class can also be extended in regular ways. In English, adverbs can be derived from adjectives by means of the suffix *-ly*, and in French by means of suffixation with *-ment*, as in *lente-ment* "slowly". Nouns are the bases of adverbs such as English *group-wise*, and Latin *articulat-im* "piecemeal" derived from the noun *articulus* "member". Adverbs are special in that they tend not to feed other word-formation processes, unlike words of the three other open categories. Inflection of adverbs is also rare, but the comparative form of an English adverb such as *sooner* suggests that inflection is not completely excluded (note that *soon* functions as an adverb only, not as an adjective).

The description of each process of derivation consists of a specification of the properties of the input words, and those of the output words. The first set of examples in (1) consists of cases of **nominalization** (the derivation of nouns from words of other word classes). Such derivation processes usually impose constraints on the lexical category of their input words, for instance that they have to be adjectives. Besides nominalization, we distinguish **verbalization, adjectivalization**, and **adverbialization** as types of **category-determining** processes.

All derivational suffixes in (1) appear to determine the lexical category of the complex words that they form, and hence, they are category-determining. This generalization holds for all Germanic languages. For instance, it is the diminutive suffix -*(t)je* of Dutch that determines the lexical category of diminutives, which are always nouns. This suffix does not only attach to nouns, but also to adjectives and verbs. In the latter cases the derived words are also nouns: *blond* "blond" (A)—*blondje* "blond girl" (N), *speel* "to play" (V)—*speeltje* "toy" (N).

A suffix may be category-determining even if it does not change the lexical category of its input words. When Dutch diminutive nouns are derived from nouns, they do not change the category. Yet, we can see that they are category-determining because they always have neuter gender even if the input noun is non-neuter, as illustrated by the word pair *zaal* "room, NON-NEUTER"—*zaaltje* "small room, NEUTER". That is, the diminutive suffix determines the lexical subclass of its derived words.

This category-determining role of suffixes has led some linguists to extend the notion **head**, an important notion in syntax, to the domain of morphology. In syntax, phrases consist of minimally a head, and it is the syntactic category of the head that determines the category of the phrase. A phrase with an adjectival head is an Adjective Phrase (AP), a phrase with a noun as head is a Noun Phrase (NP), etc. For instance, *very good* is an AP with the adjective *good* as its head, and *hard work* is an NP with the noun *work* as its head. By analogy, we may say that the Dutch diminutive suffix is the head of the diminutive noun since it determines the syntactic category of this type of complex word. This morphological use of the notion 'head' has been advocated in particular in the morpheme-based approach to morphology. In that framework, affixes get their own lexical entry in the lexicon, in which their class-determining properties are specified. The morphological structure of the Dutch diminutive noun *blondje* might then be represented as in Figure 3.1. The lexical category N and the gender feature

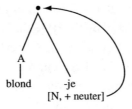

Fig. 3.1 Percolation of head features

[+neuter] are taken to be properties of the suffix *-je*, and percolated to the dominating node, thus classifying this word as a neuter noun. The **percolation** procedure will percolate the properties of the head to the dominating node of the whole word (Lieber 1980, 1989). Additional evidence for the headship of the Dutch diminutive suffix is that it governs the selection of the correct plural suffix. Whereas simplex nouns ending in [ə] take either *-s* or *-n* as their plural suffix, the diminutive nouns in *-je* [ə] always select *-s*.

Williams (1981: 248) proposed the following rule for the identification of the head constituent of complex words:

(2)   **Right-hand Head Rule** (RHR): In morphology, we define the head of a morphologically complex word to be the right-hand member of that word.

This rule will identify suffixes as heads, and hence, they will determine the lexical (sub)category of the words they create. The rule is supposed to be applicable to both derived words and compounds. In English compounds it is indeed the lexical category of the right constituent that determines the lexical (sub)category of the compound: a *bottle factory* is a kind of factory, not a kind of bottle. Similarly, English derivational suffixes are category-determining. However, the Right-hand Head Rule cannot be a universal rule because there are languages with left-headed complex words, as illustrated in section 4.1.

You should realize that the notion 'head' as used here is different from its standard use in syntax. In syntax, a head is not identified by its linear position in the phrase, but by the hierarchical configuration in which it occurs. Moreover, the RHR is at best a language-specific principle since there are also languages with category-determining prefixes or category-neutral suffixes. In the list (1) given above we see examples of both **category-neutral** prefixes (the negative prefix *on-* that derives adjectives from adjectives, and nouns from nouns), and of category-determining prefixes such as *ver-* that derives verbs from adjectives. The latter prefix thus forms a problem for assuming the RHR to be generally applicable to Dutch. There are many other languages with category-determining prefixation.

The generalization expressed by the RHR has a historical explanation. In languages with right-headed phrases, the univerbation of such phrases has led to the emergence of right-headed compounds. Subsequently, some right constituents of compounds have developed into suffixes. The English suffix *-dom* (as in *kingdom*) with the meaning "domain" derives from the Old English word *dom* "fate, destiny", and the Dutch suffix *-loos* "-less" (as in *hulpe-loos* "helpless") derives from the adjective *loos* "being without", words that once occurred in the head position of compounds. Thus, such suffixes could start functioning as morphological heads. On the other hand, prefixes often derive from words functioning as left, non-head constituents of compounds or from preverbal adverbs. The English prefix *over-* (as in *to overdo*) derives historically from the word *over* and the Latin prefix *ab-* (as in *abducere* "to take away") from the preposition *ab*. Due to their origin from words in a (morphological or syntactic) non-head position, such prefixes do not function as heads either (Hall 1991).

The category-neutral evaluative suffixes of Italian and other Romance languages also pose a problem for the universal applicability of the RHR (Scalise 1988). The Italian diminutive suffix *-ino*, for example, derives nouns from nouns, but adjectives from adjectives, and adverbs from adverbs. Hence it is category-neutral as illustrated by the following examples: *tavolo* "table"— *tavolino* "small table", *giallo* "yellow"—*giallino* "yellowish", *bene* "well"— *benino* "reasonably well". That is, these suffixes do not function as heads.

In lexeme-based morphology, the category-determining nature of a particular affix can be expressed in the template for that affix. The Dutch diminutive suffix will thus occur in the following template:

(3) $[[x]_Y \text{ tje}]_N$ "small entity with Y-related property" where Y = N, A, V

The variable Y used here stands for the lexical categories, N, A, and V. Words from these categories may serve as base words (and a few other words and phrases as well). The output category is always N. The Dutch category-neutral prefix *on-* "un-" will be specified as follows:

(4) $[\text{on}[x]_Y]_Y$ 'not-Y', where Y = N, A

This template expresses that *on-* is a prefix, not a lexeme since the prefix does not carry a category label of its own. It specifies that the prefix *on-* takes nouns and adjectives as base words, and that it is category-neutral since the variable Y recurs as category of the whole word.

Morphological rules do not necessarily apply to existing lexemes: possible words may also function as inputs. Dutch negative adjectives prefixed with *on-* "un-" often have a possible, but non-existing deverbal adjective ending in *-baar* "-able" as base word. Similar observations can be made for English adjectives in *-ible* and *-able: undefatigable* is an existing word, unlike its base word *defatigable*.

(5) aanraakbaar "touchable"   onaanraakbaar "untouchable"
     uitstaanbaar "tolerable"   onuitstaanbaar "intolerable"
     verwoestbaar "destroyable"   onverwoestbaar "undestroyable"
     corrigible   incorrigible
     delible   indelible
     defatigable   indefatigable

The positive adjectives in *-baar*, *-ible*, and *-able* in the left column of (5) do not occur by themselves. However, intuitions about existence versus non-existence of a particular positive adjective may vary from speaker to speaker, and sometimes the positive adjective crops up in usage. The crucial point is that existence is not a necessary condition for these adjectives to be used as base words. In the case of Dutch, we cannot assume, as a way out for this problem, that the prefix *on-* has been attached before the suffix *-baar*, because the prefix *on-* does not attach to verbs. It is the adjectival suffix *-baar* that makes the attachment of this prefix possible.

We might interpret these facts, the co-occurrence of two word-formation processes, as showing that the use of one morphological operation may imply the use of a second one. A formal representation of this co-occurrence is the assumption of a conflated morphological template $[on[V\text{-}baar]_A]_A$, a **conflation** of the template $[on\text{-}A]_A$ and the template $[V\text{-}baar]_A$. This simultaneous attachment of a prefix and a suffix is called **parasynthetic word-formation**. The formation of Italian verbs from adjectives by adding both a prefix and a verbalizing suffix to an adjectival stem might be seen as another instance of this kind of word-formation (Scalise 1984: 146):

(6) brutt-o "ugly"   im-brutt-i-re "to make ugly"
     rozz-o "crude"   di-rozz-a-re "to make less crude"
     vecchi-o "old"   in-vecchi-a-re "to age"

Note that this kind of word-formation is different from circumfixation. In the latter case we have to do with one, discontinuous affix, whereas in the examples in (6) two independently occuring affixes are used simultaneously.

Rules or templates for derivational patterns describe both the formal (phonological and syntactic) properties and the semantic properties of the class of output words. The semantic interpretation of a complex word is determined by the template, and includes the meaning of the base word. Hence, the meaning of a complex word is in principle a **compositional function** of the meaning of its base word and its morphological structure, as illustrated by the templates (3) and (4).

The meaning contribution of the affix, or more generally, the derivational process, might actually be pretty vague. English (and many other languages) make use of a number of suffixes to derive **relational adjectives** from nouns:

(7) *Noun*   *NP with relational adjective*
    atom   atomic bomb
    music   musical performance
    ocean   oceanic winds
    parent   parental refusal
    president   presidential speech

The suffixes *-ic*, *-al* and *-ial* are used to form denominal adjectives that serve to express that there is some relation between the base noun of the adjective and the head noun of the phrase. The precise nature of that relationship is not specified, and needs further interpretation by the language user. In the case of *parental refusal*, the parents are engaged in refusing, in *musical performance* it is the music that is being performed. The same semantic vagueness in the relation between base word and derived word can be observed when we compare the differences in meaning between the following denominal verbs ending in *-ize: hospitalize* "to put someone in hospital", *burglarize* "to do the work of a burglar", *vaporize* "to turn something to vapour".

Conversion can be subsumed under derivation, although there is no phonological change involved, because it serves to coin new lexemes on the basis of existing ones. The examples in (8) illustrate the conversion of nouns to verbs.

(8)	*Noun*	*Verb*
English	bed	bed "to put to bed"
	bottle	bottle "to put into a bottle"
	bomb	bomb "to throw bombs on"
Dutch	kaas "cheese"	kaas "to produce cheese"
	melk "milk"	melk "to extract milk from"
	stof "dust"	stof "to remove dust from"

Other input categories involved in conversion in English are adjectives and verbs:

(9) A > V: calm > to calm, clean > to clean, wet > to wet
     V > N: to cheat > (a) cheat, to take > (a) take, to approach > (an) approach

How can we be certain about the direction of the conversion given the fact there are no phonological indications for this direction? Arguments for determining the direction are often (but not always) provided by the semantics of the conversion pair. In the examples in (8), the meaning of the verb is a compositional function of that of the noun, and that is why we interpret the relation in terms of verbs being derived from nouns. The phonological make-up of words may also form an indication. Dutch simplex verbs consist of either one syllable, or two syllables, the second of which contains a schwa. Yet, we find verbs such as *papegaai* "to imitate" and *domino* "to play dominoes" that do not exhibit this phonological make-up since they consist of three syllables. This can be explained by these verbs being conversions of the nouns *papegaai* "parrot" and *domino* "dominoes" respectively, which accounts for their marked phonological structure.

The template for the conversion cases in (8) will be as follows:

(10) $[[x]_N]_V$ "to perform an action in which $[x]_N$ plays a role"

Again, the semantic description is vague; the precise role of the N, and hence the nature of the action expressed, is not defined exactly. These are determined by non-grammatical knowledge. Thus, the actual meaning of the conversion verbs may be quite varied, which increases the semantic flexibility, and hence the usability of this pattern of lexeme formation.

The interpretation of conversion as a case of lexeme formation is supported by the observation that languages may differ in that one language uses an affix to coin a verb from a noun, whereas another language creates the corresponding lexeme by means of affixation. For instance, the Dutch de-adjectival conversion verb *wit* "to make white" corresponds to English *whiten*, coined by addition of the suffix *-en* to the adjectival stem *white*. Even within a single language one may find both types exemplified; compare the English verbs *to wet* and *to dampen* to their adjectival bases *wet* and *damp*.

The coinage of middle verbs is another instantiation of lexeme formation without overt phonological effect. Middle verbs express a generic property and hence are stative verbs, whereas their source verbs indicate an action. This process is used in Dutch and English, whereas Russian requires a suffix *-sja* to perform the same semantic operation (Spencer and Zaretskaya 1998):

(11)   Dutch   Vurenhout   zaagt   gemakkelijk
              Pine   saws   easily
              "Pine saws easily"

Russian Sosna   legko   pilit-sja
        Pine   easily   saw-SJA
        "Pine saws easily"

Middle verbs often require the presence of an adverbial expression such as
easily: a sentence like *Pine saws*, without an adverbial expression, is odd.
This can be explained by the **Non-Redundancy Constraint** (Ackerman and
Goldberg 1996: 21; Goldberg and Ackerman 2001) that forbids morphological operations expressing redundant information. Since you know that
pine is a kind of wood that can be sawn, it does not make sense to state this,
unless you add a modification with some informational content to that
statement, in this example the adverb *easily*. For the same reason, an adjective such as *eyed* does not make much sense as a specification of the properties of human beings since they normally have eyes, whereas the adjective
blue-eyed expresses a non-redundant piece of information about human
beings. This illustrates that there is a difference between the well-
formedness of a complex word, and its semantic or pragmatic
appropriateness.

The interpretational versatility that we observed for relational adjectives
can also be found in the case of reduplication. Reduplication is often (but
not always!) a case of **iconicity** in language. This means that the formal
structure is iconic for the meaning expressed. This applies particularly to
full reduplication in which the form is doubled; the corresponding meaning
also appears to be doubled in the sense that it may express repetition,
intensity, plurality, distributivity, etc. Afrikaans has borrowed reduplication, an unusual word-formation process in Germanic languages, from
Malay, and this process is used frequently (Botha 1988: 1–2):

(12)   Die   kinders drink   bottels-bottels   limonade
       the   children drink   bottles-bottles   lemonade
       "The children drink bottles and bottles of lemonade"

       Die   leeu   loop   brul-brul   weg
       the   lion   walk   roar-roar   away
       "Roaring repeatedly, the lion walks away"

       Hy   dra   tien-tien   boek   die   trap   op
       he   carry   ten-ten   books   the   stairs up
       "He carries the books up the stairs ten at a time"

Derivation is not only used in a category-changing fashion, but also to
create other semantic subcategories of the same lexical category. Italian has
a lot of category-neutral evaluative suffixes that serve to create nouns with

an evaluative meaning component, as illustrated by the following examples (Scalise 1988: 233):

(13)   albero "tree"   alber-ino "little tree"
       giardino "garden"   giardin-etto "nice little garden"
       libro "book"   libr-one "big book"
       ragazzo "boy"   ragazz-accio "bad boy"

In the domain of adjectives we find many affixes that can be attached to adjectives without changing their syntactic category, in order to modify their meaning: weakening (English *-ish* as in *reddish, oldish*), negation or reversal (English *dis-, in-, un-, non-*), or intensification of the meaning of the adjectival base, as in the following examples from Dutch:

(14)   bang "afraid"   doods-bang "lit. death-afraid, very frightened"
       mooi "beautiful"   bloed-mooi "lit. blood-beautiful, very beautiful"
       sterk "strong"   bere-sterk "lit. bear-strong, very strong"
       triest "sad"   in-triest "lit, in-sad, very sad"

Formation of the middle verbs mentioned above illustrates that derivational processes are used to create specific subclasses of verbs. Middle verbs in English are intransitive verbs, whereas their base verbs are transitive, that is, require a direct object to be present. Middle verb formation is therefore a case of change in **syntactic valency**. With the latter term we refer to the syntactic combinatorial properties of words. Whereas intransitive verbs only require the presence of a subject, transitive verbs require the presence of a second noun phrase that functions as direct object. In many languages, causative verbs are created from base verbs that mention an event or action. The causative verbs have a subject that mentions the causer of the event or action. Here are two examples from Bolivian Quechua, in which the causative suffix *-chi* is attached to the verbs *llank'a* "to work" and *awa* "to knit", and thus induces a change in valency of these verbs. The derived causative verbs take a subject that mentions the causer, in addition to the NPs required by the base verb. For instance, in sentence (15a) the presence of the NP *churi* "my son" is required by the base verb *llank'* "work" (van de Kerke 1996: 195–6):

(15)   a.   churi-y-ta   llank'a-chi-saq
            son-1SG-ACC   work-CAUS-1SG.FUT
            "I will make my son work"

       b.   warmi-wawa-y-wan   chompa-ta   awa-chi-saq
            woman-child-1SG-COM   sweater-ACC   knit-CAUS-1SG.FUT
            "I will make my daughter knit a sweater"

The Semitic languages are well known for their system of creating related verbal lexemes by combining a consonantal root with a specific pattern of C and V positions, and a vowel melody. In addition, prefixes may be used. Such a set of verbal lexemes with the same morphological pattern is called a **binyan** ("building", plural *binyanim*). The root *qtl* "to kill" as used in biblical Hebrew has the five active binyan forms shown in (16) (Aronoff 1994: 124). In addition to these five binyanim, there are two binyanim with a passive meaning, the Pu'al as a passive variant of the Pi'el, and the Hof'al as the passive of the Hif'il. Each of these seven binyanim has a paradigm of inflectional forms, part of which, the 3SG.MASC.PERF paradigm, is illustrated in (16). As the glosses indicate, the binyan system mainly serves to create related verbs with differences in syntactic valency. However, the semantics of the different binyanim is more complicated and less transparent than this example suggests.

(16)	*Binyan name*	3SG. MASC.PERF	*Gloss*
	Qal	qâtal	to kill
	Nif'al	ni-qtal	to kill oneself
	Pi'el	qittel	to massacre
	Hif'il	hi-qtil	to cause to kill
	Hitpa'el	hit-qattel	to kill oneself

3.2 Templates and idiosyncrasies

As discussed in section 1.4, complex words are listed in the lexicon for two reasons. In the case of a fully regular complex word, it may be necessary to list it because it is the conventional way of expressing a particular meaning. For instance, the Dutch action noun for the verb *concretiseer* "to make concrete" is *concretiser-ing*; the alternative noun *concretis-atie* is also well-formed, but not the word that Dutch speakers in the Netherlands use. Thus, established complex words may have a blocking effect on the coinage of new complex words. The second reason why we need to list complex words is that they may have properties that are not predictable by rule. Thus, morphological rules or templates have two functions: stating the predictable properties of established complex words, and indicating how new complex words can be formed.

This raises the issue of how to formally express the relation between the regularities as stated in a rule or template, and the listed properties of individual complex words. Consider the following German deverbal adjectives in *-bar* "-able", and their idiosyncratic properties (Richemann 1998: 54):

(17)   additional aspect of meaning:
   essen "eat"   *essbar* "safely edible"

   obligation instead of possibility:
   zahlen "pay"   *zahlbar* "payable, must be payed"

   lexicalized meaning:
   halten "hold, keep"   *haltbar* "non-perishable"

Fully regular adjectives in *-bar* are derived from transitive verbs, and their meaning is predictable. This meaning can be circumscribed as "can be V-ed". The three adjectives in (17) are derived from transitive verbs as well, but they have an additional meaning or slightly different meaning. For instance, *essbar* does not just mean "can be eaten", but "can be eaten safely". The meaning component "safely" is the additional unpredictable meaning component. The adjective *zahlbar* does not mean that something can be paid, but that it has to be paid. The meaning "non-perishable" of the adjective *haltbar* is more specific than just "can be kept".

The relation between the properties that hold for all deverbal adjectives ending in *-bar*, and the properties of the individual adjectives can be expressed by an **inheritance tree**. In such a tree, each node inherits all the properties of the dominating nodes, and may have additional unique properties, which are then also specified on that node. The following (simplified) inheritance tree may be constructed for these German *bar*-adjectives. The unpredictable properties of the three adjectives discussed are printed in italics. All other properties of these three adjectives

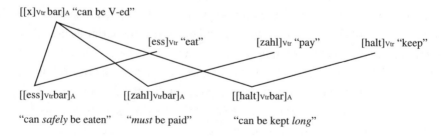

Fig. 3.2 Inheritance tree for *-bar*-adjectives

are predictable, and are inherited from the dominating nodes of the base verbs and the dominating node with the template for regular *bar*-adjectives. That is, these properties count as redundant information. The predictable properties are partially inherited from their base verbs, and partially from the word-formation template for adjectives ending in *-bar*. The inheritance tree shown here is a multiple inheritance tree since the lower nodes for the individual words are connected to two different layers of dominating nodes, the nodes of the base verbs, and the node of the morphological template of *-bar* adjectives.

This kind of modelling of the lexicon enables us to specify which complex words exist, and which of their properties have been generalized into patterns, expressed as morphological templates. A morphological template thus coexists with the individual complex words formed according to that template. The templates will also be used to create new complex words of that type which in their turn will be added to the lexicon. This model reflects the way in which language users acquire the morphological system of a language. First, individual complex words are learnt, and subsequently, more abstract patterns can be discovered on the basis of form-meaning correspondences between sets of words.

Instead of providing each individual adjective with a specification of all its properties, one might also restrict this specification to the unpredictable properties that are not inherited from the dominating nodes. In that case, the inheritance tree is redundancy-free. For instance, the specification of the regular English adjective *doable* will then consist of a node without any specification, linked to the nodes for *to do* and the relevant word-formation template. In this case, the empty node at the bottom only specifies that the adjective *doable* is an existing adjective of English. All other properties can be derived from the dominating nodes.

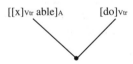

Fig. 3.3 Non-redundant specification of *doable*

From a psychological point of view the full specification approach is more plausible since human memory is so vast that a massive amount of redundant information is memorized, even though that information is predictable. It is important to bear in mind that the existence of a particular rule in a language does not imply that the outputs of such a rule cannot be stored individually in the lexicon of that language. Note, finally, that this point about the relation between rules and lists does not only pertain to derivation, but also to compounding and inflection.

3.3 Constraints on derivation

Derivational processes impose constraints on the kind of base words they take as their inputs. Examples of such **input constraints** are syntactic class requirements, as illustrated above. Some derivational processes require a more specific syntactic subclass. The Dutch suffix *-baar* "-able" can only be used for deriving new adjectives from verbs that are transitive, as in *drink-baar* "drinkable" derived from the transitive verb *drink* "to drink".

Does an affix always require one specific syntactic category for its input words? As we saw above, this is not the case for the Dutch negative prefix *on-* that can be attached to adjectives and nouns. The Italian evaluative suffixes mentioned in section 3.1 can be added to nouns, adjectives, and adverbs. Even category-determining suffixes sometimes attach to words of more than one category. The Dutch diminutive suffix attaches mostly to nouns, but other categories are not excluded (section 3.1). The English nominalizing suffix *-er* combines with both verbs and nouns (*work-er, London-er*).

Input constraints may also be phonological in nature. The Dutch nominalizing suffix *-aar* can only be attached to stems ending in a coronal sonorant consonant preceded by a schwa. In other cases, the suffix *-er* has to be used:

(18)   luist[ə]r "to listen"   luister-aar "listener"
       duik[ə]l "to tumble"   duikel-aar "tumbler"
       bez[ə]m "to sweep"   bezem-er "sweeper"
       veeg "to sweep"   veg-er "sweeper"

The German diminutive suffix *-lein* is not attached to nouns ending in /l/; instead, the synonymous suffix *-chen* is used. In Dutch, the suffix *-ig* /əɣ/ "-ish" is not added to words ending in /ɣ/; instead, the synonymous suffix *-achtig* is used. For instance, the denominal adjective **berg-ig* "mountainous" is ill-formed, whereas *berg-achtig* is fine. These German and Dutch examples illustrate the cross-linguistic tendency to avoid sequences with (almost) adjacent identical sounds in the phonetic forms of complex words.

The English verbalizing suffix -en that is attached to adjectives must be preceded by exactly one stem-final obstruent. This excludes a verb *greenen*, but allows for *blacken, whiten, harden, fasten*, and *soften*. In the latter two examples, the /t/ is deleted in order to comply with this phonological constraint. The constraint is an output constraint, because the input *soft* ends in two obstruents, instead of one. Yet, it does not mean that *soft* cannot be an input word; instead, its phonetic form is adjusted. Thus, this verb is pronounced as [sɔfən].

In sum, the possibility of using an affix and the choice of a particular affix may be determined by considerations concerning the optimal phonetic shape of the complex word that is being created. That is, **output constraints** on the phonetic form of a complex word can govern the choice or usability of a particular affix, as these examples from German, Dutch, and English illustrate.

Prosodic restrictions may also play a role in restricting productivity. The term **prosody** refers to properties of words and sentences, such as stress, tone, intonation, and the organization of sounds in larger units such as syllables. These properties are not linked to specifc segments, and hence they are called suprasegmental properties.

An example of a prosodic constraint is the following. It has been observed for Dutch that a word almost never begins with two unstressed prefixes. A stressed prefix, however, can easily be attached before an unstressed one. Nominalization of prefixed verbs by means of the stressless prefix *ge-* /ɣə/ tends to be avoided, whereas the addition of the stressed category-neutral prefix *her-* /hɛr/ "re-" is without problems:

(19) ?ge-ont-dek "discovery", ?ge-ont-bos "deforestation", ?ge-be-loof "promising"
hér-ont-dek "to rediscover", hér-be-gin "to re-begin", hér-ge-bruik "to re-use"

This difference in behaviour between the two prefixes has to do with the tendency of Dutch to avoid sequences of unstressed syllables, in particular at the beginning of a word. Therefore, the prefix *ge-* cannot be used before another unstressed prefix.

Derivational processes may also be subject to **stratal constraints**. A **stratum** is a layer of the lexicon of a particular historical origin. Germanic languages have borrowed many words from Greek and Latin, often with

French as an intermediary language, words that form the non-native stratum of the vocabulary. Since language users are able to discover affixes on the basis of recurrent form–meaning patterns in sets of borrowed words, these languages acquired a set of non-native affixes. These affixes have not been borrowed directly. It is words that are borrowed, and sets of borrowed non-native words may give rise to non-native suffixes. Thus, the non-native suffix -*ity* emerged in English, like its etymological cognates -*iteit* and -*ität* in Dutch and German respectively. This suffix can now be used for coining new de-adjectival nouns, for which there is no counterpart in Latin or French. However, the use of such non-native affixes (that is, **neo-classical word-formation**) is mostly restricted to base words of the non-native stratum. The Dutch suffix -*iteit* "-ity" can be attached to non-native adjectives, but not to native ones. For native adjectives, the synonymous native suffix -*heid* "-ness" (of Germanic origin) has to be used. These native affixes combine in principle both with native and non-native stems. So the following asymmetry can be observed:

(20) *Non-native adjectives*   *Derived nouns*
      absurd "absurd"   absurd-iteit/absurd-heid "absurdity"
      stabile "stable"   stabil-iteit/stabiel-heid "stability"

      native adjectives
      groen "green"   *groen-iteit/groen-heid "green-ness"
      zeker "certain"   *zeker-iteit/zeker-heid "certainty"

One may wonder how language users, most of whom have no knowledge of the historical origin of the words of their mother tongue, are able to comply with such constraints. A feature such as [-native] cannot be seen as an etymological feature, but only as a non-historical property of words. A possible answer to this question is that non-native words tend to differ systematically from native ones in terms of their phonological make-up, and thus they are recognizable. Dutch non-native adjectives, for instance, are always polysyllabic and end in a stressed syllable (*absúrd* "absurd", *stabíel* "stable"). This makes them different from native adjectives that are either monosyllabic (*groen* "green") or end in an unstressed syllable (*zeker* "certain").

The choice of a particular affix may also be determined by the morphological make-up of the base. For instance, when we want to nominalize an English verb ending in -*ize*, the obvious choice is the suffix -*ation*, and not some other suffix such as -*ion* (*verbalization*, not **verbaliz-ion*). Adjectives in -*able* prefer the suffix -*ity* to -*ness*, hence *parsability*, not *parsableness*.

These are **base-driven restrictions** since it is the base that imposes constraints on the suffix to be attached.

Such base-driven restrictions show that the internal morphological structure of a complex word is accessible to morphological rules, whereas the internal structure of complex words is not accessible for rules of syntax (the Lexical Integrity Principle). Generally, the application of morphological rules may be sensitive to morphological structure. For example, conversion of nouns to verbs in English and Dutch applies to simplex nouns and compounds, but not to suffixed nouns.

An example of a semantic constraint is that the English suffix *un-* when applied to verbs, indicates the reversal of a situation, as in *unfold* and *unscrew*. Because of this meaning of *un-*, you cannot *unswim* or *unkill*. Or, as the teacher warned my neighbour when he was taught how to make proper holes in a flute, "*You can't undrill a hole*". This constraint should not be interpreted as a constraint on a specific word-formation process. The impossibility of *unkill* and similar verbs follows from the incompatibility between the meaning of the deverbal suffix *un-* and that of the base verb. In fact, there are possible worlds in which *kill* is not an irreversible action, and where *unkill* could be used. That is, *un-* imposes an interpretation of reversibility on the verb. This kind of semantic effect is called **type coercion**: the prefix forces the base verb to belong to a particular semantic type of verbs, and thus imposes a particular interpretation on the prefixed verb as a whole.

Derivational processes may also be subject to particular pragmatic, stylistic, or sociolinguistic constraints. The use of the diminutive suffix *-ie* in Dutch, as in the phrase *lekker soepie* "nice soup" and in *liev-ie* "love, darling" is characteristic of an informal register, or is used between lovers or in mother–child conversation. A more appropriate interpretation of these pragmatic limitations on certain derivational patterns is to consider them as linguistic means of defining the communicative situation.

3.4 Productivity

The notion **productivity** is used quite frequently in morphological descriptions of languages. It presupposes the idea of rule-governed morphological creativity, the ability of language users to create new well-formed complex words. Although this chapter deals with derivation, you should realize that the notion 'productivity' is also relevant in the domains of compounding and inflection. When we call a morphological pattern productive, we mean that this pattern can be extended to new cases, can be used to form new words. When we say that a morphological pattern is unproductive, this means that it is not used for coining new words. The formation of plural nouns by means of vowel change, as in English *foot–feet* has become obsolete, and is an example of unproductive morphology. The same applies to the use of vowel alternations for past tense verb formation in the Germanic languages. You have to learn which verbs exhibit which particular vowel alternation, and the pattern is almost never used for making the past tense of new verbs.

Within the class of productive morphological templates, we find differences in degree of productivity. Morphological patterns are not used to the same degree. The basic opposition presupposed in using the notion 'degree of productivity' is that between possible words and actual words. Leaving inflection aside for a moment, one might say that the word-formation templates of a language define the set of possible complex words of that language. Not all these possible words are also actual words, that is, belong to the lexical norm or convention of that language. For instance, my English dictionaries do not mention the verb *unblacken* although it is a possible word with a transparent meaning, "undoing the effect of blackening".

The degree of productivity of a word-formation pattern thus refers to the degree to which the structural possibilities of a word-formation pattern are actually used. This can be illustrated as follows. Both in German and in Dutch female nouns can be coined by means of suffixation, in German by means of suffixation with *-in*:

(21)   Dozent "teacher"   Dozent-in "female teacher"
      Minister "minister"   Minister-in "female minister"
      Professor "professor"   Professor-in "female professor"
      Student "student"   Student-in "female student"

Dutch has the same female suffix *-in*, and some other female suffixes as well. Yet, it does not have equivalent words for these German female nouns. A German speaker may begin his speech with the phrase *Liebe Hörerinnen und Hörer* "dear female listeners and listeners" whereas Dutch speakers will never say the equivalent, well-formed expression *Geachte toehoorsters en toehoorders*. This shows that German requires more awareness of there being a sex difference between the people addressed than Dutch that does not exploit this word-formation possibility very much. So you see it makes sense to say that certain morphological processes are more productive than others. The actual use of structural possibilities may have to do with language-external factors such as cultural habits and politeness rules. In addition, there are language-internal factors such as the existence of competing word-formation processes.

Morphological processes can lose their productivity in the course of time. The Dutch suffix *-lijk* "-able" used to be productive in earlier stages of Dutch, but has now become completely unproductive, and its role has been taken over by the synonymous suffix *-baar*. So the set of Dutch adjectives ending in *-lijk* has become a closed set of words that cannot be extended any more.

How can we measure the degree of productivity of a morphological pattern, and how can we rank the different patterns on a scale of productivity? We might count the number of different words (word types) of a certain morphological type, i.e. its **type frequency**, to be distinguished from the notion **token frequency**. The token frequency of a morphological class of words is the summed frequency of use of all the words of that particular type in a sample of language use. For example, if there are 100 different English adjectives in *-able* in a certain language sample, the type frequency of *-able* adjectives is 100, but the token frequency will be much higher because the individual adjectives in *-able* will have been used more than once.

Type frequency is best calculated on the basis of a large corpus instead of a dictionary. A **corpus** is a collection of data concerning actual language use, these days mainly in electronic form. A corpus is a better source of information than a dictionary. A dictionary is always lagging behind with respect to the use of productive morphological patterns because it only registers, after some lapse of time, which new complex words have become established words. Morphological productivity manifests itself most clearly in the appearance of complex words that never make it to the dictionary. However, a high type frequency of a morphological pattern, even when based on a proper corpus, does not tell us that much about degree of productivity: the class of words of that type may be a more or less closed set that is (almost) never expanded. Therefore, we need another way of computing productivity.

A basic property of a productive word-formation process is that it may lead to **hapaxes**, new word types that occur only once in the corpus, and clearly do not belong to the set of established words. Therefore, one might define the degree of productivity P of a particular morphological process as the proportion between the number of hapaxes of that type (n_1) to the total number of tokens N of complex words of that type in the sample (Baayen 1992: 115):

(22) $P = n_1/N$

The use of P as a measure of productivity is illustrated by the data in Table 3.1. These data are from the English Cobuild Corpus, a corpus of 18 million word forms of British English. N stands for the number of word tokens ending in these affixes, and V for the number of types. The table shows that the number of tokens in *-ity* is higher than that of the tokens in *-ness*. However, the number of types with *-ness* is higher, and—what is more important—the number of hapaxes as well. Hence, the suffix *-ness* is more productive than *-ity*. This is in accordance with the observation that the use of *-ity* is restricted to being attached to non-native stems, whereas *-ness* can be used with all kinds of stems. Whereas both *stability* and *stableness* are well-formed, we do not have a well-formed word *reddity* besides *redness*.

Table 3.1. *Productivity measure for the English suffixes* -ity *and* -ness

Affix	N	V	n_1	P
-ity	42,252	405	29	0.0007
-ness	17,481	497	77	0.0044

Source: Baayen 1992: 116.

   The data in this table concern two rival affixes with the same meaning. Thus it is possible to compare them because they have the same potential of being useful for the language user, and to rank them on a scale of productivity. However, it may be the case that an affix has a relatively high proportion of hapaxes in the set of token words with that affix, without that affix creating a lot of new words, simply because that kind of complex word is not very useful, has no high pragmatic potential. If we want to get a more precise idea of the contribution of a particular type of complex word to the growth of the lexicon, we might use another measure, referred to as the global productivity measure P*, which is the number of hapaxes of that morphological type in a given corpus divided by the total number of hapax words in that corpus. This measure gives us a ranking for all affixes on one scale, and indicates their relative contribution to the growth of the lexicon. Thus, we have at least three measures for quantifying three different aspects of productivity: the number of attested types (V), the potential to make new word types (P), and the actual contribution to the growth of the lexicon (P*).

The existence of rival affixes may also affect the token frequency of the corresponding types of complex word. Once a complex word with one of these affixes has been formed and established, the language user will tend not to use a rival process for creating another complex word with the same meaning. This is called the blocking effect. However, if the rival processes are very productive, blocking is not a very strong factor. As illustrated by the examples (20), pairs of complex words with exactly the same meaning are possible. In other cases, complex words with the same base exhibit semantic differences. For instance, there is a semantic difference between *admission* and *admittance*, both derived from the verb *to admit*. If there is such a difference, it is obvious that there cannot be a blocking effect.

3.5 Affix ordering

Complex words may contain more than one prefix or suffix, and we would therefore like to know which principles govern the order of affixes. Given the distinction between derivation and inflection (derivation creates lexemes, inflection creates forms of lexemes), we expect the following schema to apply, and this is indeed basically correct (although there are some complications, see Chapter 5):

(23) Inflectional prefixes—Derivational prefixes—Root—Derivational suffixes—
      Inflectional Suffixes

As to ordering restrictions within a sequence of derivational affixes, it is clear that the input constraints often predict which order is the correct one. For instance, the suffix order in *read-abil-ity* is determined by the fact that the suffix *-ity* selects adjectives as bases and creates nouns, whereas *-able* takes verbs as inputs in order to form adjectives. Therefore, *-able* must be attached before *-ity*.

Stratal restrictions account for the generalization that in Germanic languages native suffixes are peripheral with respect to non-native ones. As we saw, it is only non-native suffixes that require their inputs to be of a specific stratum, the non-native one. Native suffixes combine with both non-native and native inputs. Once a native suffix has been added to a stem, the new word is [+ native], which blocks the attachment of non-native suffixes. Therefore, the only possible order is: non-native root + non-native suffixes + native suffixes. For instance, the Dutch native suffix *-baar* "-able" can be attached to verbal stems ending in the non-native suffix *-iseer* (as in *stabiliseer-baar* "stabilizable"), but not vice versa: **drag-bar-iseer* "port-able-ize" is ill-formed because the non-native suffix *-iseer* has been added to a native stem.

Affix order might also be determined by the intended semantic scope of the affixes used. Thus, derivational affixes may appear in different order, with different interpretational effects, as illustrated here for Quechua which allows for both the suffix sequence *-schi-rpari-* and the suffix sequence *-rpari-schi-* (Muysken 1988: 267–8):

(24)   a.   llank'a-schi-rpari-n
            work-help-effect-3SG
            "He really helped him work"
       b.   qunqa-rpari-schi-wa-n
            forget-effect-help-1OBJ-3SG
            "He helped me forget completely"

The ordering of, in particular inflectional, affixes is sometimes described in terms of templates or position classes (Chapter 5).

Summary

Derivation is the formation of lexemes by means of affixation, conversion, reduplication, and root-and-pattern morphology. These different morphological operations serve a large number of semantic and syntactic functions, including that of valency change. Such derived words, once they are formed, may exhibit idiosyncratic properties. Word-formation templates function as redundancy statements with respect to established, listed complex words, which can be modelled by inheritance trees.

The application of a particular word-formation process may be governed by rule-specific and general input constraints with respect to syntactic, phonological, morphological, stratal, and semantic properties of the base words.

Morphological rules differ in their degree of quantitative productivity, which can be estimated by counting the number of hapaxes of the relevant morphological type in a sample of words.

An important topic of morphological analysis is the investigation of principles and constraints with respect to the ordering of affixes in a multiply complex word.

Questions

1. The English verb *to ride* has as its past tense form *rode*, whereas the past tense of the denominal verb *to joyride* is *joyrided*. Suppose that the use of vowel change for making past tense forms is triggered by the presence of a diacritic feature [+ ablaut]. How can the difference between *rode* and *joyrided* be explained?

2. The English suffix *-able* is of non-native, Romance origin. Can you provide evidence to prove that this suffix has become a native suffix in present-day English?

3. Do the following English denominal verbs form a problem for the Right-hand Head Rule for English: *enamour, encage, enchain, encircle, encourage, enfeeble*? (Bear in mind that possible words can form an intermediate stage in word-formation.)

4. The Italian default conjugation is that of verbs in *-are*, as can be seen in Italian loan verbs from English such as *dribblare* "to dribble" and *scioccare* "to shock". How can this fact be used for interpreting the formation of the Italian verb *invecchiare* in (6) as a case of prefixation only instead of considering it a case of parasynthetic word-formation?

5. A number of Dutch prefixed verbs have a corresponding noun without additional overt morphology. Such nouns, derived from prefixed verbs through conversion, are always neuter:

be-roep "to appeal"	beroep "appeal"
ge-bruik "to use"	gebruik "use"
onder-wijs "to teach"	onderwijs "teaching"
over-leg "to deliberate"	overleg "deliberation"
ver-val "to decay"	verval "decay"
ver-raad "to betray"	verraad "betrayal"

   Nouns derived from simplex verbs through conversion (such as *val* "fall"), however, tend to be non-neuter. Why are these facts a problem for a percolation account of gender assignment to complex nouns?

6. In Malagasy, reduplication is often used for attenuation or diminution. Thus, *fòtsifótsy* "white-white" means "whitish" (compare the simplex word *fótsy* "white"; Keenan and Polinsky 1998: 571). Do you think it is possible to explain this interpretation of reduplicated forms by means of the notion of 'iconicity'?

7. English has at least the following prefixes with some negative meaning: *de-*, *dis-*, *in-*, *non-*, and *un-*. Make a list of the (phonological, syntactic, semantic, and stratal) constraints that each of these prefixes imposes on its base words. What is the division of labour between these five prefixes?

8. a. In Polish, the diminutive suffix *-awy* can be attached to adjectives only, resulting in adjectives with the meaning "somewhat A", as in *czarny–czarnawy* "black–blackish" and *czerwony–czerwonawy* "red–reddish". Is this a counterexample to the RHR if that rule is assumed to be valid for Polish?

   b. This diminutive suffix cannot be attached to relational adjectives such as *domowy* "of a house" derived from *dom* "house", or *szkolny* "of a school" derived from *szkoła* "school". How might this be explained?

9. The English negative prefixes *a-* and *an-* borrowed from Greek can both be attached to adjectives. What determines the choice between these prefixes?

10. The relational adjective *American* can be modified by the adverb *very*, as in *a very American attitude*, or prefixed, as in *an un-American attitude*. What kind of change in the interpretation of *American* does this bring about?

Further reading

General discussions of constraints on word-formation are found in Aronoff (1976), Booij (1977, 2002*b*), Plank (1981), Plag (1999, 2003), Scalise (1984), and Rainer (2000). Plag (1999) advocates base-driven restrictions. Anderson (1992) defends the position that word-internal structure is inaccessible to morphology (the theory of A-morphous Morphology), whereas Carstairs-McCarthy (1993) defends the opposite view. A survey of cases of cross-categorial morphology is given in Plank (1981: 43–65).

The binyanim of Classical Hebrew are treated in Aronoff (1994) and Verheij (2000).

Bauer (2001) presents a survey and analysis of the discussions on the notion 'productivity'; quantitative measures of productivity are proposed in Baayen (1992, 1993). The different quantitative measures of productivity are also discussed in Plag (1999: ch 2) and in Baayen (2003).

Affix ordering is discussed in the framework of lexical phonology, in terms of so-called level ordering (cf. Fabb 1988; Plag 1996; Booij 2000). Affix ordering principles for English and German are discussed in Aronoff and Fuhrhop (2002), and in a number of articles in *YoM 2001*. Hay (2002) relates affix ordering restrictions in English to the degree of parsability of the affixes. Rice (2000) proposes semantic principles for affix order in Athapaskan languages.

4

Compounding

4.1 Compound types

In many languages, compounding (also called **composition**) is the most frequently used way of making new lexemes. Its defining property is that it consists of the combination of lexemes into larger words. In simple cases, compounding consists of the combination of two words, in which one word modifies the meaning of the other, the head. This means that such compounds have a binary structure. Here are some examples from a number of European languages:

(1)   Dutch   huis-vrouw "house wife"
      German   Rot-licht "red light"
      Greek   organo-pektis "instrument player, musician"
      Hungarian város-háza "city hall"
      Latin   perenni-servus "perennial slave, slave forever"

The productivity of compounding in many languages is largely due to its semantic transparency and versatility. When a new compound is formed, we already know the meaning of its constituents, and the only task we face is to find out about the semantic relation between the two parts. The general semantic pattern of a compound of the form XY is that it denotes a Y that has something to do with X, or vice versa, depending on the language. The exact nature of the semantic relation between the two constituents receives no formal expression, and is a matter of interpretation by the language user. As language users, we have to interpret that relationship on the basis of the meanings of the compound constituents, our knowledge of the world, and sometimes the context in which the compound is used. The role of context can be illustrated by a situation in which we tell a guest who enters the room and looks for a seat: *You may take the apple-juice chair*. This means that this person should take the seat at the table in front of which a glass of apple juice is standing (Downing 1977). The recently coined compound *butt call* denotes a call on your mobile phone from someone who calls you unintentionally by sitting on her/his own mobile phone and thus pressing a button. This is by nature a contextual compound, but even these can get lexicalized.

The process of compounding can be applied recursively, and thus we might get pretty long compounds. This is another cause of its productivity. A famous long compound is the German word *Donau-dampf-schiff-fahrts-gesellschaft* "lit. Danube-steam-ship-travel-company", the name of a shipping company that used to be active on the Danube; an English example is *White House travel office staff*. The structure of this latter compound can be represented as follows:

(2) [[[[White]$_A$ [House]$_N$]$_N$ [[travel]$_N$ [office]$_N$]$_N$]$_N$ [staff]$_N$]$_N$

Instead of labelled bracketing we may also use trees to represent the morphological structure of compounds. In the case of multiply complex words, this notation is easier for understanding the structure of a word. The tree representation of the compound in (2) is as shown in Figure 4.1.

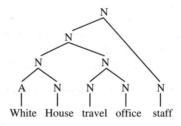

Fig. 4.1 Morphological tree of *White House travel office staff*

The morphological notion 'head' discussed in Chapter 3 is very relevant for the analysis of compounding. In Germanic languages like English, for instance, the right constituent of a compound is normally the head, and hence almost all compounds conform to the following scheme:

(3) $[X\,Y]_Y$, Y = N, A, V

As shown by words such as *underdog* and German *Um-welt* "lit. around-world, environment" (*um* "around" is a preposition), not only content words may occupy the non-head position *X*, but function words such as prepositions as well. As we will see shortly, phrases may also occur in the non-head position. Almost all compounds in these languages belong to one of the major lexical categories, in particular N and A. Compounds with a verbal head (Y = V) do occur, but are exceptional in Germanic languages.

The scheme in (3) indicates that the syntactic category of the compound as a whole is that of the right constituent. This also holds for subclass features, such as gender for nouns. In Dutch, the distinction between neuter and non-neuter gender manifests itself in the choice of the DEF.SG determiner (*het* and *de* respectively), and so we get pairs like the following:

(4) het soepvlees "the soup meat" (neuter)   de vleessoep "the meat soup" (non-neuter)
      het modefeest "the fashion party" (neuter)   de feestmode "the party fashion" (non-neuter)

The headedness of a compound is not only relevant for its formal properties, but also for its semantic interpretation. The compound *soepvlees* in (4), for example, denotes a particular kind of meat, not a particular kind of soup, whereas the inverse applies to the compound *vleessoep*. In other words, the left constituent of such compounds functions to modify the meaning of the head constituent.

The notion 'head' is also relevant for the application of inflectional rules, since it is the head that determines how the inflectional properties of the whole compound are realized. Since the Dutch noun *kind* "child" has the irregular plural form *kinderen*, this plural form recurs in the plural form of the compound *kleinkind* "grandchild", namely *kleinkinderen*. This is why the process of noun pluralization is sometimes called a **head operation**. An alternative interpretation of these facts is that the pluralization of a compound is determined by its paradigmatic relationship with its head noun. In this example, the compound *kleinkind* is then paradigmatically related to the noun pair *kind–kinderen* "child–children", and hence its plural is *kleinkinderen*.

Compounds are not universally right-headed since there are also languages with left-headed compounds. The following examples of left-headed compounds are from Maori, spoken in New Zealand (Bauer 1993: 518–20):

(5)   roro   hiko
      brain   electricity
      "computer"

      maarama   taka
      month   revolve
      "calendar"

      wai   mangu
      water   black
      "ink"

      whare   heihei
      house   hen
      "hen-house"

This difference with respect to the position of the head in compounds might suggest that the position of the head is a parametrical difference between languages. For Germanic languages, the value of the parameter is 'right', whereas it is 'left' for Maori.

Is it possible for a language to have both left-headed and right-headed compounds? Italian appears to have both left-headed compounds such as *capo-stazione* "lit. master station, station master" and *croce-rossa* "lit. cross red, red cross", and right-headed compounds such as *gentil-uomo* "kind man, gentleman" (Scalise 1992*a*). However, one could also interpret the left-headed compounds as lexicalized phrases. This interpretation is supported by the observation that the plural form of *capostazione* is *capistazione*, with an internal plural suffix -*i*. So the answer to the question raised in this paragraph depends on your criteria for word-hood. If we want to stick to the rule that inflection cannot appear word-internally, *capostazione* is a phrase (and thus Italian might be a language with right-headed compounds only), but if we think this is not a relevant criterion, it can be classified as a (left-headed) compound with inflection on its head *capo*, that is, a case of head inflection.

The scheme in (3) above is a bit too general for Germanic languages such as English, in that it predicts too many compounds to occur. A robust generalization for Germanic languages is that VV compounds such as *to freeze-dry*, AV compounds such as *to whitewash*, and NV compounds such as *to machine-wash* are pretty rare. They have often been coined through back formation from nominal compounds (*to babysit* from *babysitter*) or adjectival compounds (*to machine-wash* from *machine-washable*). Hence we have to specify which instantiations of (3) are well formed in a particular language, and which can be formed productively.

Another source of compound verbs is the conversion of nominal compounds into verbs. For instance, the Dutch nominal compound *voetbal* "soccer" has been converted into the verb *voetbal* "to play soccer". Note that this verb has no right verbal constituent as its head. Therefore, we have to specify for each language with right-headed compounds which particular combinations of lexical categories in scheme (3) can be used for coining compounds.

The left, non-head position X of scheme (3) allows for all kinds of constituents, and hence is left unspecified. Phrasal constituents need not be excluded from the left head position, as the following examples from English illustrate:

(6) [French history]$_{NP}$ teacher
[20th century]$_{NP}$ welfare state
[wages or employment]$_{NP}$ protection
['one size fits all']$_{S}$ mass production public service

It is obvious why phrases can only occur in the left, non-head position: if they appeared in the head position, such constructions would be phrases themselves, and not words. However, the possibility for phrases to appear within compounds does not mean that all kinds of phrases are allowed in this position. Definite NPs with a determiner are clearly excluded, as illustrated by the ungrammaticality of the phrase *a [the French history] teacher*.

Compounds with a head are called **endocentric compounds**. The term 'endocentric' means that the category of the whole (syntactic or morphological) construction is identical to that of one of its constituents. There are also **exocentric compounds** for which this is not the case. Consider Romance compounds consisting of a verbal stem followed by a plural noun (Scalise 1992*a*; Rainer and Varela 1992):

(7) Italian   porta-lettere "lit. carry letters, postman"
        lava-piatti "lit. wash dishes, dish washer"
    Spanish   lanza-cohetes "lit. launch rockets, rocket launcher"
        limpia-botas "lit. clean boots, bootblack"

These compounds are nouns, but there is no head. In this respect, they are comparable to English compounds like *pickpocket* and *cut-throat* that also lack a head. The plural nominal constituents do not function as heads. For instance, *portalettere* does not denote certain kinds of letters. The left constituent is a verb in its stem-form. The nouns in the right position of these compounds have plural endings, whereas the compounds themselves are neutral with respect to number, and can be used both as singular and as plural forms. Therefore, these nouns cannot be the heads of the compounds of which they form a part. So this kind of compound is a clear case of exocentric compounding.

A special semantic interpretation is required for compounds such as German *Kahlkopf* "lit. bald-head, person with a bald head", and English *blue-stocking*. In these cases, the compound denotes the person who is in possession of the entity mentioned by the compound. The traditional term for compounds with this special interpretation, taken from Sanskrit, is **bahuvrihi-compound**. They are sometimes considered to form a subset of the exocentric compounds, since they do not refer to the entity mentioned by the head of the compound: a *baldhead* is not a type of head. However, this special use is not unique for compounds. When a teacher wants to address a pupil whose name she does not know, she might say: *That red sweater should shut up*, meaning that the pupil with the red sweater should keep his mouth closed. Hence, this use of compounds appears to be a conventionalized use of words, in which the word for a part denotes the whole (pars-pro-toto). Therefore, we do not have to consider them as a special structural category. The conventional interpretation might however influence its formal behaviour. The Dutch bahuvrihi-compound *spleet-oog* "slit-eye" is used to refer to people of Chinese appearance. Its gender is non-neuter, although its head *oog* "eye" is a neuter noun. So the formal gender class of the head noun is overruled by the special semantic interpretation of this compound.

Another type of bahuvrihi-compounds is exemplified by the Latin adjectival compounds *auri-com-us* "having golden hair" and *magn-anim-us* "magnanimous". Here the noun *aurum* "gold" and the adjective *magnus* "great" combine with a noun (*coma* "hair" and *animus* "soul" respectively) into a compound that is an adjective (Oniga 1992). The exocentricity of these compounds cannot be explained in terms of semantic interpretation in the same way as *baldhead*, because they behave formally as adjectives, although there is no adjectival head.

A special class of compounds is formed by **copulative compounds**. In these compounds there is no semantic head, and the relation between the constituent is a relation of coordination. Examples of such compounds are the Sanskrit **dvanda compounds**, and similar compounds in Punjabi (Olsen 2001; Bhatia 1993: 320):

(8) candrā-dityā-u
     moon-sun-DUAL
     "the moon and the sun"

     devā-sura-s
     god-demon-PL
     "three or more gods and demons"

     raat-din "night and day"
     maa-pio "mother and father"
     sukh-dukh "happiness and sorrow"

These compounds function as dual or plural expressions, and are therefore quite similar to NPs with coordination, which also receive a plural interpretation.

   Copulative compounds also occur in European languages, as illustrated by the following words:

(9) German   Österreich-Ungarn "Austria and Hungary"
              Fürstbischof "prince and bishop"
     English blue-green, washer-dryer
     Dutch   rood-wit-blauw "red-white-blue"

The last example is an adjectival compound with three constituents of semantically equal status. Yet, it is only the last of the three constituents that receives the inflectional ending -e in attributive position (as in *rood-wit-blauw-e vlag* "red-white-blue flag"), which shows that this is not a case of syntactic coordination of words. If that were the case, all adjectives would be inflected, as in *rode-witte-blauwe vlag*. However, the copulative compounds in (9) are different from dvanda compounds because their number is singular. A *Fürstbischof* is a person who is simultaneously a prince and a bishop, and this word does not refer to a combination of persons. Therefore, such compounds are sometimes classified as **appositive compounds**.

4.2 Compounds and phrases

An important issue in the analysis of compounds is their demarcation from phrasal expressions. There are two reasons why it is not always easy to distinguish the two. First, phrases can have the same function as words, that of labels for name-worthy categories. Secondly, phrases and compounds look quite similar because compound patterns often derive historically from phrasal word combinations.

Let us now have a look at formal correlates of the distinction between compounds and phrases. The German word for "red cabbage" is the Adjective–Noun compound *Rotkohl*, whereas Dutch uses the NP *rode kool* to express the notion "red cabbage". In this example it is not difficult to see that the Dutch expression is a phrase, since the adjective is inflected (the stem *rod-* "red" is followed by the inflectional ending *-e*). This type of inflection is a case of **agreement**: the adjective has to agree with the noun that it modifies for properties such as gender, number, and definiteness. The German expression, on the other hand, is a compound because the adjective *Rot* is not inflected (compare this to the German noun phrase *ein rot-er Kohl* "a red cabbage", with the adjectival ending *-er*). This reasoning presupposes that word-internal constituents cannot be affected by a syntactically conditioned rule such as agreement. Independent evidence for the different status of German *Rotkohl* compared to Dutch *rode kool* is found in the stress differences between these expressions. In German and Dutch noun phrases, main stress is normally on the head, whereas in nominal compounds main stress is on the non-head. Indeed, the main stress locations are different: *Rótkòhl* (compound stress) versus *ròde kóol* (phrasal stress). In English there is no adjectival inflection of this kind, and hence stress is the only criterion that we can use to distinguish phrases from compounds. Thus, we consider *bláckbòard* a compound, and *blàck bóard* a phrase.

This use of A + N phrases as labels for categories implies a certain formal restriction: the adjective cannot be modified. A phrase such as *heel rode kool* "very red cabbage" cannot function to classify *kool* "cabbage". This latter phrase functions as a description instead of a name for a particular kind of cabbage.

The potential functional equivalence of compounds and phrases of the Adjective + Noun type is particularly clear in the case of noun phrases with relational adjectives. Consider the following data from English (Levi 1978: 38):

(11)   a.   atom bomb   b.   atomic bomb
            industry output   industrial output
            language skills   linguistic skills
            city parks   urban parks
            ocean life   marine life

We see NN compounds in the left, and AN phrases in the right column. The adjectives used are denominal relational adjectives. We consider the expressions in the right column as phrases because they carry main stress on their right constituent. The last two examples illustrate that these relational adjectives do not necessarily have to be the adjectival derivatives of nouns: *urban*, for instance, is the only available relational adjective for expressing the meaning "related to cities". These relational adjectives can normally only be used in attributive position. We can speak of *urban parks* or *rural police*, but not of *parks that are urban* or *police that is rural* (we might, however, speak of *parks that are urban in nature*). In sum, AN phrases with relational adjectives are functionally equivalent to NN compounds. Yet, these two constructions have to be kept apart as far as their formal properties are concerned, as phrases versus compounds.

Another illustration of this demarcation problem are the so-called genitive compounds in English of the type *women's magazine, girls' school, Down's syndrome* and *Murphy's law*. These expressions must be considered phrases given the presence of the internal inflectional suffix or clitic *-s*. Yet, they function in the same way as compounds. These expressions instantiate a lexicalized syntactic pattern that functions to create new labels. Note also that many of these expressions have main stress on their first constituent, just like English compounds: *Dówn's syndrome* and *Múrphy's law*. We therefore assume an idiomatic pattern or **constructional idiom** *N's N* for English that serves to create new lexical expressions. A constructional idiom is a fixed syntactic pattern in which some positions may be filled by all kinds of words of the right category, whereas other positions are filled by specific morphemes or words. In this case, there is only one morpheme lexically specified, the morpheme *-s*. The two N positions are variable, and can be filled by all sorts of noun.

Certain lexical expressions in Romance languages are sometimes incorrectly called compounds although they have in fact a phrasal form. This applies to French *salle à manger* "dining room" and *chambre d'hôtes* "guest room". The structures *N à N* and *N de N* are instantiations of the syntactic structure [N PP]$_{NP}$, a noun phrase consisting of a head N followed by a PP complement, and have developed into constructional idioms. Such phrases are functionally equivalent to compounds in Germanic languages, and that is why the mistake is made to consider them compounds. Note, however, that their plural forms are *salle-s à manger* and *chambre-s d'hôtes* respectively, with an internal plural ending. This proves their phrasal nature since the plural form of a French word is expressed by a suffix at its right edge. Another type of apparent French compound is *homme-grenouille* "lit. man frog, frogman". Its plural form requires both constituents to be pluralized (*hommes-grenouilles*) which suggests that we have to do with an NP in which the phrasal head is followed by a noun with an appositional function.

The word-or-phrase problem also shows up in the formal analysis of **separable complex verbs**. These are verbal expressions that look like verbal compounds, but do not have the formal status of words since their constituents can be separated in syntax. Consider the following Hungarian noun–verb combinations (Kiefer 1992):

(**12**) levelet   ír
       letter   write
       "be engaged in letter writing"

       újságot   olvas
       newspaper   read
       "be engaged in newspaper reading"

       tévét   néz
       television   watch
       "be engaged in television watching"

Similar separable complex verbs occur in Dutch:

(**13**) stof   zuigen
       dust   suck
       "to vacuum-clean"

       bier   brouwen
       beer   brew
       "to brew beer"

       piano   spelen
       piano   play
       "to play the piano"

These Hungarian and Dutch expressions are different from regular verb phrases in that the object NP is a bare noun and cannot be preceded by a determiner. This makes them look like verbal compounds. However, these expressions are phrasal in that they can be split in certain syntactic contexts. In Hungarian, the negative particle *nem* "not" can appear between the noun and the verb:

(**14**)   Levelet nem ír "He is not engaged in letter writing"

In the case of the Dutch separable complex verbs, their phrasal nature can be concluded from the fact that the participle prefix *ge-* does not appear before the particle, but in between the particle and the verb. The relevant participles of the verbs mentioned above are *stof-ge-zog-en, bier-ge-brouw-en* and *piano-ge-speel-d* respectively.

Phrasal patterns with a word-like function such as these separable complex verbs can be qualified as constructional idioms. The constructional idiom 'bare Noun + V' in Hungarian and Dutch has the specific meaning "to be engaged in a particular institutionalized activity" (such as writing letters or playing the piano). Such constructional idioms may serve the same function as morphological patterns: expanding the set of lexical units of a language. Recall that the concept of constructional idiom is also applicable to the cases of apparent compounds in French discussed above. These are syntactic patterns such as *N de N*, with open positions for the nouns, and a fixed preposition *de*, patterns that can be used to coin new expressions to designate classes of entities.

4.3 Compounds and derived words

The crucial distinction between compounds and derived words is that in compounds each of the constituents is a form of a lexeme, whereas derivation involves affixes, that is, non-lexemic morphemes. However, the distinction is not always so clear-cut, because a lexeme may develop into a derivational morpheme. An example is the Dutch noun *boer* "farmer" that occurs in complex words such as the following:

(15)   groente-boer "lit. greens farmer, green-grocer"
       melk-boer "lit. milk farmer, dairy man"
       sigaren-boer "lit. cigars farmer, cigar seller"
       tijdschriften-boer "lit. magazines farmer, magazine seller"

In the first two examples, the original meaning of "farmer" still makes some sense since farmers may sell their produce such as greens and dairy. However, these words are nowadays used to refer to persons who sell vegetables or dairy without producing these goods themselves. The last two examples show even more clearly that the morpheme *boer* has developed into a morpheme with the meaning "seller", but only in combination with another noun. Hence, we may conclude that *boer* has developed into a suffix. In fact, many affixes derive from lexemes. An example of a prefix that derives from a lexeme is Dutch *oud* "old" that has the meaning "former, ex-" when added to a noun as in *oud-burgemeester* "ex-mayor". Note that this word cannot receive the interpretation "old mayor". The phenomenon of lexemes becoming affixes is a cross-linguistically widespread phenomenon, and an instance of **grammaticalization**, the historical process in which lexical morphemes become grammatical ones. Grammatical morphemes are either function words or bound morphemes. Affix-like morphemes such as *boer* and *oud* that still correspond to a lexeme are called **affixoids**.

The boundary between compounding and derivation is also blurred in the domain of neo-classical compounding. In this kind of compounding one or both of the constituents of a word are roots borrowed from Greek and Latin that do not correspond to lexemes, so-called combining forms. Consider the following English words:

(16)   a. bio-logy, psycho-logy, socio-logy, geo-graphy, tomo-graphy
       b. tele-camera, tele-graph, tele-gram, tele-kinesis, tele-matics, tele-phone, tele-vision
       c. bureau-crat, magneto-metry, magneto-hydro-dynamic

The examples in (16a) consist of two combining forms. Combining forms are divided into initial combining forms (*bio-, psycho-, socio-, geo-, tomo-*), and final combining forms (*-logy, -graphy*). The root *graph* is found as a final combining form in *telegraph* in (16b). There is also a lexeme *graph*, a word used in mathematics. However, the lexeme *graph* has a specific mathematical meaning that does not show up in *telegraph*.

Neo-classical compounds are different from normal compounds in that the meanings of the constituent parts cannot be derived from the meaning of corresponding lexemes. For instance, when a language user is able to assign the meaning "life" to the morpheme *bio-*, this is either based on comparison of a number of words that begin with *bio-* (in the same way in which we discover the meaning of affixes), or because she has been taught this at school, maybe since she took Ancient Greek as a subject. The reason why we call such words neo-classical compounds is that in most cases they have not been borrowed as a whole directly from the classical languages Greek and Latin. Instead, they have been coined in the course of time by combining these root morphemes which the language user can discover through comparison of existing already existing complex words. In fact, neo-classical compounding has given rise to a huge pan-European lexicon. European languages share huge parts of the set of neo-classical compounds which are used in science, government, culture, and business.

The example *tele-camera* in (16b) shows that an initial combining form can also combine with words. We are not always sure if the second constituent is a lexeme or a combining form that corresponds in form to a lexeme. In the case of *television*, for instance, there is a lexeme *vision*, but this lexeme has a more specific meaning than just "sight" (the meaning of *-vision* as a combining form). The same applies to *graph*, as pointed out in the preceding paragraph. This is why English dictionaries may have two entries, one for *-graph* as a combining form, and one for *graph* as a word.

The words in (16c) show that there are also cases in which a lexeme is followed by a final combining form. In *bureaucrat*, the first constituent *bureau* is a lexeme, unlike *-crat*. The word *magneto-metry* is another instantiation of this pattern since there is a lexeme *magnet*. Note, however, that the form of the lexeme *magnet* is special in that it is followed by the linking vowel *o*. Indeed, most words when used in the first position of a neo-classical compound have a linking vowel. The word *magneto-hydro-dynamic* shows that we also find neo-classical compounds with more than two constituents.

Final combining forms such as *-logy* and *-graphy* are perhaps not to be considered as one, but as two morphemes since they lend themselves to further morphological analysis, and may be divided into *log-y* and *graph-y* respectively, as suggested by a comparison with words such as *bio-log-ist* and *geo-graph-er*.

When a combining form is combined with a lexeme, the lexeme is usually taken from the non-native stratum of the lexicon. This is particularly the case for final combining forms. For instance, the Dutch neo-classical compound *hond-o-loog* "dog specialist" derived from the native word *hond* "dog" is felt as a jocular type of word-formation. However, initial combining forms such as the Greek roots *eco-* and *tele-* are often attached to native words as well, as illustrated here for Dutch:

(17)   eco-ontbijt "eco-breakfast"
       eco-paddestoel "eco-mushroom"
       eco-sigaret "eco-cigarette"
       tele-leren "tele-learning"
       tele-werken "tele-working"
       tele-winkelen "tele-shopping"

One might conclude from such data that these initial combining forms have become prefixes.

A lot of initial combining forms have been created by means of truncation. A good example is the pan-European initial combining form *euro-* that is a truncation of the word *Europa*. Other examples of such truncations are *afro-*, *compu-*, *crea-*, *cine-*, *cyber-*, *digi-*, *docu-*, and *flexi-* that are all used very productively to coin new words in most European languages.

In short, neo-classical compounding is a very important source of new words, even though it does not combine lexemes, and therefore does not possess the same degree of semantic transparency as regular compounds.

The observations on neo-classical compounding in the preceding paragraphs all lead to the conclusion that it is not always easy or possible to decide if a complex word is a case of compounding or of derivation.

4.4 Interfixes and allomorphy

When lexemes are used as building blocks of compounds, they may exhibit a special form. This is the case for Greek compounds: in most cases the first constituent ends in the vowel /o/ which is added to the stem-form of the lexeme. These vowels are clearly different from the inflectional endings that appear in the corresponding words (Ralli 1992: 145, 153):

(18)   pag-o-vuno "ice mountain, ice berg" < pag-os "ice", vun-o "mountain"
       psom-o-tiri "bread (and) cheese" < psom-i "bread", tir-i "cheese"
       sime-o-stolizmos "flag decoration" < sime-a "flag", stolizm-os "decoration"

Such vowels, which are called **interfixes** or **linking elements**, do not contribute a meaning of their own to the word as a whole, but only function to create stem-forms that are suitable for being used in compounds. Phonologically, they belong to the first constituent of the compound. This can be concluded from the division of such words into syllables: when possible, these vowels form a syllable together with the last consonant of the first stem, for instance *pa.go.vu.no* (the dots indicate syllable boundaries). If the linking element did not belong phonologically to the first stem, we would have expected the syllabification pattern *pag.o.vu.no*. The appearance of these linking elements can be interpreted as a case of **stem allomorphy**, the phenomenon that stems may have more than one phonological form. The selection of a particular allomorph is governed by the morphological context. In the case of Greek compounds, we thus have to state that the stem allomorph that ends in *-o* has to be used as first constituent of such words.

Stem allomorphy is also found in Dutch compounds. Consider the following cases (Booij 2002*a*: 178–80):

(19) schaap "sheep"   schaap-herder "shepherd"
                          schaap-s-kop "sheep's head"
                          schap-en-vlees "lit. sheep's meat, mutton"
       kind "child"   kind-er-wagen "lit. children's cart, pram"
       koningin "queen"   koninginn-e-dag "Queen's birthday"

These examples illustrate the use of the linking elements *-s*, *-e* (mostly spelt as *-en*), and -er. Historically, these are mainly inflectional endings. For instance, *-s* derives from a genitive suffix *-s*, and *-er* is an old plural suffix that is still used as such in German. The *-e* is historically either a case suffix or the last vowel of the stem. Synchronically, these linking elements no longer have the status of inflectional suffixes. Since they belong phonologically to the first stem, we may say that, for instance, the lexeme SCHAAP has three stem allomorphs: *schaap-*, *schaaps-*, and *schape-*. When a native speaker of Dutch coins new compounds, the choice of a particular allomorph will often be based on analogy. Since we have *koninginnedag*, we will also opt for the schwa-final allomorph in a new compound such as *koninginne-hoed* "queen's hat". In the case of SCHAAP, however, all three allomorphs may be chosen. The morphological structure of the left constituent may also play a role. For instance, Dutch diminutive nouns, which end in *-je*, are always followed by the linking element *-s* when used as the first constituent of a compound:

(20) meisje-s-lijk "girl's corpse", *meisje-lijk
       dagje-s-mens "day tripper", *dagje-mens
       rijtje-s-huis "row house", *rijtje-huis

Dutch has a plural suffix *-s* as well. However, the *-s* in these compounds cannot be interpreted as a plural suffix, given their meaning. For instance, *meisjeslijk* denotes the corpse of only one girl, and *dagjesmens* denotes a person who takes a one-day trip.

The choice of stem allomorph in Dutch compounds is also constrained by a paradigmatic factor: one can only choose the schwa-final allomorph (spelt with final *-en*) if the plural suffix for the relevant noun is the suffix *-en*. The appearance of the linking element *-s* is not subject to such a constraint. The following data illustrate this regularity:

(21)   *Noun*   *Plural form*   *Compound*
   varken "pig"   varken-s   varken-s-vlees "pig's meat", *varken-e-vlees
   leraar "teacher" lerar-en   leraar-s-salaris "teacher's salary",
                                                lerar-en-vergadering "teachers' meeting"

The use of linking elements is not restricted to nominal compounds. In Spanish the vowel *i* can be used as an interfix in coordinative adjectival compounds (Rainer and Varela 1992: 132):

(22)   roj-i-blanco "red and white" < rojo "red", blanco "white"
      clar-i-vidente "clairvoyant" < clar-o "clear", vidente "seeing"

This kind of stem allomorphy is thus a variation in the shape of morphemes that is not governed by the phonology of a language, but is regulated by its morphology.

4.5 Synthetic compounds and noun incorporation

Consider the following English nominal compounds of which the head is a deverbal noun:

(23)   sword-swallower, heart-breaker, church-goer, money-changer, typesetter

These compounds pose some analytical questions. First, some of the nominal heads such as *swallower* and *goer* do not occur as words of their own. These are possible, but not established English words. Thus, these words show that possible words can function as building blocks in word-formation. One might also argue that these words are derived by attaching the suffix -*er* to the verbal compounds *sword-swallow, heart-break*, etc. This alternative analysis is inadequate because verbal compounding is not a productive process in English, and hence does not license the possible words *sword-swallow* or *heart-break*. What we see here is that the use of one word-formation process, nominal compounding, implies the use of another word-formation process, deverbal nominalization with -*er*, which provides possible words like *swallower* and *breaker*. These words are then used as the heads of nominal compounds. The term **synthetic compounding** is trad-itionally used to indicate that this kind of word-formation looks like the simultaneous use of compounding and derivation. This instance of simultaneous use can be expressed through the conflation of the English morphological templates for NN compounds and deverbal nouns into the following one:

(24) $[[N] [V\text{-}er]_N]_N$

Such conflation of compounding and derivation is also found for other types of word-formation, as illustrated by *blue-eyed*, in which AA compounding is conflated with the formation of denominal adjectives (note that *eyed* itself is not an established word of English).

The second special property of the compounds in (23) is that the left constituent fulfils a specific semantic role with respect to the verbal base of the right constituent. For instance, in *sword swallower*, the constituent *sword* functions as the Patient-argument of *swallow*, the verbal base of the head noun. In order to understand this semantic regularity, we must look in more detail at how semantic roles are linked to verbs. Verbs assign specific semantic roles to the NPs that they occur with in a clause. The verb *to swallow* may occur with two NPs, one with the role of **Agent** (the controller of the action), and one with the role of **Patient** (the entity that undergoes the action mentioned by the verb). NPs that receive a semantic role from a verb are called the **arguments** of that verb. Similarly, in the synthetic compound *church goer*, the constituent *church* fulfils the semantic role of Goal with respect to the verbal base *go* of the head noun *goer* because *to go* assigns the semantic role of Goal. The question thus arises how we account for this semantic relationship between the left noun and the verbal base of the right noun.

Is it possible to consider these words to be cases of *-er*-affixation to VPs such as *to swallow swords*? If this were possible, we would have explained why the left nouns in these compounds have the same semantic roles as those they receive in verb phrases. The answer is negative. This guess may look adequate, but from a formal point of view it is a hopeless idea. First, in the compound, the word *sword* appears in its bare form, as a stem, which is impossible in a phrase: *to swallow sword. Secondly, the word order would be wrong. In English VPs the syntactic object follows the verb, but in *sword swallower* the opposite order is found. Therefore, it is a better option to analyse these words as regular compounds, with the special property that the argument structure of the verbal base is inherited by the derived noun with the suffix *-er*. Thus, the head noun can assign a semantic role such as Patient or Goal to the left constituent.

As mentioned before, most Germanic languages do not have productive processes for verbal compounding. However, English gerund forms and Dutch infinitival forms of verbs do occur as the heads of compounds:

(25)   *English*: mountain-climbing, word-processing
       Dutch: hard-lopen "fast walking", wedstrijd-zwemmen "competition swimming"

These words, however, do not have finite forms, and the sentence *I went mountain-climbing* is much better than *I mountain-climb every Saturday* (Mithun 1984: 847). Speakers of Dutch use the periphrastic progressive construction to solve the problem caused by the lack of finite forms, as in *Ik ben aan het hardlopen* "I am fast-walking" (compare the ungrammatical sentence **Ik hard-loop* "I fast-walk"). In another Germanic language, Frisian, occasionally new NV compounds with finite forms do occur (Dyk 1997: 29):

(26)   Hja bôle-bakt al jieren met njocht
       she loaf-bakes already years with pleasure
       "She bakes loaves already for many years with pleasure"

The combination of a noun and a verb into a verbal compound is usually called **noun incorporation**. It is used primarily to form verbs that express an institutionalized activity. These incorporated nouns do not denote specific objects, they are non-referential. In example (26), the noun *bôle* does not refer to a specific loaf, but to loaves in general. Hence such incorporated nouns are non-referential.

The difference between a verb phrase with an NP and noun incorporation is illustrated by the following example from the Micronesian language Ponapean (Mithun 1984: 850):

(27)   a.   I kanga-la wini-o
            I eat-COMP medicine-that
            "I took all that medicine"
       b.   I keng-winih-la
            I eat-medicine-COMP
            "I completed my medicine-taking"

In (27b) we see a case of noun incorporation. It has a different meaning than (27a), which has a syntactically independent object *wini-o*. In (27b), with an incorporated and non-referential object *winih-*, the sentence indicates completion of the action of medicine taking, while there may be medicine left.

Typically, the nouns in these cases of incorporation are unmarked for definiteness, number or case, and the verbal compound behaves as an intransitive verb, whereas its verbal head is transitive. Thus, noun incorporation often has the effect of creating verbs with reduced syntactic valency:

since the Patient-argument of the verb is expressed by the incorporated noun, this argument will no longer receive an independent syntactic expression.

Summary

Compounds are combinations of two or more lexemes. In many languages this word-formation process is used frequently because of its semantic transparency and versatility. The boundary between compounds and phrasal lexical expressions is not always clear. Diagnostics for the phrasal status of lexical expressions are internal inflection, and the splittability of their constituents.

The distinction between compounding and derivation is sometimes blurred because lexemes as parts of compounds may receive specialized interpretations. Such compound constituents are affix-like, since affixes also depend on occurring as part of complex words for them to receive a proper semantic interpretation. The use of Greek and Latin roots for neo-classical word-formation also relativizes the distinction between compounding and word-derivation, because classical roots that are not lexemes might be considered affixes.

Stem allomorphy is a recurrent phenomenon in compounding. The choice of a particular linking element may be determined by paradigmatic factors such as analogy to existing compounds and the shape of the plural form of the corresponding lexeme.

Synthetic compounding can be seen as the simultaneous use of compounding and derivational morphology in coining a new compound. The semantic role of the non-head in these compounds may be determined by the argument structure of the verbal base of the head noun. Noun incorporation is a similar process.

Questions

1. Which categories of words can combine in English compounds? What restrictions on possible combinations of categories do you observe?

2. Give the complete morphological structure the following English compounds: *recreation hall, book keeping, truck driver, pickpocket, underdog, homegrown*.

3. Dutch appears to make use of noun incorporation, as illustrated by the following verbal compounds (Weggelaar 1986):

   klapper-tand "to have chattering teeth" < *klapper* "to rattle", *tand* "tooth"
   stamp-voet "to stamp one's feet" < *stamp* "to stamp", < *voet* "feet".

   What problem do these compounds pose for the Right-hand Head Rule which is normally applicable to Dutch compounds?

4. Consider the following recently coined words ending in *gate* coined on analogy to *Watergate: Irangate, Monicagate, nipplegate*. These three words denote scandals. Are these words cases of compounding, or of derivation? Explain your answer.

5. Compare the following two sentences from Yucatec, a Mexican language (Mithun 1984: 858):

   a. k-in-č'ak-Ø-k   če' ičil in-kool
       INCOMP-I-chop-it-IMPF   tree in   my-cornfield
       "I chop the tree in my cornfield"
   b. k-in-č'ak-če'-t-ik   in-kool
       INCOMP-I-chop-tree-tr-IMPF   my-cornfield
       "I clear my cornfield"

   Explain the differences in interpretation between these two almost identical sentences.

6. Compare the following two adjective–noun combinations in Modern Greek:

   [aghri-o]$_A$ [ghat-os]$_N$ "wild cat" < aghri- "wild" + ghatos "cat"
   [psixr-os]$_A$ [polem-os]$_N$ "cold war" < psixros "cold" + polemos "war"

   In the first example, there is a linking element *o*, and only an inflectional ending on the second word; in the second AN combination, both constituents are inflected. How can this difference in inflectional behaviour be explained?

7. Consider the following Italian verb–noun compound: [[spazza]$_V$[camino]$_N$]$_N$ "lit. sweep chimney, chimney sweep(er)". Is this an endocentric or an exocentric compound?

8. Try to specify the semantic relation between the two constituents of the recently coined English compounds *bear jam, deprivation cuisine, flash mob, information pollution, man breasts, office creeper, salad dodger*. Which of them cannot be interpreted easily on the basis of the meanings of their constituent words? (source www.wordspy.com).

9. In Punjabi, there are noun–noun compounds that denote the superordinate semantic category of the two nouns involved (Bhatia 1993: 320):

   hatth-pair "body" < hatth "hand", pair "feet"
   múú-nakk "face" < múú "mouth", nakk "nose"
   bas-kaar "vehicle" < bas "bus", kaar "car"

   What problem do these compounds pose for the hypothesis that compounds always have one of their constituents as a head?

10. Which formal processes are involved in the formation of the following complex words in Punjabi (Bhatia 1993: 322)?

paanii "water"	paanii-shaanii "water and the like"
kamm "work"	kamm-shamm "work and the like"
gapp "silly talk"	gapp-shapp "silly talk and the rest"
ultaa "conflicting nonsense"	ultaa-shultaa "conflicting and other nonsense"

Further reading

For a survey of types of compounding, see Olsen (2000, 2001); a survey of compounding in a number of European languages is given in Scalise (1992*b*). A number of articles on separable complex verbs can be found in *YoM 2003*. The problem of stem selection is discussed in Aronoff (1994). The role of analogy in selecting a linking element for Dutch compounds is shown in Krott (2001).

There is a wealth of literature on synthetic compounds. Botha (1984) provides a survey of the debate. Specific contributions to the debate are Selkirk (1982), Hoeksema (1985), Booij (1988), and Hoekstra and van der Putten (1988). For different views of noun incorporation, see Mithun (1984, 1999, 2000) and Rosen (1989) for a lexical/morphological, and Baker (1988, 1996, 2001) for a syntactic analysis.

Part III

Inflection

5

Inflection

5.1 Inflectional properties

Inflection is the morphological marking of properties on a lexeme resulting in a number of forms for that lexeme, a set of grammatical words. In the example given in section 2.1, the inflection of the Polish lexeme KOT, each form of the lexeme has properties with respect to two inflectional dimensions, number and case. These two inflectional dimensions for nouns are found in many languages. The dimensions are referred to as **morphosyntactic categories** because they may play a role both in morphology and in syntax. For each dimension or category, there is more than one value. In the case of Polish nouns, there are two values for NUMBER: SINGULAR and PLURAL, and seven different values for CASE: NOMINATIVE, GENITIVE, DATIVE, ACCUSATIVE, INSTRUMENTAL, LOCATIVE, and VOCATIVE. These values are referred to as **morphosyntactic features**. A particular cell in the paradigm of KOT is thus filled with a word form with a specific set of morphosyntactic features. The nominative plural form *koty* "cats" can be represented as follows:

(1) kot-y NUMBER: PLURAL
           CASE: NOMINATIVE

Another category of words that plays a prominent role in inflection are verbs, which are often inflected for categories such as TENSE, ASPECT, and

Table 5.1. *Indicative forms of the Latin verb* laudāre

	INDICATIVE PRESENT	INDICATIVE IMPERFECT	INDICATIVE PERFECT
1SG	laudō	laudābam	laudāvi
2SG	laudās	laudābas	laudāvisti
3SG	laudat	laudābat	laudāvit
1PL	laudāmus	laudābāmus	laudāvimus
2PL	laudātis	laudābātis	laudāvistis
3PL	laudant	laudābant	laudāvērunt

MOOD. Some of us have been introduced to this kind of inflectional morphology through textbooks on Latin that present the whole set of verbal forms in a number of paradigms. A part of the paradigm of *laudare* "to praise" as presented in such textbooks is given in Table 5.1 (the makron over the vowel letter indicates length). The three labels PRESENT, IMPERFECT, and PERFECT are the traditional labels for these Latin verbal forms (cf. section 6.2). Each of these forms expresses a property for the categories TENSE, ASPECT, and MOOD. For instance, the form *laudat* "he praises" has the following values for these three verbal categories (in addition, it has values for the number and person of the subject of this verb):

(2) laud-a-t TENSE: PRESENT
               ASPECT: IMPERFECTIVE
               MOOD: INDICATIVE
               NUMBER: SINGULAR
               PERSON: 3

The following list presents a (non-exhaustive) survey of the different types of morphosyntactic information that are found as morphological markings on nouns, verbs, and adjectives in the languages of the world:

(3) *Nouns*: Number (singular, plural, dual, etc.), Case (nominative, genitive, accusative, etc.), Definiteness, Gender;
    Verbs: Tense (present, past, future), Aspect (imperfective, perfective, etc.), Mood (indicative, subjunctive, imperative, etc.), Voice (active, passive, etc.), Number (singular, plural, etc.), Person (first, second, third), Gender;
    Adjectives: Degree (positive, comparative, superlative), Number, Gender, Case, Definiteness.

The category Voice for verbs comprises distinctions such as that between active and passive voice. The Latin word *laudat* belongs to the active voice, but Latin also has special verbal forms with a passive interpretation such as *laudātur* "he is praised".

The category **Degree** for adjectives comprises the **positive, comparative**, and **superlative** degree, as in English *happy–happier–happiest*. Some languages also have an **equative** form for adjectives, as is the case for Finnish (Sulkala and Karjalainen 1992: 172):

(4) Jukka on   Peka-n   pit-uinen
    Jukka be.3SG Pekka-GEN   long-EQUATIVE
    "Jukka is of the same length as Pekka"

In addition, the form of an adjective may be determined by a relation of agreement with its head noun and determiner with respect to properties such as definiteness, gender, number, and case.

An additional distinction in the domain of verbal inflection is that between **finite** forms, which are inflected for the categories tense, number, and person, versus **infinite** (or **non-finite**) forms such as **infinitives, gerunds**, and **participles**. The following Dutch sentences illustrate the use of infinitive and participle forms:

(5) a. Jan   wil   kom-en
       John   want.PRES.3SG   come-INF
       "John wants to come"
    b Huil-end   vertrok   hij
       cry-PRES.PTCP   leave.PAST.3SG   he
       "He left crying"

As you can see, these non-finite verbs are used in sentences that have a finite verbal form as well. Their actual use is a matter of complex syntactic principles, and will not be discussed here.

A remarkable property of these non-finite forms is that they do not only have verbal properties, but also properties of other lexical categories such as nouns and adjectives. For instance, infinitives can be qualified as nominal forms of verbs. In some languages, they may be preceded by a determiner or a preposition, and they may function as the head of NPs, as illustrated here for the Dutch infinitive:

(6) a. Jan   houdt   van   het   lez-en   van   poëzie
       John   likes   of   the   read-INF   of   poetry
       "John likes reading poetry"
    b Jan   houdt   van   lez-en
       John   likes   of   read-INF
       "John likes reading"

The English word *reading* in the gloss of sentence (6a) is an example of a gerund form. As shown by the phrase *John's reading poetry* "the reading of poetry by John", gerunds, like infinitives, have nominal properties: the pre-ceding noun *John* has the same form *John's* that we find in the phrase *John's book*. At the same time, this gerund form still has verbal properties: it combines with the preposition-less complement *poetry*. The occurrence with preposition-less complements is a characteristic feature of verbs. When one adds a complement to a noun, that complement has to be pre-ceded by a preposition, as in *John's love of poetry* where the preposition *of* has to precede the complement noun *poetry* (**John's love poetry* is ill-formed).

Participles are verbal forms that can be used as adjectives, and are also inflected as such in relevant syntactic contexts. In the German example in (7) below, the present participle has the adjectival ending *-e* that is required for attributive adjectives in definite NPs with a masculine head noun (Haspelmath 1996: 44):

(7) Der   im   Wald   laut   sing-end-e   Wanderer
     the   in.the forest loud   sing-PRES.PTCP-e hiker
     "the hiker who is singing loud in the forest"

A less known non-finite verbal form with adverbial properties is the **converb**. Converbs are verbal forms used as adverbs, as in the following sentence from Kannada, a Dravidian language (Haspelmath 1996: 50):

(8) Yaar-ig-uu   heel-ade   eke   bande
     who-DAT-INDEF   say-NEG.CVB why   come.PRET.2SG
     "Why did you come without telling anyone?"

What is remarkable about these non-finite forms is that their inflection appears to be category-changing, from verb to noun, adjective, or adverb, without erasing the verbal properties of these forms. This is remarkable because, typically, inflection does not affect the syntactic category of a word, unlike derivation.

In many languages, nouns and verbs are classified into a number of **inflectional classes**, called **declensions** in the case of nouns and adjectives, and **conjugations** in the case of verbs. These declensions and conjuga-tions do not express morphosyntactic properties themselves, but deter-mine how such properties are expressed. Latin, for instance, has five declination classes for nouns that determine number and case marking, as illustrated in (9) for the singular forms in the nominative and genitive case.

(9) Class	NOM.SG	GEN.SG	*Words with the same inflectional pattern*
I	mensa "table"	mensae	puella "girl", colonia "colony"
II	hortus "garden"	horti	captivus "prisoner", buxus "buxus tree"
III	rex "king"	regis	onus "burden", civis "citizen"
IV	fructus "fruit"	fructūs	domus "house", manus "hand"
V	diēs "day"	diēi	rēs "thing", meridiēs "afternoon"

Latin adjectives are also divided into declension classes, but there are only three declensions for adjectives compared to five for nouns.

Latin is also a language with inflectional classes in the verbal domain. It has four conjugations for its verbs, with different thematic vowels after the verbal root. The forms listed in Table 5.1 above all have a thematic vowel *a* (except *laudō*, where the thematic vowel is absent before the ending *ō*). Thus, *laudāre* belongs to the conjugation of *ā*-verbs. Examples of verbs of the three other conjugations are *delēre* "to delete", *emere* "to buy", and *audīre* "to hear".

5.2 The roles of inflection

Consider the following German sentence that illustrates the roles of inflection in constructing a sentence of German:

(10) Der   Vater   putz-t   sein-er
     the.MASC.SG.NOM father.MASC.SG.NOM brush-PRES.3SG   his-FEM.SG.DAT
     Tochter   die   Schuh-e
     daughter.FEM.SG.DAT the.PL.ACC   shoe.MASC-PL.ACC
     "The father brushes the shoes for his daughter"

The words *Vater, Tochter*, and *Schuhe* are marked for number. The first two nouns are marked as singular, the last one as plural. These three nouns are also marked for case. Since *der Vater* "the father" is the subject of the sentence, it must be marked with **nominative** case. The noun *Tochter* "daughter" has to be marked with **dative** case, because *seiner Tochter* functions as indirect object of the sentence. Finally, the noun *Schuh-e* has the **accusative** form since *die Schuhe* functions as the direct object of this sentence. The case marking of these nouns is obviously determined by the syntactic contexts in which they occur, and hence we call this **contextual inflection**. It stands in contrast with the number marking for these nouns, which is not determined by the syntactic context. The choice of a particular number is determined by what information the speaker wants to convey, and we therefore call it **inherent inflection**. The present tense on the verb is also a case of inherent inflection: it is a matter of free choice: the verb could as well have appeared with a different tense. Below, we will see that the distinction between inherent and contextual inflection plays an important role in analysing morphological systems.

The basic role of contextual inflection is to mark the relationship between a head and a dependent in a syntactic construction. Two basic types of dependency must be distinguished: **government** and agreement. Let us first focus on government.

In languages with case systems, the verb assigns a certain case to each of its dependent NPs such as the subject, the object, and the indirect object. This is illustrated by the German sentence (10), and also by the following Latin sentence, (25) from Chapter 2:

(11)   Manu-s   manu-m   lava-t
         hand-NOM.SG   hand-ACC.SG   wash-3SG
         "One hand washes the other"

It is the verb that is the head of the clause since the verb determines that there must be a subject and, in this case, an object. The case markings in sentences (10) and (11) are instances of **dependent marking** since the syntactic relations between the verb and the nouns are marked on the dependents. This kind of dependent marking is a case of government. We speak of government when a constituent imposes requirements on a related constituent. In the example (11), the verb requires specific case markings on its subject and object. The verb itself, however, bears no corresponding case markings, and that is why we qualify this kind of case marking as government. In contrast, in the case of agreement both constituents involved are marked for the relevant inflectional properties. For instance, in the phrase *seiner Tochter* in (10) the head noun *Tochter* and the dependent modifier *seiner* have the same dative case, and hence the inflection of *seiner* is an instance of agreement rather than government.

The specific case form of the head noun of a noun phrase not only marks its dependency on the verb, but also indicates a specific semantic relation of the noun phrase to the verb. In (11), the NP *manus* denotes the Agent of the verb *lavāre* "to wash", whereas *manum* "hand" denotes the Patient that undergoes the action. When the verb governs an NP with the role of **recipient**, this NP will be marked by means of the dative case, as in (10). These cases are called **structural cases** or **direct cases**. They stand in opposition to **inherent** or **semantic** cases. Semantic case is illustrated by the following Latin sentence in which the ablative case is used for creating the adverbial instrumental phrase "with a knife", whereas the accusative case is a structural case, and marks the direct object "the bread":

(12) Cultr-o   pan-em   secat
      knife-SG.ABL   bread-SG.ACC cuts
      "He cuts the bread with a knife"

The non-nominative structural cases are sometimes called the **oblique** cases. These are the cases that are required by a specific syntactic structure (accusative and dative case), whereas the nominative is the case form that may also be used without a specific syntactic context, for instance as a citation form.

The assignment of case may be lexically governed, and is called **lexical case**. Accusative case is the default case that an NP with the syntactic function of direct object will receive. Verbs may, however, require another case on their object-NP. For instance, in eighteenth-century German, the verb *sich erinnern* "to remember" marked its object with genitive case. A famous sentence from Bach's Matthäus Passion sung by Petrus is (13a); its form in present-day German is (13b):

(13) a. Ich kenne de-s   Mensch-en   nicht
          I   know   the-MASC.GEN.SG man-MASC.GEN.SG not
          "I do not know the man"
      b   Ich kenne de-n   Mensch-en   nicht
          I   know   the-MASC.ACC.SG man-MASC.ACC.SG not
          "I do not know the man"

In (13a) the object is marked as genitive. In present-day German this lexical marking with genitive case for the object of the verb *kennen* "to know" has disappeared, and hence the default accusative case is assigned. The German verb *trauen* "to trust" requires dative case on its object, as in *Wir trauen ihm* "We trust him", with the dative form *ihm* of the 3SG personal pronoun.

Case forms that are used in structural case assignment may also function as semantic cases. For instance, *Romam*, the accusative form of the Latin noun *Roma*, can be used as a directional phrase with the meaning "to Rome", as in *Eo Romam* "I go to Rome". Both in Latin and German, the accusuative case is also used to mark durational phrases, as in German:

(14) Wir laufen den ganz-en Tag
we walk the.MASC.ACC.SG whole-MASC.ACC.SG day.MASC.ACC.SG
"We walk the whole day"

The durational phrase *den ganzen Tag* has the accusative form.

Another well-known case of dependent marking in Indo-European languages is that prepositions govern the choice of case form of the noun with which they combine. German prepositions can be classified according to the kind of case marking they require on their dependent nouns. For instance, the following German prepositions always require accusative case: *für* "for", *durch* "through", *bis* "until", *gegen* "against", *ohne* "without", and *um* "around". Other German prepositions appear with either dative or accusative case, depending on the meaning expressed:

(15) a. Ich stecke die Zeitung hinter den Spiegel
I put the newspaper behind the.ACC.SG mirror
"I put the newspaper behind the mirror"
b Die Zeitung steckt hinter dem Spiegel
the newspaper is behind the.DAT.SG mirror
"The newspaper is behind the mirror"

Although prepositions govern their NP-complement with respect to case, in some cases there is a choice, which depends on the particular semantic relation between the verb and the preposition. If the verb *stecken* "to put" denotes an action (15a), the preposition *hinter* requires accusative case, if it expresses a state (15b), the same preposition *hinter* requires dative case.

Nouns may require a particular marking on their dependent. In the phrase *John's house* the dependent NP *John* is marked as such through the presence of the possessive marker *s*, whereas the head noun *house* is not marked for this syntactic relationship. In languages with **genitive** case, this case is typically used for marking relations between nouns.

In some languages it is not the dependent, but the head that is morphologically marked for standing in a syntactic relationship to its dependent. For instance, in Hungarian, marking is on the head (Nichols 1986: 57):

(16) az ember haz-a
the man house-3SG
"the man's house"

Semitic languages are well known for their **head marking** patterns: the head noun of an NP has often a special phonological form when it is followed by a dependent NP. The word *bayit* "house" in Modern Hebrew has the form *beyt* when followed by an NP-complement like *sefer* "book" (Borer 1988: 50):

(**17**) beyt   sefer
     house   book
     "school"

This special form of the head noun is called the **construct state** since it appears when the noun is in construction with another noun. In this case, the head is marked by means of allomorphy, instead of by an additional morpheme.

The second main type of contextual inflection besides government is agreement (also called **concord**). In many Indo-European languages attributive adjectives agree with respect to a number of morphosyntactic properties with their head nouns, as is illustrated by the following examples (Latin and Hebrew are adapted from Barlow and Ferguson 1988: 3, 5). The nouns function as the source of the shared property, the adjectives and determiners as the targets.

(**18**) a. Latin: acta   vir-orum   omni-um   bon-orum
             deeds   man.MASC-PL.GEN   all-PL.GEN   good-MASC.PL.GEN
          "deeds of all good men"
     b. Hebrew: ha-isha   ha-tov-a
             the-woman. FEM.SG   the-good-FEM.SG
          "the good woman"
     c. Dutch: het   oud-e   paard
             the.DEF.SG.NEUT   old-DEF.SG.NEUT   horse.SG.NEUT
          "the old horse"
     d. French: les femme-s   enchanté-e-s
             the women.FEM-PL   delighted-FEM-PL
          "the delighted women"

In these examples it is the dependent adjective that is marked for properties of the head noun with respect to case, number, and gender. In the Hebrew and the Dutch case, the feature DEFINITE of the noun phrase assigned by the determiners *ha* and *het* respectively, is also expressed on the adjective. Example (18a) shows that in agreement contexts both inherently and contextually determined morphosyntactic properties can be expressed on the constituent that has to be marked. In addition to the inherent inflectional features MASCULINE and PLURAL, the contextually determined GENITIVE case marking of the head noun *vir* "man" is also expressed on the following quantifier and adjective.

In some languages, such as those of the Indo-European family, there is no direct morphological marking of **gender** on nouns. For such languages, we only observe direct morphological effects of gender on the form of dependent adjectives and determiners. In French, the gender of a noun (masculine or feminine) manifests itself in the choice of the SG articles (indefinite *un* or *une*, definite *le* or *la*), and in the form of the adjective (suffix -*e* in feminine forms), but not in the inflectional form of the noun itself. At first sight, it may seem as if nouns in languages such as Latin do express gender in their inflectional form. For instance, most Latin nouns ending in -*a* are feminine. Yet, the ending -*a* is no direct marking of gender, but is characteristic for a specific declension class of Latin nouns, and there is a correlation between declension class and gender: most nouns of the -*a* declension class are feminine. Words such as *nauta* "sailor" and *poeta* "poet", however, are masculine notwithstanding the presence of the ending -*a*, as we can tell from gender agreement. It is *nauta bonus* "the good sailor" where *bonus* is the MASC.SG.NOM form, not *nauta bona.

When gender of nouns manifests itself indirectly, it is perhaps more appropriate to consider the marking of gender on adjectives as a case of government (instead of agreement), parallel to the government of specific case forms of nouns by adpositions. For instance, we do not say that the German preposition *durch* itself has accusative case, and that the noun governed by it agrees with respect to case. Rather, we say that *durch* requires a specific case form of the noun. Similarly, we might say that a masculine noun selects a masculine form of its adjective and determiner.

Dependent marking is also found on relative pronouns that function as the subject of a relative clause. In Dutch, for instance, these pronouns have to agree in number and gender with their antecedents:

(19) a. de   jongen   die   ziek is
          the   boy.MASC.SG who   ill   is
          "the boy who is ill"
      b   het   meisje   dat   ziek is
          the.NEUT.SG.DEF girl.NEUT.SG who.NEUT.SG ill   is
          "the girl who is ill"

The interlinear morphemic glossing in the examples (19) shows that agreement is not a matter of identity of features, but of non-contradictoriness of features. The relative pronoun *die* can be used for non-neuter singular antecedents, and for all plural antecedents. It is only the relative pronoun *dat* that has a specific feature set, NEUTRAL and SINGULAR. The pronoun *die* is used in all other cases. It is the default form, and hence it is unspecified for the categories GENDER and NUMBER. The same applies to the article *het* which is only used in DEFINITE SG.NEUT NPs, whereas *de* is the default article for definite NPs.

These examples also illustrate that agreement is not always marked by means of morphology, but may also be marked through the choice of a specific lexical item (in this example *die* or *dat*). This was also the case for the Hebrew construct state in (17), a case of government. This is in particular true for pronouns, which often have different lexemes for different morphosyntactic properties. The examples in (19) also illustrate that 'gender' is primarily a formal, and not a semantic category: the word *meisje* "girl" denotes a person of the female sex, yet it is a neuter noun that selects the neuter relative pronoun.

As illustrated by the Dutch sentence (18c), the feature (IN)DEFINITE may play a role in agreement between an adjective and its head noun. In German, attributive adjectives have two patterns of contextual inflection, traditionally called **weak inflection** and **strong inflection**. In weak inflection there are less formal differences between the cells of a paradigm than in strong inflection. When an adjective is not preceded by an article, it is subject to strong inflection. (When it is preceded by an indefinite article it has a slightly simplified form of strong inflection, called **mixed inflection**.) After a definite article it has weak inflection. This is illustrated here for NPs with nominative case, where there is no difference between strong and mixed inflection (Eisenberg 1994: 235):

(20) *strong* heiss-er Tee   hot-MASC.NOM.SG tea.MASC.NOM.SG "hot tea"

             heiss-e Suppe   hot-FEM.MASC.SG soup.FEM.MASC.SG "hot soup"

             heiss-es Wasser   hot- NEUT.MASC.SG water.NEUT.MASC.SG "hot water"

    weak der heiss-e Tee   the hot-MASC.NOM.SG tea.MASC.NOM.SG "the hot tea"

             die heiss-e Suppe   the hot-FEM.MASC.SG soup.FEM.MASC.SG "the hot soup"

             das heiss-e Wasser   the hot-NEUT.MASC.SG water.NEUT.MASC.SG "the hot water"

As the examples show, there are more formal differences in the adjectival forms of strong inflection than in those of weak inflection.

Agreement is not always a case of dependent marking, as we saw above. A frequent type of agreement in Indo-European languages is subject–verb agreement. The relevant morphosyntactic properties are those of number and person. This is a case of head marking since the verb is the head, and the subject is the dependent. Subject–verb agreement is therefore an exception to the tendency for Indo-European languages to have dependent marking rather than head marking. Subject–verb agreement is illustrated by the Latin sentence (11): the form *lavat* agrees in number and person with the subject *manus*.

Head marking in Indo-European languages can also be illustrated by quantifiers that denote a quantity higher than 1. These quantifiers require the plural form of the head noun if it is countable, as in English *two books*. This is a case of government in which the number of nouns (normally a case of inherent inflection) plays a role in contextual inflection. In the non-Indo-European language Hungarian, on the other hand, the noun in such phrases is forbidden to have a plural marking, and the whole noun phrase behaves as singular with respect to verb agreement (Corbett 2000: 211):

(21)   Két   lény   beszé
       two   girl.SG   chat.SG
       "two girls are chatting"

In several Slavonic languages, numerals require specific morphological markings on their nouns. For instance, the Russian numerals for 2, 3, and 4 require the nouns with which they combine to appear in the genitive singular form.

In some languages the verb is not only marked for the properties of its subject, but also for its dependent NPs such as the accusative or dative object, as illustrated here for the Austronesian language Kambera spoken on the island of Sumba, Indonesia (Klamer 1998: 63):

(22)   a.   (Na   tau   wútu)   na-palu-ka   (nyungga)
            the   person   be.fat   3SG.NOM-hit-1SG.ACC   I
            "the big man hit me"
       b.   (I   ama)   na-kei-nya   ri
            ART   father   3SG.NOM-buy-3PL.DAT   vegetable
            "Father buys them vegetables"

The parts of these sentences that are between parentheses can be omitted. Therefore, the affixes on the verb are best interpreted as pronominal affixes that indicate the subject and the object of the verb. These affixal pronouns can then be said to have a relation of co-reference with the NPs in the sentence. In other words, you might paraphrase a sentence such as (22a) as 'As to the big man and me, he hit me'. Such sentences are therefore comparable to an English sentence such as *John, he hit it, the ball*.

In a number of languages with subject–verb agreement, the subject with which the verb is supposed to agree in person and number can be absent. For instance, the Latin verb form *laudat* in (2) can function as a sentence by itself, with the meaning "he praises". Thus, the verb form suffices to identify the number and person of the subject of a clause. That is, the choice of one and the same inflectional form is sometimes determined by syntactic context, as in *Carolus laudat* "Charles praises" (where the verbal form has to agree in person and number with the subject *Carolus*), whereas in other cases that choice is not required by another element in the syntactic context, as in the sentence *Laudat* "He praises". The same observation can be made for gender agreement in French. In this language, predicatively used adjectives must agree in gender with the subject, as illustrated in the following sentences:

(**23**) a. Mon   mari   est   heureux
           My.MASC.SG   husband.MASC.SG is   happy.MASC.SG
      b. Ma   tante   est   heureus-e
           My.FEM.SG   aunt.FEM.SG   is   happy-FEM.SG
      c. Je suis heureux
           I   am   happy.SG.MASC
      d. Je suis heureus-e
           I   am   happy-SG.FEM

In (23a, b) the features of the subject are imposed on the adjective. In (23c, d) on the other hand, the pronoun *je* "I" has no inherent features for gender, and it is the gender expressed on the adjective that determines the gender value assigned to the subject *je*. These facts imply that agreement should not be interpreted as the transfer of certain features from one word or constituent to another, but as a checking device that checks if the features of the constituents in the relevant syntactic configuration do not contradict each other. In (23a, b) the features are identical, and hence non-contradictory. In (23c, d) the features of *je* are non-contradictory (though not identical) to those of the predicate: *je* has no specification for gender, whereas the predicative adjectives do have such a specification.

An effect of agreement is to indicate which words belong together in a phrase. This may have the effect that constituent words of a phrase with agreement can be separated by other words, as is frequently the case in Latin texts. In the following example, the complement *mundi* separates the adjective and the head noun with which it agrees in gender, number and case (Virgil, *Georgics* 1.5):

(24)   O   clar-issim-a   mund-i   lumin-a
       O   clear-SUPERL-NEUT.PL.VOC   world-GEN.SG   light-NEUT.PL.VOC
       "O, clearest lights of the earth"

Australian languages such as Warlpiri are also well-known for this kind of
freedom in word order, made possible by the case-marking system. Both
case marking and agreement patterns make it possible for a language to
have more or less free word order because they may serve to find out which
words belong together, and which function they have. However, this is not
an automatic consequence: the presence of rich inflection does not necessarily imply that a language has free word order. German, for instance,
has pretty rigid word order principles notwithstanding its rich case and
agreement system.

Contextual inflection introduces a large degree of redundancy, and it
may therefore come as no surprise that contextual inflection erodes much
more frequently in the course of history than inherent inflection. The
Romance languages French, Italian, and Spanish, descendants of Latin, all
kept the number distinction for nouns, whereas these languages no longer
have case markings on nouns. Afrikaans has lost its verbal endings for
number and person (contextual inflection), whereas it has kept the tense
distinction between present and past. This shows that the distinction
between inherent and contextual inflection is important for understanding
patterns of language change.

5.3 Inflection and derivation

As we saw in Chapter 1, the primary distinction between inflection and
derivation is a functional one: derivation creates new lexemes, and inflection
serves to create different forms of the same lexeme. Yet, this is not always
sufficient to determine in concrete cases of morphology to which domain a
particular morphological form belongs. Consider English comparatives.
How do we know if *bigger* is a different lexeme than *big*, or another form of
the lexeme BIG?

We might define inflection as 'the kind of morphology that is relevant to
syntax'. According to that demarcation criterion, the morphological properties that play a role in agreement and government are clear cases of
inflection. This comprises all contextual inflection, but also those morphological properties of words that function as controllers for this kind of

inflection. The marking of number on nouns is often not an instance of contextual inflection itself, but it may play a role in determining the shape of adjectives and determiners with which it combines. Note, however, that we cannot say that derivation is completely irrelevant to syntax. For example, when we create causative verbs by means of derivation, we create transitive verbs, and transitivity is certainly a property that is relevant to syntax.

A second possible criterion is that inflection is obligatory, whereas derivation is optional. This criterion does apply to contextual inflection, but at first sight not always to inherent inflection. In the case of verbal conjugation, inflection is always obligatory: you have to choose a specific form of a verb in a clause. This seems not to apply to nouns: a noun can be used without any morphological marking for number. In fact, for many nouns the need for a plural form will (almost) never arise, as is the case for the English nouns *attention, accordance*, and *adolescence*. However, one may claim that English words are always inflected for the relevant categories because an English noun is always either singular or plural. After all, these latter three nouns behave as singular nouns in subject–verb agreement. So these nouns are singular "by default". In this sense, inflection for number is indeed obligatory in English.

An important criterion that might distinguish inflection from derivation is the essential role of the paradigm in inflection. The cells of the paradigm are defined by the inflectional categories of a particular word class. In Chapter 6 the role of paradigms in making morphological generalizations is discussed. A clear example of the role of paradigms can be found in **periphrasis**. We have to do with periphrasis if for certain cells of the paradigm no **synthetic** morphological form is available. Instead, a combination of words, an **analytic** or periphrastic form, has to be used. Latin has no synthetic forms for the perfective passive of verbs, as illustrated in Table 5.2 for the 3SG forms of *laudāre* "to praise". The cells for the perfective passive are a combination of the passive participle (that, like adjectives, agrees with the subject of the clause with respect to case, gender, and number) and a form of the verb *esse* "to be". If these word combinations were not considered part of the verbal paradigm, Latin verbs would have a paradigm with a gap for the perfective passive forms. These periphrastic forms have a perfective interpretation, although the forms of the verb *esse* "to be" are that of the imperfect tense.

An additional argument for considering these word combinations as

Table 5.2. *Imperfective and perfective 3SG forms of laudāre*

IMPERFECTIVE	ACTIVE	PASSIVE
PRESENT	laudat	laudātur
PAST	laudābat	laudābātur
FUTURE	laudābit	laudābitur

PERFECTIVE	ACTIVE	PASSIVE
PRESENT	laudāvit	laudātus/a/um est
PAST	laudāverat	laudātus/a/um erat
FUTURE	laudāverit	laudātus/a/um erat

filling paradigm cells is the following. Latin has a number of so-called **deponent verbs**, verbs with a passive form but an active meaning. For instance, the verb *loquor* "to speak" is such a deponent verb. The crucial observation is that a word-sequence such as *locutus est* receives an active interpretation as well, and means "he has spoken". This parallelism in interpretation as active forms is to be expected if these analytic forms belong to the inflectional paradigm of verbs.

The notion 'suppletion' also presupposes the idea of a paradigm. We speak about the grammatical words *am, are, is, was*, and *were* as forms of the English lexeme BE although they are quite different in phonological shape, and show (almost) no phonological relatedness. These words fill specific cells in the paradigm of *to be*. The same applies to *worse*, the suppletive comparative form of BAD.

A fourth criterion for distinguishing inflection and derivation is that derivation may feed inflection, but not vice versa. Derivation applies to the stem-forms of words, without their inflectional endings, and creates new, more complex stems to which inflectional rules can be applied. This is the main reason for keeping the two kinds of morphology distinct. It is a cross-linguistic generalization that inflection is peripheral with respect to derivation, formulated by Greenberg as follows:

(25) 'Universal 28. If both the derivation and inflection follow the root, or they both precede the root, the derivation is always between the root and the inflection' (Greenberg 1963: 93)

Greenberg's universal excludes the morpheme order patterns *Derivation–Inflection–Root and *Root–Inflection–Derivation. It might also be interpreted as saying that derivation cannot apply to inflected forms. Yet, there are exceptions to this universal tendency, cases in which inflectional forms appear to feed derivation. For instance, the comparative form of some Dutch adjectives has functioned as the base for derivation with the prefix *ver-*, as in

(26)   erg-er "worse"   [ver-[erg-er]$_A$]$_V$ "to worsen"
       oud-er "older"   [ver-[oud-er]$_A$]$_V$ "to get older"

Strictly speaking, this morphological pattern is not excluded by Greenberg's Universal 28 because the derivational morpheme is a prefix, and the inflectional morpheme is a suffix. A real exception to this universal is the use of verbal participles (which may function as adjectives) for de-adjectival word-formation, which is quite common in Indo-European languages. For example, English past participles show up in de-adjectival word-formation, as in *affect-ed-ness* and *relat-ed-ness*. Here we find the "wrong" order Root–Inflection–Derivation, since *-ed* is an inflectional suffix, and *-ness* a derivational one. However, this kind of de-inflectional word-formation is only found with instances of inherent inflection such as comparatives and participles as bases.

Another demarcation criterion that might be invoked is that derivation is potentially category-changing, unlike inflection. Although it is true that most cases of inflection do not change syntactic category, there is a change of category involved for infinitives, gerunds, participles, and converbs, which keep their verbal potential, but also have properties of other syntactic categories (section 5.1).

In sum, the best criteria for distinguishing inflection from derivation are the obligatoriness of inflection, the fact that it is organized by means of paradigms, and that it is normally a word without its inflectional endings (= the stem) that forms the basis for word-formation. It will be clear that the boundary between the two is not extremely sharp, and that there are similarities between inherent inflection and derivation.

5.4 Theoretical models

The inflectional phenomena discussed above pose two specific questions for the theory of grammar: (i) what is the best formal representation of inflectional processes, and (ii) where in the grammar should inflectional rules apply?

Let us first focus on the formal nature of inflectional rules. For simple cases, one might think of inflection as the attachment of inflectional morphemes to the stem-forms of lexemes. For instance, in English we create plural forms of nouns by suffixing the stem with the suffix *-s*. Similarly, past tense forms of verbs are made by suffixation of the verbal stem with *-ed*. Such cases of agglutinative morphology can therefore be dealt with in a model in which morphology is seen as the concatenation of morphemes. This model is called **Item-and-Arrangement Morphology**.

There are two basic problems for this model of inflection. The first is that in many languages there is no one-to-one relation between inflectional properties and their expression by morphemes. Consider once more the paradigm of the Polish noun KOT in Chapter 2, repeated as (27) here for

(27)	SINGULAR	PLURAL
NOMINATIVE	kot	kot-y
GENITIVE	kot-a	kot-ów
DATIVE	kot-u	kot-om
ACCUSATIVE	kot-a	kot-y
INSTRUMENTAL	kot-em	kot-ami
LOCATIVE	koci-e	kot-ach
VOCATIVE	koci-e	kot-y

convenience. Each inflectional suffix in this paradigm expresses features (is an **exponent**) for two categories, NUMBER and CASE. There are no distinct morphemes for these two categories, and the inflectional endings are portmanteau morphemes. This is a case of **cumulative exponence**: each ending in the paradigm of KOT is the expression of more than one inflectional category (the formal correlate of a morphological category is called its **exponence**). There is also the opposite phenomenon that one inflectional category may receive more than one morphological expression. This is illustrated by the Latin word form *laudāvisti* in Table 5.1: the inflectional category PERFECT is expressed by both the morpheme *-vi-* after the stem *laudā* and the selection of a 2SG ending *-isti* that is unique to the PERFECT, and hence also expresses this category. This is called **extended exponence**.

The second problem for an Item-and-Arrangement model of inflection is that inflectional categories may be expressed by other means than morpheme concatenation. In Germanic languages, for instance, the past tense forms of so-called strong verbs are formed by changing the vowel of the verbal stem (ablaut), not by suffixation.

These problems for the Item-and-Arrangement model have led to a different view of inflection in which inflectional rules are operations of various sorts: affixation, vowel change, reduplication, etc. This process-variant of morphology is called **Item-and-Process Morphology**. Thus, the rule for computing the PL.INSTR. form of Polish nouns like KOT might be formulated as follows:

(28) $[x]_N \rightarrow [x\text{-ami}]_{N[+pl.,instr]}$

This rule states that if we add the ending *-ami* to the stem form of a noun, we thus create a noun with the features PLURAL and INSTRUMENTAL.

A third model for inflection, which shares the processual view of morphology with the model of Item-and-Process morphology, is the **Word-and-Paradigm** model. This model takes the lexeme and its paradigm of cells as its starting point. The different forms of the paradigm of a lexeme are computed by a set of **realization rules**. The realization rule for the INSTR.PL. form of nouns like KOT will have the following form:

(29) $[x]_{N\ [+pl,\ instr]} \rightarrow [x\text{-ami}]_N$

The difference between rule (28) and rule (29) is the following. Rule (28) introduces a morphosyntactic property hand-in-hand with its exponent, while rule (29) treats the property set as a precondition for the introduction of its exponent. Rules such as (29) are therefore called realization rules or **spell out rules**, and this kind of morphological analysis is called **realizational morphology**.

One advantage of using the format of spell out rules for inflection is that it can easily account for cases in which there is no overt phonological expression for certain morphosyntactic features. In English and Dutch, there is no overt ending for singular nouns. Yet, nouns must be specified for number in order for agreement rules to apply properly. One might therefore assume a zero suffix or prefix for singular nouns, but this is an *ad hoc* assumption. It is even impossible to determine if the zero is a prefix or a suffix, since you cannot hear it. In a realization approach one can account for this straightforwardly. Since the cell with the feature [– plural] of a Dutch or English noun will not trigger a realization rule, the singular form of the noun will be identical to the stem-form. This makes the introduction of a zero affix superfluous.

The basic analytical problem posed by inflectional systems discussed above is that there is no neat mapping of form and (morphosyntactic) content in a one-to-one-fashion. A related problem is that there is quite often competition between different realization rules for the same morphosyntactic content. In Germanic languages, for instance, the past tense form of verbs is created either by vowel change, or by suffixation. In the case of *sing*, with the past tense form *sang*, we have to take care that the grammar will not specify its past tense form as *singed*. This will be achieved as follows. The rule that applies to ablauting verbs such as *sing* will not only be conditioned by the presence of the feature PAST TENSE, but also by the **diacritic feature** [ablaut] that is assigned to these ablauting verbs in the lexicon. A diacritic feature refers to an arbitrary class of lexical items. From the synchronic point of view it is an arbitrary property of a verb that it belongs to the class of verbs that makes use of vowel alternations to express past tense. The additional presence of the feature [ablaut] in the condition for vowel change makes this rule more specific than the rule for suffixation with -*ed*, which only requires its inputs to be verbs. It is a generally accepted idea in linguistics that, in the case of competition between two or more rules, the more specific rule will be applied first, and then pre-empts the application of the more general rule. This is called **Panini's Principle**, after the Sanskrit grammarian Panini who introduced this idea.

Another theoretical model that should be mentioned here is that of **Distributed Morphology**. This model is not process-based, but morpheme-based: morphemes are the atoms of morphosyntactic representations, and to that extent it is a (sophisticated) variant of Item-and-Arrangement Morphology. At the syntactic level, the structure of a sentence is represented as a syntactic tree that includes abstract morphemes such as [+plural], [+past], etc. These abstract morphemes form terminal nodes in the syntactic tree, just like lexical morphemes. The phonological content of these morphemes is then spelt out through the insertion of vocabulary items that specify the phonological correlate of an abstract morpheme. An example of a vocabulary item is the English plural suffix /z/ for nouns (as in *dog–dogs*):

(30)   /z/ ↔ [_, +plural]

This vocabulary item states that the phonological piece /z/ can be inserted in the context of the feature [+plural]. In this approach, there is no lexicon that provides full words, to be used in syntactic structure. The task of providing fully inflected words is distributed over other components of the grammar, hence the name Distributed Morphology.

How does the model of Distributed Morphology deal with cumulative exponence, the phenomenon that poses a problem for Item-and-Arrangement Morphology? In such situations, in which one phonological piece expresses a set of morphosyntactic features, the morphosyntactic tree will be restructured before lexical insertion takes place. For instance, the abstract morphemes for number and case in Latin and Polish may be fused into one terminal node through a **fusion rule**. Subsequently, the vocabulary item that matches with that feature combination is inserted, for instance the Latin suffix *-i* for the NOM. PL form of second declension nouns:

(31)   /i/ $\leftrightarrow$ [_, +plural, +nom]$_{\text{N, class II}}$

In English plural nouns such as *geese* and *men*, the plurality is expressed by vowel change, not by the addition of a morpheme. In Distributed Morphology, this is taken care of by assuming a zero suffix for these plural nouns, followed by the application of **readjustment rules** that perform phonological operations triggered by the presence of the feature [+plural] for a specified number of lexical items.

5.5 Morpheme order

The issue of morpheme order deserves special attention in the domain of inflection. In the case of derivation the basic idea is that each morphological operation adds a new layer of structure, and a corresponding semantic interpretation, as was illustrated in section 1.1 for the word *tranquillizer*, the morphological structure of which could be represented by means of a hierarchical structure. In the domain of inflection, however, a flat structure might be more appropriate. When there are different endings for TENSE and for PERSON, with the second ending being more peripheral, there may be no particular reason for assuming a hierarchy in which PERSON is higher than TENSE. This is why some linguists assume that with respect to inflection we have to do with a set of unordered features, and why the expression "set of morphosyntactic features" is used. The order in which inflectional elements appear is sometimes expressed by means of templates. Well-known examples of languages with such **templatic morphology** (also called **position class morphology**) are the Bantu languages. For instance, the following (partial) template can be assumed for Bemba, a Bantu language of Zambia:

(32) Negation—Subject marker—Tense—Aspect—Object marker—Stem—Final vowel

This template is exemplified by the following sentence (Kula 2002: 33):

(33) ta-   tu-   aku-   laa-   ba-   bombel -a
      NEG   SUBJ.1PL   FUT   PROGR   OBJ   work   FINAL VOWEL
      "We will not be working for them"

   The assumption of templates does not mean, however, that morpheme order is completely arbitrary, and that there are no tendencies in the ordering of inflectional morphemes. One clear generalization is that contextual inflection is peripheral to inherent inflection. Thus, in the case of nouns, affixes for CASE are peripheral to affixes for NUMBER (Greenberg's Universal 39, Greenberg 1963: 95), and in the case of verbs PERSON endings tend to be peripheral to TENSE endings. A second generalization concerns the order of morphemes of inherent inflection such as those for tense and aspect. Generally, aspect morphemes appear closer to the root of a word than tense morphemes (Bybee 1985).

   If word-formation and inflection are indeed different subsystems of morphology, does this imply that they are located in different parts of the grammar? This is the second main issue for theoretical models of inflection: where in the grammar is inflection?

   One possible view is that word-formation is pre-syntactic, and inflection is post-syntactic. Word-formation (compounding, derivation, etc.) serves to enlarge the set of lexical items that can be inserted into syntactic structure. Inflection, on the other hand, may be claimed to be post-syntactic because the specific form of a lexeme may depend on its syntactic context (contextual inflection). This is the **split morphology** model:

(34) word-formation → syntax → inflection

   However, the dependency of inflection on syntax does not necessarily imply that inflection is post-syntactic. The alternative view is that the morphological component of the grammar computes new lexemes and the different inflectional forms of lexemes, the theory of **strong lexicalism:**

(35) morphology → syntax

Rules of contextual inflection like those of agreement will then have the function of checking mechanisms: they check if the morphosyntactic features of the words in a particular syntactic configuration can go together. If not, the sentence is qualified as ungrammatical. For instance, if we insert the word form *books* with the feature [+ plural] in the context — *is interesting*, we get the ungrammatical sentence **Books is interesting*. The English rule of subject–verb agreement will find a clash between the number specifications of *books* and *is*, and hence, the grammar will qualify it as an ungrammatical sentence. Moreover, as we saw above, the choice of a particular inflected form like the French FEM.SG adjective *heureuse* does not always depend on the presence of a syntactic source for the feature [feminine]. In *Je suis heureuse* "I am happy", this form is selected because the speaker is female. Hence, it cannot be created post-syntactically through agreement with the gender features of the subject, because the subject *je* is unspecified for gender.

Another advantage of the strong lexicalist position is that we can account for the fact that certain kinds of (inherent) inflection feed word-formation. For instance, in many languages participles may function as adjectives, and feed de-adjectival word-formation (as in English *affectedness*). In the split morphology model it is impossible for inflectional forms to be used as bases for word-formation since inflection is post-syntactic, whereas word-formation comes before syntax.

An additional consideration for dealing with word-formation and inflection in the same component of the grammar is that derived words and inflected forms of words may be subject to the same phonological rules or constraints. These phonological regularities within words are referred to as the **lexical phonology** of a language. For instance, all Dutch words are subject to the rule that the vowel schwa [ə] disappears before an adjacent vowel. In the case of vowel-initial suffixes that trigger this schwa-deletion, it does not matter if the suffix is inflectional or derivational in nature:

(36) *derivation* zijde-ig "silky"   /zɛɪdə-əɣ/ [zɛidəx]
      inflection bode-en "messengers"   /boːdə-ən/ [boːdən]

The rule of schwa-deletion should not apply twice, both pre-syntactically and post-syntactically, because that would complicate the grammar of Dutch beyond necessity. This duplication would be necessary if we followed the theory of split morphology, unless all phonology would be post-syntactic. In Chapter 7 it is shown that this latter position cannot be correct.

These considerations lead to the conclusion that morphology should not be split into a pre-syntactic and a post-syntactic component, and that it is only the strong lexicalist position that can do justice to the facts discussed here.

Summary

Inflection is the expression of morphosyntactic properties of lexemes. These properties either serve to express a particular meaning (inherent inflection), or are required in specific syntactic contexts (contextual inflection). In contextual inflection the relation between two elements in a syntactic configuration is marked either on the head or on the dependent. Contextual inflection indicates syntactic relationships between words. Word order also has the function to indicate these relationships. Hence, a language with a rich system of contextual inflection may have relatively free word order.

The main criterion for distinguishing inflection from derivation is that only inflection is obligatory: each word must be specified for the relevant inflectional properties of its word class. Each lexeme thus has a paradigm of inflectional forms. It is normally the word without its inflectional endings that forms the starting point for word-formation. However, certain types of inherent inflection may feed derivation.

The complications in the relation between phonological form and morphosyntactic properties have given rise to a number of theoretical models that are alternatives to the Item-and-Arrangement model that analyses (inflectional) morphology as morpheme concatenation. These alternative models are processual models of inflection.

Questions

1. Give an explanation for the fact that the German phrase *Guten Morgen* "good morning" has the accusative form although there is no verb that assigns accusative case to this phrase.

2. What are the rules for choosing between a synthetic and a periphrastic expression of the comparative of the English adjective?

3. In English, the infinitival form of the verb is identical to that of the stem. Is it therefore necessary to assume a zero ending for this form?

4. In Dutch we find compound pairs such as the following: *school-*

gemeenschap "school community" versus *schol-en-gemeenschap* "schools community, comprehensive school", and *stads-raad* "city council" versus *sted-en-raad* "cities' council" (-*en* is a plural morpheme). Which conclusion can you draw from the existence of such compounds about the relation between inflection and word-formation?

5. Which kinds of inherent and contextual inflection can be observed in the following Finnish sentence?

Anno-i-n   vet-tä   kahde-lle   koira-lle
give-IMPF-1SG   water-PART   two-ALL   dog-ALL
"I gave water to two dogs"

6. Melčuk (2000: 515) gives the following examples of Russian male–female noun pairs that he qualifies as suppletion: *byk* "bull"–*korova* "cow", *petuch* "rooster"–*kurica* "hen". Do you think it makes sense to use the notion "suppletion" in the domain of word-formation?

7. Identify instances of cumulative and extended exponence in the following forms of the Hebridian Gaelic word *clach* "stone" (Coates 2000: 623):

	SG	PL
NOM	clach [khlax]	clachan [klaxan]
GEN	cloiche [khloçe]	clachan [klaxan]
DAT	cloich [khloç]	clachan [klaxan]

8. Consider the following sentences from British English and American English respectively:

The police are investigating the case
The police is investigating the case

What conclusion can you draw for the difference in specification of *police* between the lexicons of British and of American English?

9. French has two genders, masculine and feminine. The following French noun phrases illustrate gender agreement between the head noun and the following attributive adjective:

un   père   excellent
a.MASC.SG   father.MASC.SG   excellent.MASC.SG
"an excellent father"
une   mère   excellent-e
a.FEM.SG   mother.FEM.SG   excellent-FEM.SG
"an excellent mother"
une   mère   et   une   sœur   excellent-e-s
a.FEM.SG   mother.FEM.SG   and   a.FEM.SG   sister.FEM.SG   excellent-FEM-PL
"an excellent mother and sister"
un père   et   une   mère   excellent-s
a father.MASC.SG   and   a   mother.FEM.SG   excellent-MASC.PL
"an excellent father and mother"

Formulate the rule of 'gender resolution' that is needed to compute the gender feature of the attributive adjective when the head of the phrase is formed by two conjoined nouns.

10. Dutch has fifteen nouns with a plural suffix *-eren* instead of the regular *-en*, for example *kind–kinderen* "child–children". The regular suffix for monosyllabic nouns is *-en*, as in *boek–boeken* "book(s)". Which principle can be invoked to block the formation of **kinden*?

Further reading

The distinction between inherent and contextual inflection has been made in Anderson (1985) as the distinction between inherent and relational inflection; the importance of this distinction for morphological theory is discussed in Booij (1994, 1996a). Panini's principle is discussed in Pinker (1999).

The Word-and-Paradigm model has been defended in a classic article by Robins (1959), and in Matthews (1972). A survey and classification of inflectional theories is given in Stump (2001: ch 1). Realization rules for inflection are defended in Anderson (1992) and Stump (2001), which are detailed studies within the Word-and-Paradigm approach. Börjars *et al.* (1997) and Sadler and Spencer (2001) deal with the theoretical status of periphrasis.

Key publications on the model of Distributed Morphology are Halle (1992) and Halle and Marantz (1993). A survey of the model is presented in Harley and Noyer (2003).

The split morphology model is defended in Anderson (1992). Objections to this model are raised in Booij (1994, 1996a).

Templatic morphology is discussed in Inkelas (1993), Rice (2000), and Hyman (2003).

6

Inflectional systems

6.1. Nominal systems: gender, number, and case

The previous chapter has introduced you to the roles of inflection in constructing sentences, and its position in the grammar. In this chapter, we will zoom in on the details of inflection. The formal regularities involved are sometimes quite complicated. Moreover, the relationship between inflectional forms and their semantic interpretation is not that straightforward. Thus, inflectional phenomena give a perfect illustration of how complex the relation between form and meaning in natural languages can be.

Let us first have a more detailed look at how inflection manifests itself in the forms of nouns. The best known cases of noun inflection are the marking on nouns of number and case properties. In an agglutinative language such as Finnish, number and case are marked by means of separate suffixes. In most languages, case markings are external to number markings, in line with the generalization that contextual inflection tends to be peripheral to inherent inflection. In Finnish, nouns have either singular or plural number. As in many other languages, there is no overt marking for the singular. The plural suffix is -*t* in the nominative form and -*i* elsewhere. The latter suffix is realized as the glide [j] when it appears between two vowels. A subset of plural case forms of the Finnish noun *kissa* "cat" is given in (1) (Sulkala and Karjalainen 1992: 267):

(1) NOM.PL   kissa-t
     GEN.PL   kisso-j-en
     PART.PL kisso-j-a
     ABL.PL   kisso-i-lta

This example illustrates that both stems and affixes in inflectional forms may exhibit phonological variation of various kinds, a topic that is discussed in Chapter 7.

The number system of English nouns has two characteristic features: number marking is obligatory, and the only choice that we have is that between singular and plural. For many languages, expression of number on nouns is not obligatory. This is the case for Austronesian languages such as Malay. Such languages have a general form for nouns which is unspecified as to number, and stands outside the number system. Other languages might express number obligatorily, but not on nouns. In Maori, for instance, it is expressed on possessive markers and determiners only. Languages may have more distinctions than just singular versus plural. In fact, cross-linguistically, number marking is not restricted to the distinction between singular and plural. Some languages also distinguish a dual form, referring to precisely two entities, a **trial** form (three entities), or a **paucal** form (referring to a few entities). There is a cross-linguistic hierarchy involved here (Corbett 2000: 38):

(2) Number hierarchy: singular > plural > dual > trial

This hierarchy indicates that, if a language has a trial, it also has a dual and if it has a dual, it also has a plural form, etc. The dual and trial may be different from the plural in not being obligatory. That is, in some cases, the plural can be used for denoting a set of two and three entities respectively, in addition to larger numbers of entities.

Bayso, a Cushitic language spoken in southern Ethiopia, exhibits optional number marking: a noun can be used without any overt marking for number, and then receives a general interpretation, as shown in the first example in (3). This language features singular, plural, and paucal number (Corbett 2000: 11):

(3) lúban   foofe
     lion.GENERAL watched.1SG
     "I watched lion" (one or more than one)

     lubán-titi   foofe
     lion-SG   watched.1SG
     "I watched a lion"

luban-jaa   foofe
lion-PAUCAL watched.1SG
"I watched a few lions"

luban-jool foofe
lion-PL   watched.1SG
"I watched (a lot of) lions"

When a language has a number distinction for nouns, this is not necessarily expressed on all nouns. In this respect, number marking is certainly not the inflectional category *par excellence*, since we consider obligatoriness as a relevant criterion for the demarcation of inflection and derivation (section 5.3).

A second typological dimension of number marking is that languages may differ as to which nouns are marked for number. A language may mark number on animate nouns only, or only on nouns that denote human beings. The cross-linguistic variation involved obeys the **Animacy Hierarchy** (Corbett 2000: 56):

(4)   speaker > addressee > 3PERS > kin > human > animate > inanimate

Each language can be characterized by a particular cut-off point on this hierarchy for number marking. For instance, it may be the case that in a certain language only personal pronouns (all three persons) and nouns denoting kinship relations are marked for number. This hierarchy can be used to formulate certain constraints on the cross-linguistic variation found. For instance, if the singular–plural distinction is made for animate nouns, it will also be made for kinship nouns (but not necessarily vice versa).

In English, there is no overt morphological marking for SINGULAR, only for PLURAL. In other languages both singular and plural may be expressed phonologically. The inverse situation, no overt marking for plurals, and overt marking for singular forms is also found (see section 2.3).

Number marking on nouns, although primarily a case of inherent inflection, may also be required by a specific syntactic context, in particular in combination with number names. In English we must use the plural form of nouns after number names higher than 1. In Finnish and Hungarian, on the other hand, the singular form of a noun is required after such number names.

Through agreement, number can also be marked on words of other word classes such as adjectives, determiners, and verbs, as discussed in section

5.2. This kind of number marking is to be distinguished from inherent marking of number on verbs used to express the plurality of the event denoted by the verbs, or the number of participants involved. The following examples are from Ngiti (Kutsch Lojenga 1994: 285, transcription simplified):

(5) ma m-i   indri nadha
     1SG SC-AUX goat   pull.NOM1
     "I am pulling one goat, or a group of goats simultaneously"
     ma m-i   indri nudha
     1SG SC-AUX goat   pull.PL.NOM1
     "I am pulling several goats one by one"

(The plural verbal form here differs from the unmarked form by having a different vowel.) This plural verbal form denotes that the action takes place more than one time.

In languages with different inflectional classes such as Latin (see Chapter 5, example 9), number and case receive different morphological markings dependent on the inflectional class to which a noun belongs. This is also illustrated by the inflectional paradigms of some Icelandic nouns of class I (the default class) in Table 6.1. In these paradigms, three classifications of nouns are involved in computing the form for each number–case combination: the distinction between weak and strong nouns, gender, and arbitrary

Table 6.1. *Inflection of Icelandic class I nouns*

	MASCULINE		FEMININE		NEUTER	
	strong	weak	strong	weak	strong	weak
	"horse"	"time"	"needle"	"tongue"	"table"	"eye"
SINGULAR						
NOM	hest-ur	tím-i	nál	tung-a	borð	aug-a
ACC	hest	tím-a	nál	tung-u	borð	aug-a
DAT	hest-i	tím-a	nál	tung-u	borð-i	aug-a
GEN	hest-s	tím-a	nál-ar	tung-u	borð-s	aug-a
PLURAL						
NOM	hest-ar	tím-ar	nál-ar	tung-ur	borð	aug-u
ACC	hest-a	tím-a	nál-ar	tung-ur	borð	aug-u
DAT	hest-um	tím-um	nál-um	tung-um	borð-um	aug-um
GEN	hest-a	tím-a	nál-a	tung-na	borð-a	aug-na

Source: Thráinsson 1994: 153.

class markers. The words in Table 6.1 are all class I nouns, but there are three other classes (for non-neuter nouns only) and some irregular nouns. The phonological form of a noun may help to determine the (sub)class of a noun. For instance, if the NOM.SG form of a masculine noun ends in -*i* (as in *timi* "time"), it always follows the weak inflection pattern.

A closer look at the paradigms in Table 6.1 will reveal that the number of differences between the paradigms of Icelandic class I nouns is restricted. For instance, the dative plural marker is always -*um*, and the genitive plural always ends in -*a* (with an additional *n* in *tung-na* and *aug-na*). Another generalization is that all feminine and neuter nouns have the same form for the nominative and the accusative, in the plural. That is, the accusative forms can be computed by referring to the nominative forms. To give another example of such paradigm regularities, in Russian the accusative form is identical to the genitive form for most animate nouns, and for inanimates, the accusative is like the nominative (Corbett and Fraser 1993: 130). Such generalizations that refer to different cells of a paradigm are called **rules of referral** since one form can be computed by referring to another form of the same paradigm. It is important to note that rules of referral do not refer to word forms, but to different cells in the paradigm of a word. For instance, the following regularity holds for the masculine nouns in Table 6.1: if the nominative plural form ends in -*ar*, the accusative plural and the genitive plural end in -*a*. Rules of referral underscore the important role of the paradigm as a pattern of cells, each with it is own set of morpho-syntactic features.

When different slots of a paradigm are filled by the same phonological form, this is referred to as syncretism or **inflectional homonymy**. In Table 6.1 we see that the nominative and accusative plural forms of feminine and neuter nouns of class I are always identical. This is a case of systematic syncretism that may be expressed by the following rule of referral:

(6) [Noun, Class 1, Non-masc] → [Nom = Acc in Plural]

Rules of referral can thus be used to express systematic patterns of syncretism.

The classification of nouns into different genders is quite an intriguing phenomenon because of its strong arbitrariness. Some Indo-European languages have three genders: **masculine, feminine**, and **neuter**. Romance languages such as Italian and French have lost the neuter gender, whereas in the Germanic language Dutch there is only a distinction between neuter and **non-neuter** gender (also called **common gender**). There is a relation between gender and biological sex, to be sure. If a language distinguishes between masculine and feminine gender, morphologically simplex nouns denoting male and female beings tend to be masculine and feminine respectively. But why are some nouns for body parts in Dutch neuter (for instance, *oog* "eye"), whereas others are non-neuter (for instance *neus* "nose")? Linguists assume that originally there must have been some semantic motivation behind the different classes, a motivation that became opaque in the course of history.

Morphological structure may also be involved in computing the gender of a noun. The heads of nominal compounds, and most suffixes determine the gender of the words they create. As we observed earlier, Dutch and German diminutive nouns, for instance, are always neuter, even if they denote male or female beings:

(7)   *Dutch* het jonge-tje "the boy"; *German* das Mütter-chen "the little mother"

Another system of noun classes involved in the morphological expression of number is found in languages of Africa, in particular (but not exclusively) Bantu languages. The examples in Table 6.2 illustrate the noun-class system of Swahili. These data suggest that Swahili has six classes (genders), each class being a particular pair of singular and plural forms.

Table 6.2. *Noun classes in Swahili*

	SINGULAR	PLURAL	
I	m-tu	wa-tu	"person"
II	m-zigo	mi-zigo	"load"
III	Ø-tofali	ma-tofali	"brick"
IV	ki-tasa	vi-tasa	"lock"
V	n-dizi	n-dizi	"banana"
VI	u-bao	m-bao	"plank"

Source: Welmers 1973: 161.

The first two singular (sub)classes look as if they are one class because they have the same prefix *m-*. However, they correlate with two different plural prefixes. Moreover, they also behave differently in agreement. This is illustrated by the pattern of subject agreement prefixes in the verbal forms in (8), in which the nouns listed in Table 6.2 function as subjects, and are followed by the verbal form *mepotea* "is/are lost" (Welmers 1973: 162):

(8)   SINGULAR   PLURAL
      m-tu a-mepotea   wa-tu wa-mepotea
      m-zigo u-mepotea   mi-zigo i-mepotea
      Ø-tofali li-mepotea   ma-tofali ya-mepotea
      ki-tasa ki-mepotea   vi-tasa vi-mepotea
      n-dizi i-mepotea   n-dizi zi-mepotea
      u-bao u-mepotea   m-bao zi-mepotea

The singular nouns *m-tu* and *m-zigo* select different subject agreement prefixes. Therefore, they must be treated as belonging to two different classes. Thus, as in the case of gender in Latin (remember *nauta bonus* in section 5.2), classification of nouns in these languages may have to be based on agreement patterns rather than direct morphological properties.

The classification of nouns in these languages may have some semantic correlates. Class I includes most personal nouns, class II names of trees, plants, and a number of inanimate entities. The singular prefix of class IV is often used for the names of languages. Thus, Swahili is also referred to as Ki-Swahili.

The noun-class system of Bantu languages is very important for agreement patterns. A nice example of this pervasive agreement is the following sentence from Swahili (Welmers 1973: 171):

(9)   ki-kapu   ki-kubwa   ki-moja   ki-lianguka
      basket   large   one   fell
      "One large basket fell"

However, this kind of **alliterative concord** in Swahili is exceptional: it is not necessarily the case that the same prefix appears on all agreeing constituents of a clause. In fact, it is only the class prefix for attributive modifiers that always has the same prefix as the head noun. In other cases there are different prefixes involved as illustrated here for the class I noun *m-tu* "person" (Welmers 1973: 171):

(10) ATTRIBUTIVE   m-tu m-moja   "one person"
      ASSOCIATIVE   m-tu w-a Utete   "a person from Utete"
      DEMONSTRATIVE   m-tu yu-le   "that person"
      SUBJECT   m-tu a-likuja   "a person came"

The African noun-class system certainly has a pretty complicated appearance. Yet, just like gender, it is deeply rooted in the language system and the language user. Loan words are incorporated into that system (sometimes accompanied by reinterpretation of the phonological form of the loan). For instance, the English instruction *keep left* has been adapted in

Swahili as *kipilefti*, and is used to denote a roundabout. The first syllable *ki* has been interpreted as a class prefix (class IV), and hence the plural form of this word is *vipilefti*. A similar case is the Arabic loan word *kitabi* "book" with the plural form *vitabi*.

The other important inflectional category for nouns is case. Like number properties, case properties of nouns are transferred to words of other classes through agreement. The Icelandic paradigm in Table 6.1 is quite characteristic of Indo-European case systems with respect to the number of cases. Languages may differ considerably in the number of cases they have, if any. Finnish and Hungarian are well known for their large number of cases. There are four cases with a clearly grammatical function: nominative, accusative, genitive, and partitive. The **partitive** case is used to mark patient objects that are partially affected by the action, as the following sentence from Hungarian illustrates (Blake 1994: 153):

(11)   Olvasott   a   könyv-böl
       read.3SG   the   book-PART
       "He read some of the book"

This language and its relatives are well known for its large set of **local cases**. The Finnish nouns in (12) all have a particular local case. These local cases have similar functions as locative prepositions in languages with less elaborated case systems such as Latin. In addition to the local cases, there are also cases such as the **abessive** with the meaning "without", and the **comitative**, with the meaning "accompanied by".

(12)	*Case label*	*Meaning*	*Example*
	allative	to(wards) (the exterior) of	pöydä-lle "onto the table"
	illative	into	laitokse-en "to the institute"
	ablative	from (the exterior of)	kadu-lta "out of the street"
	elative	from (the inside of)	kaupa-sta "out of the shop"
	inessive	in(side)	talo-ssa "in the house"
	adessive	at	roof-ade "on the roof"

The elative and the partitive case are both used in quantifying expressions. Consider the following examples from Finnish (Sulkala and Karjalainen 1992: 234):

(13)   kaksi   poji-sta   kaksi   poika-a
       two   boy.PL-ELATIVE   two   boy-PARTITIVE
       "two of the boys"   "two boys"

Note that in the second example, the noun is not marked for plural. The number word functions as the head of the phrase, and assigns partitive case to the following noun. These examples show that there is no one-to-one relation between particular case labels and their semantic interpretation since the elative is used for semantically partitive expressions.

The case labels here are primarily formal notions. A particular case may be used for a number of different meanings. The Latin ablative case, for example, may be used with an instrumental meaning, but also to indicate removal from somewhere. In Finnish, the instrumental meaning can be expressed by the adessive case, as in (Sulkala and Karjalainen 1992: 224):

(14)   Tein   leivä-n   konee-lla
       make.IMPF.1SG bread-ACC   machine-ADESSIVE
       "I made bread with the machine"

The genitive case is well known for its vague meaning: it may specify a relation between the noun marked with genitive case and another noun (the head noun), but the specific interpretation of that relation is a matter of interpretation. The Latin phrase *amor parentum* "the parents' love", with the word *parens* "parent" in the GEN.PL form, can either denote the love that parents have (for their children), or the love that they receive from their children. In the first case, they are the subject of love, in the second case the object. Hence, one finds the corresponding semantic distinctions **genitivus subjectivus** and **genitivus objectivus** in traditional descriptions of Latin. The general meaning of the genitive is clearly "relation". The linguist Roman Jakobson has tried to derive such specific semantic interpretations of each of the Russian cases from a general, vague meaning, referred to as the **Gesamtbedeutung** (Jakobson 1936).

6.2 Categories of verbal inflection

There are three important categories of inherent inflection for verbs: tense, mood, and aspect. Many languages have overt marking for these categories, and in language descriptions one usually finds a description of the Tense–Mood–Aspect system or **TMA system** for short. In addition, there is a category Voice (such as Active versus Passive forms) that is sometimes considered as part of verbal inflection. However, since this category has effects on the syntactic valency of verbs, it is treated in Chapter 8. Verbs may also carry features of the participants of the event they denote. Hence, we also find number, person, and gender marking on verbs.

The tense of a verb locates the situation denoted by the relevant clause on a time axis with, in most cases, the moment of speaking as the point of reference. The notion **tense** is to be distinguished from the notion 'time'. With tense we refer to the grammatical expression of time notions in a language, through morphology or periphrastic forms. Time, on the other hand, can be expressed through all kinds of phrases, such as *the previous day*. The **past tense** indicates that the situation obtained before the moment of speaking, the **present tense** indicates that the situation obtains at the moment of speaking, and the **future tense** signals that the situation denoted is located on the time axis after the moment of speaking. Some languages have specific morphological forms for these three tenses, as is the case for Lithuanian (Chung and Timberlake 1985: 204):

(15) a. dirb-au
          work-1SG.PAST
          "I worked/was working"
      b. dirb-u
          work-1SG.PRES
          "I work/am working"
      c. dirb-s-iu
          work-FUT-1SG
          "I will work/will be working"

The function of tense is a deictic one, because its interpretation depends on some external point of reference in the speech situation, the time axis. With the notion **deixis** we refer to the link between elements of an utterance and entities in some extra-linguistic reality. In the sentence *He is ill*, for instance, the personal pronoun *he* is used deictically: the speaker assumes that the hearer is able to identify the referent of that pronoun in the speech situation.

The interpretation of tense forms is sometimes more complicated than sketched above. A well-known example of a mismatch between form and interpretation is the use of the present tense in referring to the past. This use is traditionally called **praesens historicum**. In this kind of language use, we use present tense forms in speaking about the past, in order to make our report on what has happened more lively, and incisive.

Another salient feature of tense is that, although it is marked on the verb, its semantic scope is the whole clause to which it belongs. In the sentence

Suzanne told the children a fairy-tale, the whole situation of Suzanne telling the children a fairy-tale is claimed to have been true at some moment before the moment of speaking. The statement *John met the Tsar* can therefore be true now, at the moment of speaking, even though there is no Tsar any more.

The notion **aspect** refers to the way in which situations (states or events) can be presented. The term is used as a semantic notion, but also to refer to the grammatical expression of that semantic notion. As Comrie (1976: 3) stated, 'aspects are different ways of viewing the internal temporal constituency of a situation'. **Perfective aspect** presents a situation as completed, whereas **imperfective aspect** presents the situation as ongoing. This kind of aspect is referred to as **grammatical** aspect.

Grammatical aspect has to be distinguished from **predicational aspect**, the kind of aspect that is determined by a verb and its arguments. Consider the following English sentences:

(16)   a. John reads a lot
       b. John reads the book

The action of reading does not necessarily have an inherent endpoint, and hence the verb *to read* in its intransitive use in (16a) receives a **durative** (or **atelic**) interpretation. This durative aspect is the inherent lexical aspect of this verb. In (16b), the same verb is used as a transitive verb, with a definite direct object, and hence this sentence receives a **telic** interpretation, in which the endpoint of the action is implied. Predicational aspect thus not only depends on the nature of the verb, but also on that of its arguments such as the object NP, and is therefore compositional in nature

For other verbs, telic aspect is an inherent property, as is the case for the verb *to die* that denotes a punctual event. Hence, we call it **lexical aspect** (also referred to by its German label, **Aktionsart**). A punctual event by definition implies that the endpoint of the event is reached, and hence its lexical aspect is telic. Verbs with inherent telic aspect can also be created by means of derivational morphology, as we will see in Chapter 9.

In sum, there are at least three different layers involved in the aspectual properties of a sentence: (i) lexical aspect, (ii) predicational aspect, and (iii) grammatical aspect, the latter being a property of the proposition expressed by the clause.

The necessity of distinguishing between grammatical aspect and predicational aspect is illustrated by the following sentence:

(17) John is reading the book

The predicate *reading the book* has telic aspect, since there is an implied endpoint for the action denoted. Yet, its grammatical aspect is imperfective: it presents the situation as ongoing, marked by the periphrastic **progressive** form of the English verb.

The notion **perfect** must be distinguished from the notion perfective aspect. The perfect relates two different points on the time axis, and 'indicates the continuing relevance of a past situation' (Comrie 1976: 52). Therefore, the perfect is often considered a temporal rather than an aspectual distinction. Compare the following two English sentences:

(18) a. PAST TENSE: Herry read the last novel by McEwan
     b. PRESENT PERFECT TENSE: Herry has read the last novel by McEwan

The first sentence denotes an individual event. In the second sentence, it is indicated that the event in the past of Herry reading a particular novel is added to the inventory of achievements by Herry. This explains why a temporal adverbial such as *yesterday* can be used in combination with the past tense, but not in combination with the present perfect: a time specification is only correct for an individual event.

In some European languages the differences between past and present perfect have become blurred. For instance, in Dutch, unlike English, it is possible to use the present perfect form in combination with *gisteren* "yesterday", as in

(19)   Gisteren heeft Herry de laatste roman van McEwan gelezen
       Yesterday has Herry the last novel by McEwan read
       "Yesterday, Herry read the last novel by McEwan"

In Afrikaans, the simple past tense forms of its mother language Dutch have disappeared completely and the periphrastic present perfect forms are used to express the simple past.

The distinction between imperfective and perfective aspect is most common for past tense forms; present tense denotes an ongoing event, and hence is imperfective by nature. The following examples from Spanish illustrate the differences in interpretation between the two aspects (González 2003: 112):

(20)   a.   Laura beb-ió una Coca-Cola
            Laura drink-PAST.PERF a Coca-Cola
            "Laura drank a Coca-Cola"

    b. Laura beb-ía una Coca-Cola
        Laura drink-PAST.IMPF a Coca-Cola
        "Laura drank a Coca-Cola"

In (20a), the situation is presented as closed off, whereas in (20b) the event is interpreted as ongoing, with a progressive or habitual interpretation. These examples also illustrate that, quite often, the different forms of a verbal paradigm express both tense and aspect by means of the same ending, that is, by means of cumulative exponence.

The third category associated with verbal paradigms is that of mood. **Mood** describes the actuality of an event. For instance, a language may use morphology to distinguish between actual and non-actual events by having a **realis** and an **irrealis** mood. The **indicative** mood is typically the mood for realis, whereas **subjunctive** and **imperative** forms denote some sort of non-actuality. Subjunctive forms are found, for instance, in embedded clauses with a matrix verb of hoping, ordering, or claiming. The following example illustrates this for German:

(**21**) Er behauptet er   sei   dort   gewesen
        he claims   he   be.CONJUNCTIVE there   been
        "He claims he has been there"

If you hope or think that something will happen, ·or if you order something to happen, it has not yet happened, so the event is not part of the actual world. Mood may also be used to indicate the epistemic status of the proposition. Latvian, for instance, has an **evidential** mood to report hearsay knowledge, as in the following sentence (Nau 2001: 189):

(**22**) Cit-i   saka   tu   es-ot   visai   skarb-s
        other-PL   say.PRES.3 2SG   be-EVID   very   harsh-NOM.SG.MASC
        tip-s
        fellow-NOM.SG
        "Some say—you are a rather harsh fellow"

Although tense, aspect, and mood are qualitatively different notions, they are often intertwined in the form of a verb. For instance, past tense and perfective aspect are related, because for an event to be completed, it cannot be ongoing, and thus excludes present tense. There is also a relation between past and irrealis: the event denoted is not an actual one. Hence, past tense forms are used to express irrealis, as in

(**23**) I would have come, if I had been able to

In combination with the future modal auxiliary, a counterfactual interpretation is invoked.

Because these three notions are so intertwined, one often finds the term TMA-system to refer to the verbal system for expressing these three categories and related ones such as speaker's attitude. In so far these three categories are expressed by different morphemes, the following tendency has been observed concerning their ordering and that of person markers with respect to the verbal stem:

(24)   aspect > tense > mood > person (Bybee 1985: 35)

This hierarchy means that aspect markers tend to be found more closely to the stem than tense markers, tense markers more closely than mood markers, etc. As argued by Bybee (1985), this ordering may reflect the degree to which the meaning expressed by the verbal root is affected by these different markers. For instance, aspectual markers, which are closest to the verbal root, have a direct effect on the kind of event that is denoted by the verb. Tense markers, on the other hand, do not affect the meaning of the verb directly, but express the location of the state or event denoted by the verb on the time axis with respect to the moment of speaking.

In addition to these three categories of inherent inflection on verbs, verbs may exhibit contextual inflection in the form of person, number, and gender marking. The distinction between three persons for both singular and plural number is quite pervasive in the languages of the world. **Person** marking is found for the subject, and sometimes also for other dependents of the verb such as the object. The number of distinctions made by a particular language can sometimes be read off its system of pronouns. The next step is to see how, and to what extent, these distinctions are also encoded in verbal forms. Many pronominal systems have up to six different forms for these six possible combinations of person and number. The semantic interpretation of the distinction between the three persons is as follows:

(25)   1 = speaker, 2 = addressee, 3 = any other entity than speaker or addressee

These semantic qualifications make clear that PERSON is a deictic notion. The referential value of personal pronouns, for instance, is not fixed, and depends on the situation in which the sentence is uttered. That is why the Danish linguist Jespersen called these pronouns **shifters**. The referential value of, for instance, *I* will shift continuously in the course of a dialogue.

For a child, it sometimes takes some time before it has mastered that system, and understands that *I* can refer to someone else than the child itself.

The notion plural has a particular interpretation in connection to person, namely that of "group". The following combinations are logically possible (after Cysouw 2001: 70);

(26)   1 + 1 "we", mass speaking
        1 + 2 "we", including addressee, excluding other
        1 + 3 "we", including other, excluding addressee
        1 + 2 + 3 "we", complete
        2 + 2 "you-all", only present audience
        2 + 3 "you-all", addressee(s) and others
        3 + 3 "they"

The English pronoun *we* allows for all four logically possible interpretations; the first one is only appropriate when people speak or sing together as in the soccer stadium where the audience sings *We are the champions*. Some languages have different forms for **inclusive** *we* (1 + 2) versus **exclusive** *we* (1 + 3), as illustrated here for the possessive pronouns of Cuzco Quechua (van de Kerke 1996: 121):

(27)   wasi-y   "my house"
        wasi-yki   "your house"
        wasi-n   "his house"
        wasi-nchis   "our (speaker's and hearer's) house"
        wasi-yku   "our (speaker's and not hearer's) house"
        wasi-ykichis   "your house"
        wasi-nku   "their house"

Many languages that have six formal distinctions in their pronominal system do not have the same number in their verbal inflection. In the English singular present tense forms of regular verbs we only find a formal morphological distinction between third person versus first/second person (*walk-s* versus *walk*); in the plural, there are no morphologically marked person distinctions whatsoever. This kind of syncretism can be accounted for by considering such forms as underspecified for certain morphosyntactic features. The English plural forms are not specified for the category PERSON, and hence they combine with subjects of all three persons. When combinations of finite verbal forms and subjects are checked by the rule of Agreement, these plural forms will be discovered to be compatible with their subject with respect to these categories. The form *walk* can be specified as [-3SG], and will therefore be combinable with 1SG and 2SG, and with all kinds of plural subjects. Italian, on the other hand, has distinct present tense forms for all six person–number combinations.

Some linguists have claimed that there is a relation between the omissability of the subject and the richness of the verbal paradigm. Italian, for instance, has six different present tense forms, and allows for omission of the subject. This idea is referred to as the **Pro-drop-parameter**: languages differ as to the obligatory expression of the subject, depending on the degree of richness of the verbal paradigm. However, it appears that there is no necessary connection between the two since there are also languages that do not have different forms for each of the six cells, and yet do allow for omission of the subject, as is the case for Indonesian (Cysouw 2001: 52).

In many languages, politeness conventions affect the selection of a particular person form. In Italian, for instance, the 3sG form is used as the form for addressing persons in a polite way:

(28)   Come   sta-i?   vs   Come   sta?
        how   be-2sG   how   be.3sG
        "How are you?"   "How are you?" (polite)

The 3sG form creates a larger distance between speaker and addressee than a 2sG form. This distance or indirectness receives the value of politeness. Other languages use plural forms for that purpose, or a combination of both, as in German where both the 3PL subject pronoun and the corresponding verbal form are used to refer to a singular or plural addressee in order to convey politeness:

(29)   sie kommen "they come"   Sie kommen "you (sG/PL) come" (polite)
                                  du komm-st "you (sG) come" (informal)

The use of a capital initial for the pronoun in the politeness form is an orthographic marker of this use of the pronoun. In old-fashioned Dutch, the 1PL verbal form in combination with the pronoun *wij* "we" can be used as a **pluralis majestatis**, as in the opening line of Dutch law texts which are formulated as a decision of the Dutch queen: *Wij Beatrix, bij de gratie Gods Koningin der Nederlanden* "We, Beatrix, by the grace of God Queen of the Netherlands". The 1PL form can also be used by writers to express modesty, since written *Ik* "I" might be felt as the author imposing him/herself too much on the reader. Thus, the use and interpretation of person–number features is governed by language-specific conventional pragmatic rules.

6.3 Autonomous morphology

In the realm of inflection, the relationships between form and meaning are quite complex, with much formal variation that does not serve to directly express a specific grammatical content. The existence of declensions and conjugations means that there is a many-to-one relationship between form and meaning. We might refer to these phenomena as 'autonomous morphology' since morphology has its own formal systematics that does not bear upon the other modules of the grammar. Let us have a closer look at these complexities in the domain of verbal inflection.

Many Indo-European languages have a number of verbal conjugations. Italian, for instance, has three conjugations, each with a different thematic vowel after the root, *a, e,* or *i*. The third conjugation has two subclasses because some of the *i*-verbs have a special allomorph with an augment *isc*. We call this string *isc* an augment since it does not express some inflectional property. The verbal forms in Table 6.3 constitute only a subset of the different verbal paradigms, and are meant as a modest illustration of the possible richness of verbal inflectional systems. The occurrence of the augment *isc* is lexically governed but not completely arbitrary. It only appears in those forms in which otherwise the stress would fall on the root (SG and 3PL forms).

In Italian, the infinitive form is the form used to refer to a particular verb. This form contains the thematic vowel that we have to know in order to compute the whole set of forms in a paradigm. So the infinitive form has the structure 'root + thematic vowel + ending', and it is the stem (root + thematic vowel) that is the basis for computing the different forms. These different thematic vowels show up in a systematic way in the imperfective past tense forms, which are completely regular once you know the thematic vowel.

In order to compute the whole verbal paradigm, you may actually need more than one stem-form for the computation of the whole verbal paradigm. Consider the Latin data in Table 6.4. As these data show, the best way to compute the future participle is deriving it from the perfect participle by adding the suffix *-ūr*. In those cases in which the perfect participle has an irregular form, that irregularity recurs in the future participle. The clearest case of this argument is the verb *ferre* that has a suppletive stem for the perfect participle. This suppletive stem *lāt-* recurs in the future participle.

Table 6.3. *The Italian verb paradigm*

INFINITIVE	parlare "speak"	temere "fear"	dormire "sleep"	capire "understand"
PRESENT				
1SG	parlo	temo	dormo	capisco
2SG	parli	temi	dormi	capisci
3SG	parla	teme	dorme	capisce
1PL	parliamo	temiamo	dormiamo	capiamo
2PL	parlate	temete	dormite	capite
3PL	parlano	temono	dormono	capiscono
PAST IMPERFECTIVE				
1SG	parlavo	temevo	dormivo	capivo
2SG	parlavi	temevi	dormivi	capivi
3SG	parlava	temeva	dormiva	capiva
1PL	parlavamo	temevamo	dormivamo	capivamo
2PL	parlavate	temevate	dormivate	capivate
3PL	parlavano	temevano	dormivano	capivano
PAST PERFECTIVE				
1SG	parlai	temei	dormii	capii
2SG	parlasti	temesti	dormisti	capisti
3SG	parlò	temè	dormì	capì
1PL	parlammo	tememmo	dormimmo	capimmo
2PL	parlaste	temeste	dormiste	capiste
3PL	parlarono	temerono	dormirono	capirono
FUTURE				
1SG	parlerò	temerò	dormirò	capirò
2SG	parlerai	temerai	dormirai	capirai
3SG	parlerà	temerà	dormirà	capirà
1PL	parleremo	temeremo	dormiremo	capiremo
2PL	parlerete	temerete	dormirete	capirete
3PL	parlaranno	temeranno	dormiranno	capiranno

However, from a semantic point of view, there is no ground for claiming that the future participle is derived from the perfect participle. Obviously, the future participle does not carry a perfect meaning. So we have to say instead that Latin verbs have (at least) two stems. Stem-1 is the stem-form on which the infinitive is based. Stem-2 forms the basis for both the perfect participle and the future participle. This is represented in Figure 6.1. For regular verbs such as *laudāre*, Stem-2 can be computed from Stem-1

Table 6.4. *Latin verbal stem-forms*

INFINITIVE	PERFECT PARTICIPLE	FUTURE PARTICIPLE	*gloss*
laudā-re	laudāt-	laudāt-ūr-	praise
monē-re	monit-	monit-ūr-	warn
duce-re	duct-	duct-ūr-	lead
prem-ere	press-	press-ūr-	press
fer-re	lāt-	lāt-ūr-	carry

Source: Aronoff 1994: 32.

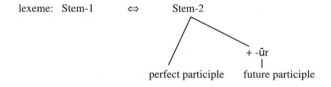

Fig. 6.1 Stems in Latin

(through the addition of *-t*). For irregular verbs, Stem-2 has to be stored as part of the lexical information on that verb. Aronoff (1994) introduced the term **morphome** as a label for categories such as Stem-2 which have no grammatical relevance beyond the functioning of morphology. Stem-2 is a morphome, a morphological function that specifies the stem form for particular morphosyntactic forms.

Different verbal stems also play a role in word-formation. For instance, the stem of Italian perfect participles is also used for coining deverbal agent nouns (Vogel 1994: 233), see (30).

(30)	*Verb*	*Past participle*	*Agent noun*
	corregg-ere "to correct"	corrett-o	corrett-ore
	dirig-ere "to direct"	dirett-o	dirett-ore
	distrugg-ere "to destroy"	distrutt-o	distrutt-ore
	scriv-ere "to write"	scritt-o	scritt-ore

Another kind of formal variation in paradigms is that of suppletion. Suppletion underscores the importance of the notion 'inflectional paradigm': forms belong together, not always because they are phonologically similar, but because they fill the cells of the paradigm of the same lexeme.

Table 6.5. *Singular present forms of 'to be'*

	English	Dutch	French	Italian
1sg	am	ben	suis	sono
2sg	are	bent	es	sei
3sg	is	is	est	è

Classic cases of suppletion are the different forms of the verb *to be* in English. In many languages, the equivalent of this verb has a suppletive paradigm (Table 6.5). Suppletive forms usually occur in particular with lexemes with a high frequency of use. In a number of languages, the verb for "to give" has different stems depending on the person of the recipient: first and second person versus third person. In Kolyma Yukaghir, a language of northeastern Siberia, the following pair of suppletive forms is found (Elena Maslova, cited in Comrie 2001):

(32)   tadi- "give to 3PERS", kej- "give to 1/2PERS"

In languages with a number of conjugations, there is usually one default conjugation: the inflection class taken by new verbs that enter the language. In Italian, this is the *a*-conjugation. A somewhat different situation obtains in Germanic languages. They have a default conjugation in which the past tense stem is formed through suffixation. This is called the weak conjugation, illustrated in Table 6.6.

Table 6.6. *Regular past tense and participle formation in Dutch*

VERB	STEM	PAST TENSE SG	PAST PARTICIPLE
tob "to toil"	/tɔb/	tob-de [bd]	ge-tob-d
leg "to lay"	/lɛɣ/	leg-de [ɣd]	ge-leg-d
kap "to cut"	/kɑp/	kap-te [pt]	ge-kap-t
paf "to puff"	/pɑf/	paf-te [ft]	ge-paf-t

In addition they have a number of classes of strong or stem-alternating verbs that create past tense by means of vowel alternation (Ablaut). The past participles of weak and strong verbs also differ in that those of strong verbs exhibit vowel alternations as well (Table 6.7). Weak verbs have a past tense suffix *-te* after stems ending in a voiceless obstruent, and *-de*

Table 6.7. *Stem alternating verbs in Dutch*

Alternation pattern	PRESENT TENSE STEM	PAST TENSE STEM	PAST PARTICIPLE
A-B-B			
/ɛi-eː-eː/	knijp "to pinch"	kneep	ge-knep-en
/i-oː-oː/	schiet "to shoot"	schoot	ge-schot-en
/ʌy-oː-oː/	buig "to bend"	boog	ge-bog-en
/eː-oː-oː/	weeg "to weigh"	woog	ge-wog-en
/ɪ-ɔ-ɔ/	bind "to bind"	bond	ge-bond-en
/ɛ-ɔ-ɔ/	zend "to send"	zond	ge-zond-en
A-B-A			
/aː-u-aː/	draag "to carry"	droeg	ge-drag-en
/aː-i-aː/	blaas "to blow"	blies	ge-blaz-en
/ɑ-i-ɑ/	val "to fall"	viel	ge-vall-en
/ɑ-ɪ-ɑ/	hang "to hang"	hing	ge-hang-en
/oː-i-oː/	loop "to walk"	liep	ge-lop-en
/ɔ-ɛ-ɔ/	word "to become"	werd	ge-word-en
/u-i-u/	roep "to call"	riep	ge-roep-en
A-B-C			
/ɛ-i-ɔ/	help "to help"	hielp	ge-holp-en
/ɛ-i-aː/	schep "to create"	schiep	ge-schap-en
/eː-u-oː/	zweer "to swear"	zwoer	ge-zwor-en

elsewhere. The past participle is formed by prefixing the stem with *ge-*, and suffixing it with *-t* (again, after voiceless obstruents), and *-d* elsewhere. Note that the past participles of stem-alternating verbs have another suffix, *-en*. New verbs that enter the language (through borrowing or conversion from nouns) are always inflected as weak verbs. This is independent evidence for the weak verbs—which form the largest inflectional class of all—being the default class. For instance, the Dutch verb *computer* "to use a computer" has *computer-de* as its past tense stem. The verb *prijzen* "to praise" is a strong verb. There is also a homophonous verb *prijzen* derived through conversion form the noun *prijs* "price", with the meaning "to price, to provide with price labels". This latter verb is weakly inflected, and thus we get the pair of past tense singular forms *prees* [preːs] "praised" versus *prijsde* [prɛizdə] "priced".

As in the case of suppletion, the verbs that exhibit apophony tend to belong to the verbs with the highest frequency of use. The entrenchment of these past tense stems in the memory of the language user must be an important factor for the relative stability of such complicated systems.

Finally, periphrasis is a common feature of verbal inflectional systems. For instance, in many European languages forms of the verb for "to have" and "to be" are used as auxiliaries in periphrastic forms for expressing the perfect, perfective aspect, or past tense. Historically, the use of *to have* as an auxiliary derives from its use in predicative constructions. The sentence *I have the door shut* can be interpreted as parallel to *I keep the door shut*, with *shut* specifying a property of *the door*, something like "I have the door in a shut state". Such constructions could be reanalysed as expressing that a certain state of the object has been achieved, thus providing an interpretation of "completion of the act of shutting". The combination of auxiliary and past participle thus started leading a life of its own.

Summary

Systems for the inflections of nouns, adjectives, and verbs show complicated patterns of formal variation in the expression of morphosyntactic categories. That is why often a number of declensions and conjugations have to be distinguished. The main inflectional categories for nouns and adjectives are gender, number, and case. Verbs may be morphologically marked for tense, aspect, mood, gender, person, and number.

The facts discussed in this chapter show that the notion 'paradigm' plays an indispensable role in the analysis of inflectional systems and their subsystems. Notions such as periphrasis, suppletion, and rule of referral all presuppose that inflectional forms are conceived of as filling the cells of a paradigm.

The notion 'autonomous morphology' introduced in section 6.3 pertains to the whole range of purely formal regularities involved in the proper morphological expression of grammatical content on words, and the analysis of these regularities.

Questions

1. The Animacy Hierarchy plays a role in the use of English personal pronouns. English distinguishes three genders for 3SG personal pronouns: *he, she, it* that can be used to refer to NPs. However, this threefold gender distinction is not maintained for all antecedent NPs of these pronouns. Where on the hierarchy is the cut-off point for the three-gender distinction?

2. Consider the following fourteen singular case forms of the Finnish words *käsi* "hand" and *tyttö* "girl" (Sulkala and Karjalainen 1992: 386):

NOMINATIVE	käsi	tyttö
GENITIVE	käden	tytön
PARTITIVE	kättä	tyttöä
ESSIVE	kätenä	tyttönä
TRANSLATIVE	kädeksi	tytöksi
ABESSIVE	kädettä	tytöttä
INESSIVE	kädessä	tytössä
ELATIVE	kädesta	tytösta
ILLATIVE	käteen	tyttöön
ADESSIVE	kädellä	tytöllä
ABLATIVE	kädeltä	tytöltä
ALLATIVE	kädelle	tytölle
INSTRUMENTAL	käden	—
COMITATIVE	käsineen	tyttöineen

a. List the different stem shapes of these two words, and their distribution across the cases.

b. If we wanted to make the instrumental case form of *tyttö* "girl", what would it be?

3. Lithuanian has five different declensions for nouns. Nouns with a NOM.SG form in *-as*, *-is*, or *-ys* such as *vyras* "man", *brolis* "brother", and *arklys* "horse" belong to the first declension, and have the paradigms shown in the table.

	SINGULAR			PLURAL		
NOM	vyras	brolis	arklys	vyrai	broliai	arkliai
GEN	vyro	brolio	arklio	vyrų	brolių	arklių
DAT	vyrui	broliui	arkliui	vyrams	broliams	arkliams
ACC	vyrą	brolį	arklį	vyrus	brolius	arklius
INST	vyru	broliu	arkliu	vyrais	broliais	arkliais
LOC	vyre	brolyje	arklyje	vyruose	broliuose	arkliuose
VOC	vyre	broli	arkly	vyrai	broliai	arkliai

Source: Tekorienė 1990: 221; the *y* stands for [i :], and the cedille on vowel letters indicates length.

a. What are the stem-forms of these three nouns?

b. What rule(s) of referral can be formulated for these paradigms?

4. My Latin school grammar presents the following paradigms for the words *nemo* "nobody" and *nihil* "nothing":

NOMINATIVE	nēmō	nihil
GENITIVE	nullīus	nullīus reī
DATIVE	neminī	nullī reī
ACCUSATIVE	neminem	nihil
ABLATIVE	a nullō	nullā rē

Which paradigmatic notions are presupposed in this presentation of the forms of *nemo* and *nihil?*

5. In some languages, the imperfect or past tense can be used with modal or politeness overtones, as in the following sentences from Dutch and Finnish (Sulkala Karjalainen 1992: 299) respectively:

Wat   was   uw   naam?
what   was   your   name
"What is your name, please?"
Oliko   rouvala   lippua?
be.IMPF.3SG.Q   madam.ADESSIVE   ticket.PARTITIVE
"Would you have a ticket, madam?"

How would you explain this use of past tense forms?

6. Which form of systematic syncretism may be assumed for the Polish nouns in (1) of Chapter 2?

7. In the following Latin sentences, the verbal infinitive used as subject imposes neuter gender on the predicative adjective, and person and number marking on the verb:

mentī-ri   turp-e   est
lie-INF   scandalous-NEUT   be.3SG
"Lying is scandalous"
navigā-re   difficil-e   est
saïl-INF   difficult-NEUT   be.3SG
"Sailing is difficult"

Explain why these verbal infinitives trigger agreement, although it is typically nominal elements that are the sources of the agreeing features.

8. In Turkish constructions with partitive numerals, the quantified noun receives genitive or ablative case. The numeral itself carries a nominal agreement marker (Kornfilt 1997: 236–7).

çocuk-lar-ın   iki-si   çocuk-lar-dan iki-si
child-PL-GEN   two-3SG   child-PL-ABL   two-3SG
"two of the children"   "two of the children"

Is the case marking of the word *çocuk-lar* "children" an instance of dependent marking or of head marking?

9. Compare the following Dutch sentence and its English gloss:

Morgen   breng   ik   je   het boek
tomorrow   bring   I   you   the book
"Tomorrow, I'll bring you the book"

How might it be explained that the future tense which is expressed overtly in English does not receive overt marking in Dutch?

10. The following Turkish sentence has an iterative aspectual interpretation

although there is no morphological marker for iterative aspect (Kornfilt 1997: 360):

Hasan   öksür-üyor
Hasan   cough-PRES.PROGR
"Hasan is coughing repeatedly"

How can this iterative aspectual interpretation be explained?

Further reading

There are monographs on the following morphosyntactic categories discussed in this chapter: Number (Corbett 2000), Gender (Corbett 1991), Case (Blake 1994), Tense (Comrie 1984), Aspect (Comrie 1976), Person (Cysouw 2001). Chung and Timberlake (1985) is an article with a typological survey of TMA-systems. The role of gender in natural language is discussed in Unterbeck *et al.* (2000).

For rules of referral, see Stump (1993, 2001). In a number of publications, Carstairs-McCarthy has studied the constraints on the extent of allomorphy we find in inflectional systems (for instance, Carstairs 1987; Carstairs-McCarthy 1994; Cameron-Faulkner and Carstairs-McCarthy 2000).

A formal analysis of syncretism by means of inheritance trees is proposed in Corbett and Fraser (1993). Harley and Noyer (2003) discuss syncretism in the framework of Distributed Morphology. A website with a database on syncretism is http://www.smg.surrey.ac.uk.

Part IV

Interfaces

7

The interface between morphology and phonology

7.1 Morphology and phonology

The English adjective *seléctive* can be suffixed with either *-ity* or *-ness*, resulting in *selectívity* and *seléctiveness* respectively. The acute accents on these words indicate the location of main stress. As you can see, the attachment of the suffix *-ity* has the effect that the location of the main word stress shifts rightwards, to the last syllable of the stem *selective*, whereas the attachment of the suffix *-ness* does not affect the location of the main stress on the stem. This suggests that morphological structure may play a role in determining the phonological form of a complex word. In this chapter we will zoom in on the issue how morphological structure plays a role in computing the phonological form of a word. Inversely, phonological properties of words may also play a role in selecting an affix with which it can combine. The English suffix *-al*, for example, can only be attached to verbs that end in a stressed syllable (*arríve– arríval, recíte–recítal, chátter–*chatter-al*). These kinds of interaction between morphology and phonology show that there must be an interface between the morphological and the phonological properties of words. 'Interface' means that different kinds of information about linguistic constructs (in these examples words) can 'see' each other.

In order to provide some more substance to the notion 'interface' in the domain of morphology, we will first consider what kinds of information on words the grammar needs to provide. A word is a complex piece of information. It links a particular sequence of sounds to a particular meaning, and also has formal properties such as a syntactic category label. The information contained in the English simplex word *dog*, for instance, can be represented as in Figure 7.1. The first piece of information in Figure 7.1 concerns

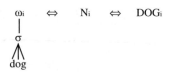

Fig. 7.1 The representation of *dog*

the phonological properties of this word: it is a **phonological word** (ω) that consists of one syllable (σ) that in its turn consists of a sequence of three sounds. This phonological word bears the same index as the syntactic information about this word (that it is a noun), and the semantic information that it expresses the predicate DOG. Coindexation is used here to specify the correspondence between the three kinds of information involved in knowing a word. We thus see that a word has a **tripartite parallel structure**.

Let us now look at a complex word such as the English word *baker*, a noun derived from the verb *bake* through suffixation with *-er*. The three kinds of information (the phonological form, the morphological structure, and the meaning) concerning this word can be represented as in Figure 7.2. The phonological structure of *baker* is that of a phonological word consisting of two syllables, (be:)$_\sigma$ and (kər)$_\sigma$, and of five phonological segments. Its

Fig. 7.2 The representation of *baker*

formal structure is that of a deverbal noun, as indicated by the tree that represents its formal morphological structure.

The representation in Figure 7.2 may be generalized into a template for nouns derived from verbs by means of the suffix -er. This is achieved by omitting the word-specific information. This morphological template thus specifies that there is the following systematic relation between the three kinds of linguistic information involved (Figure 7.3). In Figure 7.3 the level of the syllables has been omitted because the number of syllables of words ending in -er is not fixed, but depends on the phonological make-up of the base verb. The syllabification of English words is predictable, and need not be specified in morphological templates. Hence it is a computable, predictable property of each individual deverbal noun in -er. Instead of the specific predicate BAKE, the general label V is used to refer to the semantic properties of the base verb.

Fig. 7.3 The template for deverbal -er

The tripartite structure in Figure 7.3, an instance of a word-formation template, is meant to make clear that morphology is not a module of grammar on a par with the phonological or the syntactic module, which are modules that deal with one aspect of linguistic structure only. Morphology is word grammar, and similar to sentence grammar in its dealing with the relationships between three kinds of information. It is only with respect to the domain of linguistic entities that morphology is different from sentence grammar: morphology has the word domain as its primary focus.

This short introduction to the idea of tripartite parallel structure paves the way for grasping the notion 'interface'. This notion refers to the ways in which properties of one kind of structure relate to those of another structure. An example of a relation between phonological and morphological form is that the suffix -er is one of the so-called **cohering suffixes** of English. This means that this suffix forms one domain of syllabification with the stem to which it has been attached. The word *baker* is syllabified in the same way as the word *father* in which the sequence -er is not a suffix. The sound sequence -er forms one syllable with the preceding consonant in both words: *ba.ker, fa.ther* (remember that dots indicate syllable boundaries).

Thus, the morphological boundary between *bak-* and *-er* in *baker* is not respected in phonology, in the sense that it does not coincide with a syllable boundary.

There are also affixes that do influence the way that a complex word is syllabified. The English suffix *-less*, for example, is a **non-cohering suffix**. This means that this suffix forms is own domain of syllabification. The adjective *help-less*, for instance, is syllabified as *help.less*, with a syllable boundary coinciding with the internal morphological boundary. Compare the syllabification of this adjective to the syllabification of the word *staples*, which is *sta.ples*, with a syllable boundary before the consonant cluster /pl/. The distinction between cohering affixes and non-cohering ones is therefore a theoretical distinction that we need for a proper account of the interface between morphology and phonology.

These introductory remarks should give you some idea of what is meant by 'interface'. In this and the next two chapters, these interface issues are dealt with in more detail.

7.2 Interface principles

An important task of the phonological module of a grammar is computing the phonetic form of complex words. Consider the examples in (1) of plural noun formation in Dutch. The plural nouns are formed by adding the suffix *-en* /ən/ to the stem of the noun; the singular form has no overt phonological marking. The basic procedure for computing the phonetic forms of these plural nouns consists of three steps. The first step is attaching the string of segments of the plural suffix to the stem. This is a morphological operation. The next two steps are phonological operations. Step 2 is the computation of the prosodic structure of a word, in particular the way in which a word is syllabified. In step 3, we scan the singular and plural forms as to the applicability of phonological rules or constraints. A well-known phonological

(1)	SINGULAR	*Phonetic form*	PLURAL	*Phonetic form*
	hoed "hat"	[hut]	hoed-en	[hudən]
	voet "foot"	[vut]	voet-en	[vutən]
	poes "cat"	[pus]	poez-en	[puzən]
	spies "spear"	[spis]	spies-en	[spisən]

constraint of Dutch and German is that obstruents (stops and fricatives) are voiceless at the end of a syllable. Therefore, the final obstruents in the singular forms of these nouns must be voiceless. In the plural nouns *hoeden* and *poezen*, on the other hand, the stem-final voiced obstruents appear at the beginning of the second syllable, and hence they are not subject to devoicing. The three steps are illustrated here for the singular and plural forms of the word *hoed* "hat" (σ = syllable):

(2)   step 1:   morphology   hud   hud-ən
      step 2:   syllabification   (hud)$_\sigma$ (hu)$_\sigma$(dən)$_\sigma$
      step 3:   syllable-final devoicing   (hut)$_\sigma$ not applicable

In step 1 we make use of the underlying form of the word *hoed*, the abstract phonological form from which the different surface forms of this word can be derived. At the end of the derivation we have computed the phonetic form of a word. We thus see that Dutch noun stems may exhibit allomorphy, variation in their phonological shape. The lexical morpheme /hud/ has two different shapes, [hut] and [hud]. This variation is governed by a phonological constraint of Dutch, and hence this allomorphy is the predictable effect of the phonological system of Dutch.

The plural form *hoeden* [hudən] "hats" also serves to illustrate a general point concerning the interface between phonology and morphology: the potential asymmetry between morphological and phonological structure. The word *hoeden* consists of five segments that are structured in two ways, as shown in Figure 7.4. The representation of phonological structure in Figure 7.4 requires some explication. The basic idea is that the sounds of a word are organized into higher units. Sound segments combine into syllables (σ), syllables into feet (F), and feet into phonological words (ω). The foot in this word is a trochee, that is, a foot consisting of two syllables

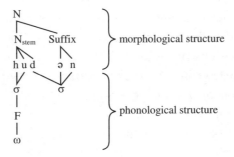

Fig. 7.4 The morphological and phonological structure of *hoeden*

of which the first is the head and carries stress (*hoeden* carries stress on its first syllable). In this case, the phonological word happens to consist of only one foot. This hierarchical organization of a word's segments is also called its **prosodic structure**, and instead of 'phonological word' the term **prosodic word** may be used.

A basic constraint on the relation between lexical words (that is, non-function words) and prosodic words is that a lexical word must consist of at least one prosodic word:

(3)   Lexical word = $_{minimally}$ prosodic word

English and Dutch require a prosodic word to contain at least one full, that is, non-reduced vowel. Hence, they cannot have schwa [ə] as their only vowel, unlike function words such as *a* and *the*. Dutch function words such as *een* [ən] "a" and *er* [ər] "there" violate a second constraint of Dutch, namely that a prosodic word cannot begin with a schwa. Hence, unlike these function words, lexical words of Dutch never begin with a schwa.

The asymmetry of phonological and morphological structure manifests itself quite clearly in Figure 7.4 with respect to the /d/: at the level of morphological structure it forms a unit with the preceding sounds, at the level of phonological structure it combines with the following sounds. The interaction between morphology and phonology in this example is, so it seems, zero. Phonology does not seem to care about the formal morphological structure of this word. However, as we will see below, there are many cases in which morphological structure does influence the phonological form of a word.

The three steps in (2) illustrate the idea of phonological derivation: the computation of the phonetic forms of words in a number of steps, which is a hallmark of classical generative phonology. There is an alternative, non-derivational model that can be used to achieve the same result. In that model, the phonology of a language is seen as a set of ranked constraints. In the case of *hoeden*, three constraints are relevant. One is the constraint which demands that obstruents are voiceless in syllable-final position. Let us refer to it as **FinDevoicing**. A second constraint is called **Faithfulness**: the phonetic realization of a word or morpheme should be identical to its underlying form, and not deviate from that underlying form. That is, allomorphy should be avoided. A third constraint that plays a role is that syllables should begin with a consonant. This is the **No Empty Onset** constraint. As the phonetic form of the singular form *hoed* [hut] shows, in

Dutch the constraint FinDevoicing is ranked higher than Faithfulness since we do get allomorphy. The existence of allomorphy shows that constraints can be violated: faithfulness is violated in the singular form in order to satisfy the higher ranked constraint FinDevoicing. The selection of the optimal phonetic form of *hoed* and *hoeden* is shown in Figure 7.5. It is represented in tables (called tableaux), and this variety of phonological analysis is called **Optimality Theory**.

/hud/	NO EMPTY ONSET	FINDEVOICING	FAITHFULNESS
(hud)$_\sigma$		*!	
☞ (hut)$_\sigma$			*
/hud-ən/	NO EMPTY ONSET	FINDEVOICING	FAITHFULNESS
☞ (hu)$_\sigma$(dən)$_\sigma$			
(hu)$_\sigma$(tən)$_\sigma$			!*
(hud)$_\sigma$(ən)$_\sigma$	*!	*	

Fig. 7.5 OT-tableaux for *hoed* and *hoeden*

The left columns mention the possible phonetic forms for the underlying forms (given between slashes). These phonetic forms are called the candidates. The left–right order of the constraints represents their ranking. The leftmost is the highest ranked one. The asterisks in the cells of the tableaux indicate that a constraint is violated by the candidate phonetic form. If a constraint is no longer relevant for choosing the optimal candidate, the corresponding cell is shaded. The pointed finger indicates the optimal phonetic form. In the case of *hoed* the second candidate is selected since the first candidate violates a higher ranked constraint than the second one. The exclamation mark indicates that a violation is fatal. That is, this violation results in the fact that the form is ungrammatical, and will never surface. For *hoeden* the first candidate will be selected since it does not violate any of the constraints, unlike the other candidates.

The potential asymmetry between morphological and phonological structure can be expressed by **alignment** constraints. If the two types of structure are to be isomorphic, the edges of stems have to be aligned with the edges of phonological constituents such as the syllable. This is what the constraints Alignment Left and Alignment Right require: align the left and right morphological stem boundaries with phonological constituent boundaries. The reason why Alignment Right is violated in the case of *hoeden* has to do with an important universal phonological constraint mentioned above: syllables should, if possible, begin with a consonant, the No Empty Onset constraint. This constraint refers to the notion 'onset' as a constituent of the syllable. Let me therefore introduce here the basic notions of **syllable structure**. The following structure of the syllable is usually assumed, illustrated in Figure 7.6 for the English word *stump*.

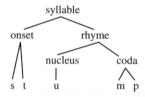

Fig. 7.6 The syllable structure of *stump*

The asymmetry between phonological and morphological structure observed with respect to *hoeden* shows that the No Empty Onset constraint is ranked higher than Alignment Right. If Alignment Right ranked higher than No Empty Onset, we would have to syllabify *hoeden* as *hoed.en* which would result in the wrong phonetic form [hut.ən]. Ranking of No Empty Onset above Alignment Right is therefore a partial specification of the interface between morphology and phonology in the grammar of Dutch.

We might be tempted to jump to a rash conclusion on the basis of the facts discussed above: phonology cannot see the internal morphological structure of words, and deals with complex words in the same way as it deals with simplex words. Hence we do not need detailed specifications of this interface. This conclusion is incorrect, however. A clear counterexample is that in many languages the morphological structure of compounds plays an essential role in the computation of their phonetic forms, with respect to both syllabification and stress patterns. Consider the following minimal pair of compounds of Dutch, with their syllabification:

(4)   [[bal]$_N$[kanker]$_N$]$_N$ "testicle cancer"   (bal)$_\sigma$(kan)$_\sigma$(ker)$_\sigma$
      [[balk]$_N$[anker]$_N$]$_N$ "beam brace"   (balk)$_\sigma$(an)$_\sigma$(ker)$_\sigma$

The difference between these two compounds, which consist of the same sequence of segments, is audible through their different syllabification patterns. This is only possible if the syllabification of compounds respects morphological structure. In particular, the requirement that the left boundary of the second constituent aligns with a syllable boundary (expressed by the constraint Alignment Left) is ranked higher than No Empty Onset. Hence, in the second example, the second syllable begins with an empty onset. Speakers of Dutch also notice this ranking through the effect of FinDevoicing: in a compound such as *handappel* "lit. hand-apple, eating apple", with the morphological structure $[[hand]_N[appel]_N]_N$ and the phonetic form [hɑnt.ɑ.pəl], the /d/ is realized as [t], and hence it must be located in coda position in order to be subject to devoicing. The example of *hoeden* with the morphological structure $[[hoed]en]$, on the other hand, shows that alignment of the right edge of a morphological stem with a syllable boundary (Alignment Right) is less important than the No Empty Onset Constraint. Hence we conclude to the following constraint ranking (>> = "ranked higher than"):

(5) Alignment Left >> No Empty Onset >> Alignment Right

This ranking for Dutch (identical to the one for English) makes correct predictions for prefixed words of Dutch, where the left stem boundary usually coincides with a syllable boundary. The complex verb *ver-as* "to incinerate" with the morphological structure $[ver[as]_N]_V$, for instance, syllabifies in careful speech as *ver.as*, not as *ve.ras*. This results in the second syllable of this word having an empty onset.

In conclusion, morphological structure may affect the computation of phonological forms. Hence, the internal morphological structure of words must be accessible to phonology, and the interface theory should specify in which ways the morphological structure of a complex word determines its phonetic form.

The representation of the phonological structure of the compounds in (4) was in fact simplified for ease of exposition. The foot boundaries and prosodic word boundaries were omitted. What should be added is that each of the compound constituents consists of a phonological word of its own (in their turn each consisting of one foot). Since the phonological word is the domain of syllabification, we will get the result that in a compound the edges of its constituents coincide with phonological word boundaries. Since the phonological word is the domain of syllabification, this implies that these morphological boundaries will also coincide with syllable boundaries. The necessity to distinguish words in the morphological sense and phonological words is a clear illustration of the asymmetry between phonology and morphology: a morphological word may correspond with more than one phonological word. In many languages this is the case for compounds. Syllabification patterns are one type of evidence for this, as discussed above.

The domain of application of phonological rules or constraints is another source of evidence for the prosodic structure of complex words. In the case of Hungarian compounds, **vowel harmony** serves to determine their prosodic structure. Vowel harmony is the phenomenon that all vowels of a word share certain properties. In the case of Hungarian, the vowels of a word are all either front vowels or back vowels. Front vowels are articulated in the anterior part of the mouth, and back vowels in the back part. Vowel harmony implies that many suffixes have two allomorphs, one with a front, and one with a back vowel, as illustrated by the following words (Siptár and Törkenczy 2000: 63):

(6) a. Buda-nak "Buda-DAT", Pest-nek "Pest-DAT"
     b. perd-ül-és-etek-töl "from your (PL) twirling around"
        ford-ul-ás-otok-tól "from your (PL) turning around"

In (6b) we observe four different suffixes. Each of them has two allomorphs, one with a front vowel, and one with a back vowel. The difference is governed by the fact that the two roots of these words have a front vowel /e/ and a back vowel /o/ respectively. (The acute accents on the vowel letters of Hungarian orthography indicate length.)

The name *Budapest* for the capital of Hungary is a compound in which the names of the two cities *Buda* and *Pest* have been combined. It seems to violate the phonological constraint of vowel harmony because the first two vowels are back, and the last one is a front one. However, there is no violation under the assumption that the domain of vowel harmony is the phonological word, not the word in the morphological sense.

After having read (6a), you may wonder which is the correct dative suffix for *Budapest*, -*nek* or -*nak*? After all, it is a suffix of the whole compound. The correct one is -*nek*, since the dative suffix is a cohering suffix, and hence forms one phonological word with the preceding material. We thus see here another instantiation of the asymmetry between morphological and phonological structure that we discussed above. Here are the two relevant structures for *Budapestnek*:

(7) morphological structure: [[[buda]$_N$[pest]$_N$]$_N$nek]$_N$
     prosodic structure: (buda)$_\omega$ (pestnek)$_\omega$

As you can see, the vowels within each of the phonological words are harmonic. In the first phonological word all vowels are front, in the second one they are all back.

The distinction between cohering and non-cohering suffixes is also relevant for Yidiɲ. In this Australian language, monosyllabic inflectional and derivational suffixes are cohering, whereas disyllabic ones are non-cohering, and form a phonological word of their own. We have to make that assumption in order to account for the distribution of stressed and unstressed syllables. Normally, words in Yidiɲ begin either with a stressed or an unstressed syllable, but always display an alternating pattern of stressed and unstressed syllables. In complex words with disyllabic suffixes, however, we find both sequences of two unstressed and of two stressed syllables across word-internal morphological boundaries, since disyllabic suffixes begin a new phonological word. The domain of stress assignment is the phonological word, not the grammatical word. Hence, Yidiɲ has words like the following (Dixon 1977: 93).

(8)   *rhythmic pattern*
      wáŋal-múday "boomerang-COMIT.ABS"   (wá.ŋal)$_\omega$(mú.day)$_\omega$
      bigú:n-mudá:y-ɲdu "shield-COMIT-ERG"   (bi.gú:n)$_\omega$(mu.dá:y.ɲdu)$_\omega$
      non-rhythmic pattern
      wáŋal-mudá:y-ŋdu "boomerang-COMIT-ERG" (wá.ŋal)$_\omega$(mu.dá:y.ɲdu)$_\omega$
      bigú:n-múday "shield-COMIT.ABS"   (bi.gú:n)$_\omega$(mú.day)$_\omega$

(The acute accents in these examples indicate stress.) The comitative suffix in the second and third word has a lengthened vowel due to the presence of stress. In the third word, both the second and the third syllable are unstressed, whereas in the fourth word the second and the third syllable are both stressed. The explanation for this disturbance of the rhythmic alternation between stressed and unstressed syllables is that the domain of this alternation is the phonological word. Since the suffixes used here are disyllabic, they begin a phonological word of their own.

In Germanic languages we find many non-cohering suffixes that derive historically from lexemes, such as English *-wise* and *-dom*. Although these two suffixes have lost their lexical status, they still behave as phonological words of their own, as can be concluded from the fact that they bear second-ary stress (*móney-wìse, kíngdòm*), just like the right constituents of most English compounds. Some examples of non-cohering suffixes of Dutch are:

(9)   -achtig /ɑxtəɣ/   rood-achtig "reddish"
       -baar /ba:r/   eet-baar "edible"
       -dom /dɔm/   adel-dom "nobility"
       -heid /hɛid/   schoon-heid "beauty"

Quite revealing is the contrast between the suffix *-achtig* and its semantic-ally equivalent competitor, the cohering suffix *-ig*; both occur with the adjectival stem *rood* "red", and contribute the same meaning "-ish", but show different phonological behaviour:

(10)   rood-achtig [roːt.ɑx.təx]   rod-ig [roː.dəx]

Since *-achtig* forms a phonological word by itself, it is an independent domain of syllabification. Hence, the /d/ of *rood* occurs in syllable-final position, and is devoiced due to the constraint FinDevoicing. On the other hand, the suffix *-ig* is cohering, and forms one prosodic word with its base. Therefore, the morpheme-final /d/ of *rood* fills an onset position in *rodig*, and will be thus exempted from being devoiced.

Non-cohering affixes are not necessarily phonological words. The English suffix *-less* /ləs/ is non-cohering, as we saw above. Yet, it does not form a phonological word of its own, and cannot bear secondary stress since its vowel is a schwa.

A characteristic of Dutch non-cohering suffixes that are phonological words is that they allow for backward gapping. In that respect, they are like compounds at the level of prosodic structure. Thus, they pattern with compounds with respect to **gapping**: of two identical phonological words, the first can be deleted (Booij 1985):

(11)   *Gapping in compounds*
       land- en tuinbouw "agri(culture) and horticulture"
       wespen- en bijesteken "wasp (stings) and bee stings"
       hoofd- of nevenaccent "main (stress) or secondary stress"

       Gapping in suffixed words
       storm- en regenachtig "storm(y) and rainy"
       zicht- en tastbaar "vis(ible) and tangible"
       christen- en heidendom "christian(ity) and heathendom"
       eenzijdig- of partijdigheid "onesided(ness) or partiality"

A cohering suffix, on the other hand, cannot be gapped since it is not a phonological word. For instance, the gapping of the cohering suffix *-ig* in the phrase *rodig en groenig* "reddish and greenish" is impossible witness the illformedness of **rood- en groenig*.

Similar things can be said about prefixes. Prefixes in Germanic languages like Dutch with at least one full vowel often form a prosodic word of their own, and hence such prefixed words are prosodic compounds, with the concomitant stress pattern (main stress on the first constituent, secondary stress on the second):

(12) *Prefix*   *Example*
    aarts- /aːrts/   áarts-vìjand "arch-enemy"
    her- /hɛr/   hér-bebòssing "reforestation"
    ex- /ɛks/   éx-vròuw "ex-wife"
    anti- /ɑnti/   ánti-betòging "anti-demonstration"

Prefixes that are prosodic words of their own lend themselves easily for being promoted to the status of lexeme. In English and Dutch, for instance, *ex* can also be used nowadays as a word to denote one's former partner. This complies with the constraint that lexical words (non-function words) must be well-formed prosodic words.

So far we have seen how the morphological and the prosodic structure of words relate. This relationship also has an effect on the phonological make-up of affixes. It is an old observation made by Roman Jakobson that the phonological make-up of affixes tends to differ from that of lexical morphemes. In Quechua, we find a number of suffixes that begin with consonant clusters that are never found at the beginning of lexical morphemes, as is illustrated by the following word (van de Kerke 1996: 126):

(13) maylla-wa-rqa-nki-ku
    wash–1OBJ-PAST-2SG-PL
    "You have washed us"

Since both the lexical root and the suffixes end in a vowel, clusters such as /rq/ and /nk/ at the beginning of a suffix will be split up in the prosodic structure, and assigned to different syllables. The syllabification of the example (13) will be *mayl.la.war.qan.ki.ku*, and hence creates no phonotactic problems.

Words must indeed be pronounceable on their own, unlike affixes. That is, words need to comply with the requirements on well-formed phonological words. Dutch requires phonological words to have at least one full vowel (that is, a vowel that is not the schwa). The schwa is a special vowel in that it cannot bear stress, and hence creates an unstressable syllable. Consequently, it is never the case that the only vowel of a Dutch word is the schwa (with the exception of function words such as determiners). On the other hand, there are many Dutch suffixes with schwa as their only vowel, such as *-er* /ər/. This is to be expected, as suffixes will not appear as phonological words themselves (note that the non-cohering suffixes listed in (9) all contain a full vowel). A related remarkable property of suffixes is that they may consist of consonants only, again unlike words. In Germanic languages most consonantal suffixes consist of /s/, /t/, or a combination thereof, consonants that can freely occur at the end of word-final syllables. To conclude, we can make the generalization that the different subclasses of morphemes of a language (lexical morphemes, prefixes, suffixes, etc.) are phonologically shaped in such a way that they can lead to phonologically well-formed words.

This relationship between morphology and phonology will also help us to understand the notion **clitic**. Clitics are 'small words' of functional, non-lexical categories such as pronouns and determiners that 'lean on' (the word *clitic* derives from the Greek verb *klinein* "to lean") a preceding or following host word, and cannot appear as phonological words by themselves. For instance, in Italian lexical morphemes have to consist of at least two syllables (there are a handful of exceptions such as *ré* "king"). Most pronouns, however, are monosyllabic. These clitics therefore take an adjacent word as their host, and form one prosodic constituent with that word. The Italian clitic pronouns precede their host word (this is called **proclisis**), except in the case of infinitival and imperative verbal forms that require the clitics to follow them (**enclisis**):

(14) proclisis: me lo racconta
                me it tell.3SG
                "(s)he tells me it"
      enclisis: racconta me lo
                tell.IMP me it
                "tell me it"

Clitics therefore share a property with cohering affixes: their phonological dependence on a host. In this respect, proclitics are like prefixes, and enclitics like suffixes. Words in the morphosyntactic sense do not always correspond in a one-to-one fashion to words in the phonological sense. Clitics form another illustration of this asymmetry between morpho-syntactic and prosodic structure, and the study of clitics belongs (partially) to the study of interface between phonological and morphosyntactic structure.

The similarity in phonological behaviour of affixes and clitics makes it sometimes difficult to determine if a morpheme is to be considered an affix or a clitic. Consider the following examples from English:

(15) a. the king of England's hat
      b. the boy across the road's cycle
      c. the man I talked about's car

The morpheme *s* used here is historically a genitive suffix, but it has developed into a clitic that can be attached at the end of the possessor phrase. Hence, it is sometimes called a **phrasal affix**. Whereas suffixes are attached to words of particular categories, the morpheme *s* attaches not only to nouns but to whatever word happens to occur in phrase-final position, so even to a preposition such as *about*, as in (15c).

Other examples of suffix-like clitics might be claimed to exist in Icelandic. In this language, the definite article may be 'suffixed' to the preceding noun. It can also occur as a free article before the noun. Both the noun and the 'suffixed' definite article are inflected for number and case. Consider the following singular forms of the word *hestur* "horse" given in Table 7.1. As you can see, both the noun and the definite article are inflected for case. The bound forms of the article differ from the full forms in that the initial /h/ is omitted. A possible interpretation of these facts is that the article is an enclitic when occurring after the noun.

Table 7.1. *The singular paradigm of* hestur

	free article + noun	*noun + suffixed article*
NOM	hin-n hest-ur	hestur-inn
ACC	hin-n hest	hest-inn
DAT	hin-um hest-i	hesti-num
GEN	hin-s hest-s	hests-ins

Source: Thráinsson 1994: 156.

The difference between affixes and clitics can sometimes be seen in the differential effect that they have on the phonetic form of words. Dutch has a clitic pronoun *er* /ər/ 'her' that is attached prosodically to a host word on its left. This causes resyllabification of the word + clitic sequence, just like vowel-initial cohering suffixes do. The difference is that attachment of a suffix pre-empts application of final devoicing to stem-final obstruents, whereas clitics with a similar phonological form do not, as shown by the following minimal pair in (16):

(16) vind-er "find-er" [vɪnd-ər] *vs* (ik) vind er [vɪn.tər] "(I) find her"

That is, final devoicing must have applied to the finite verb form *vind* before the clitic is attached. Therefore, clitics are sometimes called **postlexical affixes** since they have to be attached after the rules of word phonology (the **lexical phonology**) of the language have applied. The attachment of the clitic *er* triggers resyllabification, because the clitic forms one prosodic word with the preceding verb. Hence, the /d/ of *vind* first devoices in coda position, and subsequently, at the postlexical level, it moves to an onset position.

7.3 Allomorphy and affix competition

Morphemes may exhibit variation in their phonological shape. This variation in shape may have nothing to do with phonology. This is the case when languages have morphological systems with more than one stem-form; each stem-form has to be used for particular inflectional categories (Chapter 6). Allomorphy may also be a completely predictable effect of phonology, as shown in the previous section for the allomorphy related to final devoicing in Dutch. In other cases, the phonological alternations are regular too, but apply to a restricted set of words only. For instance, the Dutch diminutive suffix has five allomorphs, whose distribution is predictable (the letter *e* stands for a schwa, and *ng* indicates the velar nasal):

(17)   a. *-je* after stem-final obstruents;
       b. *-etje* after sonorant consonants preceded by a short vowel with primary or secondary stress;
       c. *-pje* after stem-final /m/ except in cases falling under b;
       d. *-kje* after stems ending in the velar nasal /ŋ/;
       e. *-tje* elsewhere

This allomorphy is illustrated by the words in (18):

(18)   *base noun*   *diminutive*
       a. lip "lip"   lip-je
          hek "gate"   hek-je
       b. ring "ring"   ring-etje
          seríng "lilac"   sering-etje
       c. riem "belt"   riem-pje
          bez[ə]m "sweep"   bezem-pje
       d. kóning "king"   konin-kje
          páling "eel"   palin-kje
       e. ree "deer"   ree-tje
          traan "tear"   traan-tje

The different allomorphs of the diminutive suffix might be derived from an underlying form /tjə/ that surfaces in (18e), by assuming rules that delete the /t/ (18a), insert a schwa (18b), or assimilate the /t/ to the place of articulation of the preceding nasal (18c–d). However, these rules apply exclusively to diminutive nouns. For instance, there is no general rule of schwa insertion in the context mentioned in (17b). The Dutch complex word *stil-te* "silence", for instance, is not realized as [stɪlətə]. Hence, these rules must mention the morphological property [+diminutive] in their structural description. This means that they are **morphologically conditioned** phonological rules.

In other cases, the rule applies to a fixed set of lexical items. That is, the alternation is lexically conditioned. This applies to a number of mono-syllabic Dutch nouns: in the plural form (and some derived words as well) the stem vowel is lengthened, which is a relict of the process of **Open Syllable Lengthening** (OSL) that was active in Early Germanic:

(19)   SINGULAR   PLURAL
       d[ɑ]g "day"   d[a:]gen
       h[ɔ]f "court"   h[o:]ven
       w[ɛ]g "road"   w[e:]gen

If one assumes a phonological rule for such alternations, the relevant nouns have to be marked as undergoing this rule in the lexicon as [+OSL], and this diacritic feature has to be mentioned in the structural description of the rule as well. So this rule may be formulated as follows:

(20)   V → V: in the context —)$_\sigma$
       [+OSL]

The word *dag*, for instance, will be marked as [+OSL] in the lexicon, and hence all its segments carry that diacritic feature.

It might also be the case that a rule is governed both by morphological and by lexical features, as is the case for German umlaut. This is the process in which the back vowels of stems are fronted before certain suffixes that originally contained front vowels or glides. As the examples (21a) show, application of umlaut depends on the individual stem (Wiese 1996: 188):

(21)   a.   *Umlaut*   *No umlaut*
            Vater "father"–Väter-chen "DIM"   Onkel "uncle"–Onkel-chen "DIM"
            laufen "to walk"–läuf-t "3SG"   rufen "to call"–ruf-t "3SG"
       b.   Hund "dog"–Hünd-in "dog, FEM"   Hund-e "dog, PL", Hund-chen
            Hünd-chen "dog, DIM"   "dog, DIM"

The examples *Hunde* and *Hundchen* in (21b) show that lexical items may have to be marked as exceptions to umlaut. In the case of the diminutive noun for *Hund*, the umlauted form is the standard one, but the other one also occurs. The lexical stem *Hund* does allow for umlaut, as in *Hün-din*, and the plural suffix and diminutive suffix both trigger umlaut. Yet there is no umlaut in the plural form, and umlaut is optional in the diminutive form. A useful cover term for such morphologically and/or lexically conditioned phonological rules is **morpholexical rule**.

This is not the whole story about allomorphy, however. Consider the following pairs of related words in English:

(**22**)   drama, dramat-ic, dramat-ist
       Plato, platon-ist, platon-ism

In these examples, the base words *drama* and *Plato* have a short form, whereas stem-forms with an additional consonant are used for derivation. This is a reflex of the history of these originally Greek words: the long form is the underlying form, but the stem-final consonant was dropped in NOM.SG forms. The effect for present-day English is that the long form is to be used for suffixes of the non-native learned stratum, whereas the short form is to be used before native, Germanic suffixes, and with prefixes. For instance, the plural form of *drama* is *dramas*, not *dramats*. Thus, the distribution of these allomorphs is stated in morphological terms. It is hard to see how we might provide an insightful account of this kind of allomorphy in terms of phonological rules.

Allomorphy as a reflex of history is also found in word pairs such as the following:

(**23**)   deduce   deduct-ion
       induce   induct-ion

       produce   product-ion
       reduce   reduct-ion

This allomorphy is a reflex of the system of different stems for Latin verbs: derivation takes the participial stem form of the Latin verb *ducere, duct*, as its base (cf. section 6.3).

Historically determined allomorphy is also found in the formation of French de-adjectival adverbs in *-ment*, see (24). The feminine forms of the adjectives in (24) are irregular, except the first one. The data show that the suffix *-ment* takes the feminine form of the adjective as stem for adverb formation. Note, however, that there is no feminine meaning involved in the meaning of the adverb. This is a case of **paradigmatically governed allomorphy**: the correct form of the adjectival stem is determined by referring to that of a paradigmatically related form, the feminine form. Historically, this is the effect of the suffix *-ment*. It derives from the ablative form of the Latin feminine noun *mens* "mind" that required the feminine form of the preceding adjective, as in *clara mente* "clear-ABL.SG mind-ABL.SG., with a clear mind".

(24)	MASC *adj.*	FEM *adj.*	*Adverb*
	lent "slow"	lente	lente-ment
	beau "beautiful"	belle	belle-ment
	blanc "white"	blanche	blanche-ment
	fou "mad"	folle	folle-ment

The examples discussed so far are cases of stem allomorphy. This kind of allomorphy is also found in compounds where the first constituent may have a form that cannot be used when it is used as a word of its own. Well-known cases are the linking elements in Germanic languages, illustrated here for Swedish (Anderson 1994: 277):

(25) land-s-ting "city council", läs-e-bok "textbook", kvinn-o-arbete "women's work"

Some of these linking elements are old genitive endings. Noun phrases with an inflected modifying noun became compounds, and thus the inflectional ending got trapped in between the two constituents:

(26) $[\text{N-GEN N}]_{\text{NP}} > [\text{N -linking element -N}]_{\text{N}}$

Subsequently, such compounds served as models in the coining of new compounds that, by analogy to existing compounds, got these linking elements as well. Phonologically, these linking elements form one phonological word with the first constituent of compounds, as we can conclude from word-internal gapping in Dutch compounds such as the following one:

(27) wespe- en bije-steken "wasp stings and bee stings"
$[[\text{wesp}]_{\text{N}}\text{e}[\text{steken}]_{\text{N}}]_{\text{N}}$ en $[[\text{bij}]_{\text{N}}\text{e}[\text{steken}]_{\text{N}}]_{\text{N}}$
$(\text{wes.pe})_{\omega}(\text{ste.ken})_{\omega}$ $(\text{en})_{\omega}(\text{bij.e})_{\omega}(\text{ste.ken})_{\omega}$

This example shows that the linking element is not included in the gapping and belongs to the first phonological word of compounds, as is also shown by the prosodic structure of the non-gapped compounds in (27).

Let us now have a look at another kind of allomorphy, affix allomorphy. Dutch has two counterparts to the English deverbal and denominal suffix *-er*: the suffixes *-er* and *-aar*. These two suffixes look like allomorphs in the sense that they are phonologically similar. However, it is not possible to assign them a common underlying form, and derive the two surface forms by means of well-motivated general phonological rules or constraints of Dutch. There is no general phonological constraint for Dutch that vowels in word-final unstressed syllables must be reduced to schwa. Hence, *-er* cannot be derived phonologically from *-aar*. So in fact you can see them as **competing affixes**: different affixes with the same meaning and domain of application. When the degree of phonological similarity between competing affixes is considerable, they may be considered allomorphs of one morpheme. When the similarity is less, it is better to regard them as distinct morphemes, though in a relationship that resembles the suppletive one between the stem-forms *good* and *bet-* of the lexeme GOOD.

The basis for choosing between the suffixes *-er* and *-aar* is the following: *-aar* is used after a stem ending in an unstressed syllable, with /l/, /r/, or /n/ as its final consonant (these are the coronal sonorant consonants of Dutch); *-er* is used elsewhere.

(28)   bedel /be:dəl/ "to beg"   bedel-aar /be:dəla:r/ "begger"
        luister /lʌystər/ "to listen"   luister-aar / lʌystəra:r/ "listener"
        reken /re:kən/ "to compute"   reken-aar /re:kəna:r/ "computer"
        bezem /be:zəm/ "to sweep"   bezem-er /be:zəmər/ "sweeper"
        verdedig /vɛrde:dəɣ/ "to defend" verdedig-er /vɛrde:dəɣər/ "defender"
        bak /bɑk/ "to bake"   bakk-er /bɑkər/ "baker"

It is possible to account for this pattern by assigning a phonological subcategorization feature to the suffix *-aar* that specifies its restricted distribution (only after stem-final coronal sonorants preceded by a schwa). The suffix *-er* does not need to have such a subcategorization feature: it is the default suffix that can be used elsewhere. The priority of *-aar* above *-er* for verbs ending in an unstressed syllable with /l, r, n/ can be taken care of by Panini's Principle introduced in Chapter 5. Recall that this principle states that if two or more rules compete, the more specific rules get priority over the less specific rules, and that the application of the more specific rule pre-empts application of the more general one. In the case of the base word *bedel* the suffix *-aar* wil be selected, and hence suffixation with *-er* is excluded. The base word *bezem*, on the other hand, although it ends in an unstressed syllable, does not end in a coronal sonorant since the /m/ is a labial consonant. Thus, attachment of *-aar* is impossible, and *-er* will be attached.

This analysis can be qualified as an analysis that makes use of input constraints: each competing suffix imposes certain requirements on its input forms. The drawback of such an analysis is that it does not provide any explanation for this particular selection pattern. The factor behind this pattern is most probably the avoidance of a sequence of two unstressed syllables. If we added *-er* after an unstressed syllable, we would get a sequence of two unstressed syllables. Germanic languages strive for a parsing of their words into disyllabic trochees. That is, ideally, the prosodic form of each word consists of one or more trochees. In addition, there can be monosyllabic feet if the relevant syllable has a full vowel, and is long enough. Consider the word *reken-aar* and its ill-formed counterpart *reken-er*. Their prosodic structure in terms of syllables and feet will be as follows (syllable boundaries indicated by dots):

(29)   a. $(re:.kə)_F(na:r)_F$
       b. $(re:.kə.)_F nər$

In (29b), the last syllable cannot be made part of a foot (that is, cannot be parsed into a foot), because it does not have a full vowel. Hence, (29a) is more optimal from the point of view of prosodic structure. This prosodic structure correctly implies that the last syllable also bears a degree of stress, i.e. secondary stress.

This selection process of competing allomorphs can be modelled in terms of the optimality-theoretical tableaux introduced in section 7.2: each combination of a stem and an allomorph is a candidate, and the ranked set of phonological constraints will determine the optimal candidate. The advantage of this theory is that it makes uses of output constraints. The crucial constraints involved here are ParseSyll, Foot-Min, and Foot-Max. ParseSyll requires syllables to be made part of feet, Foot-Max requires feet to be maximally binary, and Foot-Min requires feet to be minimally binary. The computation is shown in Figure 7.7.

As you can see, the ranking of ParseSyll and Foot-Max is not crucial in these cases. What is crucial is that these two are ranked higher than Foot-Min. As a result of this ranking, the first candidate is designated as the optimal one.

In the analysis outlined here, the selection of these two competing

/re:kən + a:r or ər/	ParseSyll	FootMax	FootMin
☞ (re:.kə)_F (na:r)_F			*
(re:.kə.)_F na:r	*!		
(re:.kə.)_F nər	*!		
(re:.kə.nər)_F		*!	

Fig. 7.7 OT-tableau for *rekenaar*

suffixes is done by output constraints. Such constraints thus play an important role in the interface between morphology and phonology: morphology provides a number of alternatives, equivalent from the morphological point of view, and the phonology then computes which of them is optimal from the phonological point of view.

This does not mean that phonological subcategorization constraints are superfluous. For instance, we still have to state that -*aar* can only occur after stems ending in a coronal sonorant consonant (that is, /l/, /r/, or /n/). Therefore, the deverbal noun for *bezem* "to sweep" is *bezemer* [be:.zə.mər] even though this deverbal noun ends in a sequence of two unstressed syllables. Recall also that these constraints are all violable. For instance, Dutch diminutives such as *ball-etje* [bɑlətjə] "ball, DIM" and *kamm-etje* [kɑmətjə] "comb, DIM" end in a sequence of two unstressed syllables, and hence ParseSyll will be violated. In this case there is no morphological alternative that can be used to avoid this violation. In other words, when necessary, morphology takes precedence over phonology, even if this leads to less optimal phonological structures.

Another example of the role of prosody in allomorph selection comes from Biak, a language spoken in New Guinea. This language uses either the infixes -*w*- and -*y*- or the prefixes *wa*- and *i*- for 2SG and 3SG forms of the verb respectively (Table 7.2). The choice between infix and prefix is lexically governed, as illustrated by (a–b). In the b-examples, we might have expected the infixed forms *rwov* and *ryov*, but these are not the forms used. However, if the verbal stem begins with a consonant cluster, it is always the prefix allomorph that has to be chosen since an infix would lead to phonotactically impossible consonant sequences (c–e).

In conclusion, even if allomorphs cannot be derived from a common underlying form, it is nevertheless possible to make phonological generalizations concerning their distribution.

Table 7.2. *Allomorph selection in Biak*

	stem	2SG	3SG	*gloss*
a.	ra	rwa	rya	to go
b.	rov	warov	irov	to fly
c.	kvok	wakvok	ikvok	to stand up
d.	snai	wasnai	isnai	to be clear
e.	smai	wasmai	ismai	to have

Source: W. van den Heuvel, pers. comm.

7.4 Cyclicity and co-phonologies

In many languages, the stress patterns of complex words are, at least partially, determined by their morphological structure. All Germanic languages exhibit this kind of interface between morphology and phonology. A simple example is the way in which the stress patterns of compounds have to be computed. The English compound *sugar cookie* has primary stress on its first syllable, and secondary stress on its penultimate one: *súgar còokie*. This stress pattern can be computed as follows. First, we assign stress to each constituent. Both words have penultimate stress. The second step is to determine which of these two stresses is prominent. The rule for English nominal compounds is that the stressed syllable of the first constituent has the highest prominence. A traditional way of formalizing this type of computation is to assume that phonological rules of stress assignment apply cyclically, in an outward fashion where one begins with the smallest constituents:

(30)   [[sugar]   [cookie]]
     1st cycle, Main Stress Rule   _1___   _1___
     2nd cycle, Compound Stress Rule   _1_____2____

On the first cycle, the **Main Stress Rule** of English assigns primary stress to one of the vowels of each constituent. On the second cycle, the **Compound Stress Rule** reassigns primary stress to the first primary stressed vowel, and causes all other stresses to be automatically lowered by one degree.

This formal machinery, from Chomsky and Halle (1968), is outdated by now as far as the analysis of stress patterns is concerned, but serves well to grasp the idea of cyclic application of rules. In contrast to Chomsky and

Halle's analysis, stress is considered nowadays as a property of prosodic constituents. Hence, the influence of morphological structure on stress patterns of complex words is indirect. First, we map morphological structure onto prosodic structure, and the prosodic constituents are marked for stress. One way of doing this is to use the labels 'strong' (s) and 'weak' (w). The prosodic structure of *sugar cookie* will hence look as in Figure 7.8.

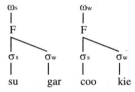

Fig. 7.8 The prosodic structure of *sugar cookie*

Strong – weak is a relation between two sister constituents. One of them is the head of a prosodic category such as the foot. The first syllable of *sugar cookie* is the strongest syllable of the strongest phonological word, and hence it carries the primary stress of this compound. The strongest syllable of the weak phonological word, *coo*, has secondary stress. In short, we do not need cyclicity as a special principle of rule application. The interface between morphology and phonology discussed here is fully covered by the following two mapping principles for English:

(i) each constituent of a compound corresponds with a phonological word;
(ii) in the case of N + N compounds, the first phonological word is the strongest.

This approach also enables us to give an adequate account of the stress patterns of complex words with non-cohering suffixes. This can be illustrated by means of the Dutch word *draagbaar* that has two meanings:

(31) compound $[[draag]_V[baar]_N]_N$ "stretcher"
      derived word $[[draag]_V baar]_A$ "port-able"

The suffix *-baar* is one of the non-cohering suffixes of Dutch. Therefore, from the prosodic point of view both words are prosodic compounds, and have the same prosodic structure $(draag)_\omega(baar)_\omega$. The first syllable carries main stress, the second one secondary stress, as is represented correctly by this prosodic structure. The same prosodic status holds for many prefixes of

Greek and Latin origin in Germanic languages that also carry stress, as illustrated here for English:

(32) a. main stress on prefix: cóunter-àrgument, súb-sèt
      b. secondary stress on prefix: ànti-relígious, nèo-classicísm,

Another aspect of the role of morphological structure in the computation of the phonetic forms of complex word is the phenomenon of **co-phonologies**. As we saw in section 3.3, the morphological system of a language may consist of more than one stratum. Each stratum may have its own phonological system, that is, its own co-phonology. In Germanic languages, for instance, words that end in non-native suffixes are stressed in the same way as simplex words. Hence, they might carry the main stress of the word. Suffixes of Germanic origin, on the other hand, are mostly stress-neutral: the addition of such a suffix does not shift the location of main stress rightward. This is illustrated here for Swedish (Andersson 1994: 278):

(33) *Non-native suffixation, stress on last syllable*: brygg-eri "brewery", individual-itet "individuality", dans-ör "dancer", *or on penultimate syllable*: prost-inna "dean's wife";
      Native suffixation, stress on first syllable: sök-ande "search", bo-ende "living", läs-ning "reading", bak-else "pastry"

These examples once more show that phonology makes use of morphological information concerning words.

7.5 The morphological use of phonology

The interface phenomena discussed so far were all cases in which phonology makes use of morphological information. The inverse situation, morphology making use of phonology, is also found in natural languages. Simple examples are cases in which the use of a particular affix is conditioned phonologically. The English comparative suffix *-er*, for example, can only—with some minor exceptions—be attached to monosyllabic adjectival stems, and to disyllabic stems ending in a light syllable. In other cases, a periphrastic form with *more* has to be used.

(34) green   greener
      silly   sillier
      obese   *obeser / more obese
      excellent   *excellenter / more excellent

Dutch is a language in which prosodic considerations play a role in the extent to which affixes can be stacked up in complex words. In the case of prefixation, a sequence of two unstressed prefixes will be avoided. Recall that Dutch parses words in trochees (section 7.1). Hence, a sequence of two unstressed prefixes at the beginning of a morphological word will violate the condition ParseSyll twice. Stressed prefixes, on the other hand can be prefixed to prefixed stems. The contrast is shown in (35):

(35)   ont-bós "to deforest"   *ver-ont-bós "to destroy through deforestation"
        ón-geluk "accident"   ver-ón-geluk "to die in an accident"

The past participles of Dutch verbs are formed through circumfixation: the prefix *ge-* and the suffix *-t/d* (regular verbs) or *-en* (irregular stem-alternating verbs). However, if the verbal stem begins with an unstressed prefix, the participial prefix is obligatorily omitted. Thus, a sequence of unparsable syllables is avoided once more:

(36)   *Verbal stem*   *Past participle*
        váng "catch"   ge-vang-en
        ont-váng "receive"   ont-vang-en
        stúur "send"   ge-stuur-d
        be-stúur "govern"   be-stuur-d
        prè-figéer "prefix"   ge-pre-figeerd
        rè-animéer "reanimate"   ge-re-animeer-d

The native prefixes *ont-* and *be-* do not receive stress at all; the non-native prefixes *pre-* and *re-* receive rhythmic secondary stress. Hence, the latter prefixes do not block the attachment of the participial prefix *ge-*.

The morphological use of phonological patterns and categories is a prominent feature in reduplication. Consider the cases in (37) of partial reduplication in the perfect tense forms of Latin and Greek (Wiltshire and Marantz 2000: 563). In these examples, the perfect stem is formed by prefixing a copy of a part of the base; the copy is called the **reduplicant**. Recall that this kind of reduplication is called partial reduplication because it is not the whole word that is copied. An example of full reduplication is given in section 2.2.

A first, informal definition of the Latin reduplication process is 'copy the first syllable of the base'. An alternative formalization is to say that Latin has a phonologically underspecified reduplicative prefix with the abstract form CV, a sequence of a consonant and a vowel. The sound segments of the base are then linked to the CV templates, from left to right. Since there are only two positions, only the first two segments of the base will be copied, as illustrated in (38) for the perfect stem *pepend-*. This is the analysis

(37)		*Base*	*Perfect stem*	*Gloss*
Latin		curr-	cu-curr-	run
		dic-	di-dic-	learn
		mord-	mo-mord-	bite
		pend-	pe-pend-	hang
Greek		lu-	le-lu-	wash
		ly-	le-ly-	loose
		graph-	ge-graph-	write
		klin-	ke-klin-	incline

proposed in Marantz (1982). It can be qualified as **autosegmental morphology**, since in this kind of analysis the abstract CV-tier of phonological structure, which is an autonomous layer of phonological structure, has a morphological role: the CV sequence has a morphological function of its own. The morphological use of abstract phonological tiers is also exemplified in section 2.2, in the analysis of the non-concatenative or root-and-pattern morphology of Hebrew verbal forms.

(38) C V   C V C C
      | | | | | |
      p e n d   p e n d

The Greek examples differ from the Latin ones in that only the initial consonant of the base is copied. That is, the vowel in the reduplicative CV prefix is a fixed one, *e*. Thus, the V of the Greek CV-prefix is already linked to a vowel /e/ on the segmental tier.

The following examples from Ilokano, a language of the Philippines, show that the reduplicative affix of this language cannot be specified as "copy the first syllable", but has to be specified in terms of a constant, abstract phonological shape (McCarthy and Prince 1998: 285):

(39) kaldí "goat" kal-kaldí "goats"
      púsa   "cat"   pus-púsa   "cats"

In the first example, the reduplicant is identical to the first syllable. In the second example, however, this is not the case, since the first consonant of the second syllable is also copied. So we have to conclude that the reduplicative affix has to be specified as a heavy (or bimoraic) syllable, that is, a syllable that either ends in a consonant, or has a long vowel. This kind of syllable is referred to as a **bimoraic syllable**: both a long vowel (VV) and a VC sequence count as two morae.

The Ilokano example serves to illustrate the basic idea of **prosodic morphology** which claims that the shape of reduplicative affixes has to be defined in terms of prosodic categories such as the syllable or the prosodic word. In the Latin case, the reduplicative prefix can be defined as a light syllable (that is, a CV syllable), and in Ilokano as a heavy syllable. Another possible form of the reduplicant is that of a minimal prosodic word. The minimal prosodic word of a language is often a disyllabic foot. Consider the following examples from the Australian language Diyari, where reduplication serves a number of morphological functions (Austin 1981; cited in McCarthy and Prince 1998: 286–7).

(40)   kanku-kanku "boy"
       kulku-kulkuŋa "to jump"
       tʲilpa-tʲilparku "bird species"

In these examples, the reduplicant consists of two syllables, which form a minimal prosodic word. The segments of the base are mapped onto this abstract prosodic pattern, and thus maximally two syllables of the base are copied. The third example is quite interesting because the last consonant of the second syllable is not copied. The reason for this is that an open syllable is the unmarked form of a syllable, and thus preferred. In the first syllable of the reduplicant, on the other hand, we find a closed syllable, a more marked syllable structure. We need this closed syllable because otherwise we would have to skip a segment of the base in the mapping of segmental structure to the prosodically defined reduplicative prefix. So it is only the second syllable that can have the unmarked form of an open syllable. The appearance of unmarked structure in this kind of morphological operation is called 'the emergence of the unmarked'. It can be nicely modelled by means of Optimality Theoretical tableaux. We need the following, informally circumscribed constraints:

(41)   Reduplicant = Minimal Prosodic Word
       Open Syllable: a syllable is open
       No Skipping

If we assume that No Skipping is ranked higher than Open Syllable, we see that of the following candidates, the first is the optimal one. This is shown in Figure 7.9. The second and the fourth candidate violate one of the two highest ranked constraints, and are therefore ill-formed. The third candidate violates the constraint Open Syllable four times, whereas the first candidate does this only three times. Hence, the fourth violation of Open

/RED + tjilparku/	RED=MinWord	No Skipping	Open Syllable
☞ tjil.pa.tjil.par.ku			***
tji.pa.tjil.par.ku		*!	**
tjil.park.tjil.par.ku			**** !
tji.tjil.par.ku	*!		**

Fig. 7.9 Reduplication in Diyari

Syllable by the third candidate is fatal. Therefore, the first candidate is qualified as the optimal one.

The morphological use of the prosodic category 'minimal prosodic word' is also found in the formation of hypocoristics (endearment forms of proper names) through truncation (see section 1.4), as the following examples illustrate (Lappe 2002: 135):

(42) German   Andreas   Andi
                 Dagmar   Daggi
      Spanish   Alexandrina   Dina
                 Ernesto   Neto
      French   Dominique   Dom
                 Valérie   Val
      English   Patrick   Pat/Patty
                 Elizabeth   Liz/Lizzy

In German and Spanish the form of these names is that of a disyllabic foot, in French the form is that of a heavy syllable, and English has both options. Both disyllabic feet and heavy syllables can function as minimal prosodic words.

A last example of the use of phonology in morphology is the use of tonal morphemes, that is, morphological operations that use tones to signal a particular morphological category. The Limburgian dialect of Maasbracht (The Netherlands) is an example of a language that makes use of tone contrasts for morphological purposes. The contrast is that between a dragging tone (High–Low–High) versus a falling tone (High–Low), either of which occurs on the stressed syllable of a word. For instance, the neuter and feminine forms of a number of adjectives differ in that the neuter form has a dragging tone, and the feminine form a falling tone, see (43). This is another example of autosegmental morphology since it is the tonal tier that is involved in expressing the morphological categories involved, whereas the segmental tier remains unchanged.

(43)	*Neuter, HLH*	*Feminine, HL*	*Gloss*
	wiis	wiis	wise
	stiif	stiif	stiff
	ɣriis	ɣriis	grey

Summary

This chapter focused on the interface between morphology and phonology. Morphological structure appeared to influence the phonetic forms of complex forms through principles of alignment that require phonological boundaries to coincide with morphological ones. Yet, this alignment is not perfect, and there are many cases of asymmetry between morphological and phonological structure. A second form of interaction is the choice between stem allomorphs or competing affixes. This choice may be governed by considerations of phonological optimality. In some cases, the choice can be insightfully modelled by means of output conditions, as in Optimality Theory.

The non-isomorphy between prosodic structure and morphological structure is also the key to the understanding of the phonological similarities between affixes and clitics.

Morphology makes use of phonology in a number of ways. Morphological operations may impose phonological constraints on the stems they operate upon. Phonological processes such as copying and truncation have morphological functions. Prosodic morphology makes use of prosodic categories such as the syllable and the prosodic word for morphological operations.

Questions

1. Show that the following English suffixes must be considered as cohering: *-able, -er, -ing*.

2. The Dutch determiners *de* "the" and *een* "a" have the phonological forms /də/ and /ən/ respectively. How can we tell from these phonological forms that these words must be function words?

3. Why would one prefer to consider the allomorphy that can be observed in noun–adjective pairs such as *Plato–Platonic* and *realist–realístic* (*-ic/-nic*) as a case of stem allomorphy, rather than as a case of suffix allomorphy?

4. The Italian negative prefixes *in-* and *non-* differ in that it is only *in-* that undergoes assimilation to a following stem-initial consonant:

ir-regolare "irregular", im-mature "immature"
non-lavabile "non-washable", non-memorizzable "non-memorizable"

How might this difference in phonological behaviour be explained?

5. Show that the syllabification pattern of English words with the suffix *-er* complies with the constraint ranking in (5).

6. Consider the following case of gapping in Dutch (the parenthesized part *beren* of the compound *ijsberen* is gapped):

ijs(beren) en bruine beren "lit. ice and brown bears, polar bears and brown bears"

How can this case of gapping be used to show that gapping in Dutch is conditioned prosodically, and not syntactically?

7. The Dutch derivational suffix *-tig*/tɔx/, used in number names such as *twin-tig* "twenty" and *der-tig* "thirty", has developed into a numeral with the meaning "umpteen". In this use, the word is pronounced as [tɪx]. How can this phonological change be explained?

8. Suppose that someone claimed that the stress pattern of the English compound *bréakfast tàble* can be computed without reference to morphological structure, by means of the following rule: in native words main stress falls on the first syllable, and secondary stress on every odd syllable going from left to right. Provide empirical evidence that speaks against such an analysis, and in favour of the role of morphological structure in computing the stress patterns of compounds.

9. Consider the following Hungarian words and their dative forms:

Vajda-né "wife of Vajda"   Vajda-né-nak (dative form)
Szoké-né "wife of Szoké"   Szoké-né-nek (dative form)

Which conclusion can you draw about the role of the suffix *-né* in vowel harmony?

10. Which prosodic constraints can be invoked to explain the choice between the English definite articles *a* and *an*?

Further reading

A classic article on the interface between phonology and morphology in Optimality Theory is McCarthy and Prince (1994). Cyclic application of phonological rules is one of the building stones of the theory of Lexical Phonology; see Booij (2000) for an overview of this theory.

Criteria for distinguishing clitics from affixes are given in Zwicky and Pullum (1983). Clitics often have a special syntactic distribution as well, cf. van Riemsdijk (1998) for studies on clitics in European languages. The necessity to distinguish between lexical and postlexical phonology in relation to clitics is argued for in Booij (1996b, 1997c)

Phonologically conditioned selection of suppletive morphemes is discussed in Carstairs (1988) The selection of allomorphs by output constraints is argued for in Booij (1998), and Rubach and Booij (2001). The role of paradigmatic relations in allomorphy is discussed in Booij (1997a, b).

A good summary of the theory of Prosodic Morphology is McCarthy and Prince (1998). Prosodic restrictions on affixation are discussed in Booij (2002b). Detailed analyses of reduplication are found in McCarthy and Prince (1998), Kager (1999), Wiltshire and Marantz (2000), and Struijke (2002).

8

Morphology and syntax: demarcation and interaction

8.1 Words and phrases

There are at least four issues that have to be dealt with when we consider the relation between morphology and syntax. One is the demarcation of the empirical domains of these two modules of the grammar: when is a multi-morphemic sequence a word, and when is it a phrase? Secondly, morphology and syntax interact in two ways: syntactic constructs may form parts of complex words, and syntax in its turn governs the use of morphological case marking on words. A third domain of investigation is how morphological operations may affect the syntactic valency of words. Finally, languages may have syntactic alternatives to the morphological expression of grammatical and semantic content, and we might therefore want to know more about the division of labour between morphology and syntax in this respect.

Let us first have a closer look at the demarcation issue. Morphology deals primarily with the structure of words, and syntax with the structure of phrases. But how do you know if a particular combination of morphemes is a word or a phrase? Is the lexical unit *hard disk* a word (that is, compound of the type A + N), or a noun phrase? How can we know?

The most important criterion for wordhood is that of lexical integrity that has already been discussed in section 4.2. The principle of Lexical Integrity has been formulated as follows:

(1) 'The syntax neither manipulates nor has access to the internal form of words' (Anderson 1992: 84).

This principle implies that if we call something a word, it should exhibit lexical integrity, that is, syntactic rules cannot refer to its parts. The importance of this criterion can be illustrated by looking at the difference between prefixed verbs and **particle verbs** in Dutch. This language has a syntactic rule of Verb Second which requires finite verbal forms in main clauses to appear in second position, after the first constituent. If the verb is prefixed, the prefix has to move along with the stem, which shows that the prefix is not a separate word. On the other hand, if the verb is a particle verb (that is a phrasal verb comparable to English word combinations such as *to look up*), the particle is left behind. The underlying word order in Dutch is SOV (Subject–Object–Verb). Hence, if the finite verb is moved to second position, the particle is stranded in the original position of the V. This shows that particles are words of their own. Hence, we get the following contrast for the Dutch prefixed verb *doorzóeken* "to search" versus the particle verb *dóorzoeken* "to continue searching":

(2) a. Jan   door-zocht   het   hele   gebouw
       John   through-seek.PAST.SG   the   whole   building
       "John searched the whole building"
    b. Jan   zocht   tot 2 uur   door
       John   seek.PAST.SG till 2 o'clock   through
       "John continued searching till 2 o'clock"

The difference between prefixed verbs and particle verbs is reflected by a difference in the location of the main stress of these expressions: particles bear main stress, whereas in prefixed verbs it is the verbal stem that carries main stress.

Lexical integrity implies that English verb particle constructions such as *to look up* are to be considered phrasal verbs because the two parts can be separated as we saw in section 1.4:

(3) John looked up the information
    John looked the information up

Lexical integrity also manifests itself in the fact that syntactically governed rules of inflection do not apply to the individual parts of a word.

Consider the following names for kinds of cabbage in Dutch, both of the form A + N:

(4) ròde$_A$ kóol$_N$ "red cabbage"
     zúur$_A$kòol$_N$ "lit. sour cabbage, sauerkraut"

The first cabbage name must be a phrase, witness the fact that the adjective *rod-e* is inflected, as is the rule for Dutch adjectives in prenominal position. Moreover, it carries phrasal stress, that is, main stress on the last constituent. The second name is an A + N compound, not a phrase, because the adjective *zuur* is not inflected. Main stress is on the first constituent, as is the rule for Dutch nominal compounds. The phrase *zure kool* is also possible, but does not denote sauerkraut. Instead, it has the literal interpretation of "sour cabbage". Determining if an A + N combination is a phrase or a compound is more difficult for English than for Dutch since English does not inflect prenominal adjectives. In the case of English, our only formal criterion is that of stress: in A + N compounds main stress is usually on the first constituent and in A + N phrases on the second, as in *gréenhouse* versus *green hóuse*. On the basis of this criterion, we may conclude that *hárd disk* is a compound since it has main stress on its first constituent.

Lexical integrity pertains to syntactic rules. Phonological rules may have access to morphological structure, as do semantic rules. In the English phrase *a hard worker*, for instance, the adjective *hard* functions as a modifier of the verbal base *work* in the noun *worker*. The phrase denotes someone who works hard, not a worker who is hard. Thus, the rules of semantic interpretation must have access to the internal structure of this deverbal noun.

It is a matter of debate to what extent rules of **anaphora** are subject to the Lexical Integrity constraint. Consider the following sentences (Bosch 1983: 154):

(5) a. John likes [the guitar]$_i$ because he thinks it$_i$ is a social instrument
     b. John became a guitarist because he thought it was a social instrument
     c. Shakespearean imitators usually fail to capture his style
     d. Fred is a New Yorker, but he has not lived there for years

In (5a) the pronoun *it* is interpreted as coreferential with *the guitar*. This is indicated by the co-indexation of these two constituents by means of a subscripted index *i*. In (5b), the pronoun *it* is also interpreted as *the guitar*. Does this mean that the pronoun is co-indexed with a part of the word *guitarist*? If so, the Lexical Integrity constraint does not hold for rules of anaphora. However, this goes against the general observation that words, when embedded in complex words, lose their referential potential (in fact, it is not words but phrases that refer to something). What is at stake in sentence (5b) is that the pronoun *it* receives an interpretation within the domain of discourse evoked by this sentence. The word *guitarist* that has a transparent meaning will certainly evoke an entity "guitar" in that discourse domain. That is, the guitar is an inferred entity here, and the pronoun *it* may be linked to that entity. The same applies to (5c, d) where *Shakespeare* and *New York* are the inferred entities that function as the referents of *his* and *there* respectively. What about the following sentence?

(6)   John is an orphan, so he never knew them

Since *orphan* means "young person whose parents have died", we may wonder if *them* in this sentence can refer to John's parents? If that is the case, we can conclude that the meaning of the simplex word *orphan* introduced parents into the discourse domain. That is, the availability of particular referents in a domain of discourse is primarily a matter of semantics. However, transparent morphological structure certainly helps to find adequate referents for pronouns in a discourse domain, and hence the sentences (5b–d) are much better than sentence (6), to say the least.

The preceding remarks pertain to the issue of demarcation between morphology and syntax: how can we determine if a particular multi-morphemic construct is morphological or syntactic in nature? It is quite clear that we need formal criteria. Semantic criteria such as semantic idiosyncrasy are not of much help. The fact that *yellow fever* denotes a specific disease is a semantic idiosyncrasy that shows that this morpheme combination must be lexically stored. It is certainly a lexical unit, but not necessarily a word in the morphological sense. Its stress pattern is that of a phrase, with main stress on the head word: *yèllow féver*.

A related question is whether phrases can be parts of words. Is there a **No Phrase Constraint** on complex words? The answer is negative: phrases do occur as parts of words, as shown in (7) for English and Dutch compounds:

(7)   a.   [special exhibitions] gallery
           [module for module] upgrade
           [drugs and rehabilitation] centre

b.   [[oude mannen]$_{NP}$ [huis]$_N$]$_N$ "old men's home"
[[gekke koeien]$_{NP}$[ziekte]$_N$]$_N$ "mad cow disease"
[[hete lucht]$_{NP}$[ballon]$_N$]$_N$ "hot air balloon"
[[God is dood]$_S$ [theologie]$_N$]$_N$ "God-is-dead theology"

In the first example in (7a), the word sequence *special exhibitions* is a noun phrase of the type A + N. This is clear from its stress pattern (stress on *exhibitions*) and the fact that the word *exhibition* is used in its plural form. In the next two English examples we see the phrases *module for module* and *drugs and rehabilitation* in the non-head position. The Dutch examples show similar patterns, and the last example illustrates that even full sentences can be embedded in a compound.

It is not the case that all kinds of phrases can feed word-formation. Noun phrases with a determiner as parts of complex words are impossible in English and Dutch:

(8)   *the [[the special exhibitions] gallery]
*het [[de oude mannen] huis] "the old men's home"

This ungrammaticality has to do with the fact that *the special exhibitions* and *de oude mannen* "the old men" with their definite determiners are referring expressions, whereas word constituents in non-head position have a modifying, classificatory function.

Affixes are not completely blocked from being attached to phrases, as shown in (9):

(9)   *English*: do good-er, do-it-your-self-er, fast-tracker, look-upper (from Ryder 2001)
Dutch: vierde klass-er "fourth grader, pupil of the fourth class", twaalfuur-tje "lit. twelve o'clock-DIM, lunch food", onderons-je "lit. between us-DIM, private chat"

Affixation of phrases is exceptional, however, and is restricted to very productive affixes such as the English nominalizing suffix *-er*, its Dutch equivalent *-er*, and the very productive Dutch diminutive suffix *-(t)je* which are the suffixes used in the examples in (9).

These examples of syntax feeding word-formation show that syntax and morphology exhibit a specific form of interaction in that syntax can feed word-formation. Of course, morphology also feeds syntax since morphology provides units that are operated upon by syntactic rules.

You should realize that interaction is not the same thing as interface. We reserve the term 'interface' for the ways in which different kinds of representations (phonological, formal, semantic) are linked to each other. Here we looked at something different, namely at constraints on the formal structure of complex words, and more specifically whether pieces of syntax can form parts of complex words.

A general observation concerning the interaction between morphology and syntax is that they make use of the same word class categories: morphological rules operate on words of a certain word class (noun, verb, adjective, etc.), and also create words or word forms of a specific category. There is thus a shared vocabulary for morphology and syntax with respect to word classes.

8.2 Grammatical functions and case marking

In most languages, the interface between the semantic properties of a clause and its morpho-syntactic structure (word order, case marking, etc.) is partially regulated by the **grammatical function** frame of the verb of that clause. This statement requires some explication, and we therefore begin by analysing the grammatical properties of a simplex verb.

Consider the English verb *to hit*. This verb denotes an event in which at least two participants are involved: the person who hits, and what is hit. We refer to these two crucially involved entities as the **core arguments** of the predicate HIT, and the **Predicate Argument Structure (PAS)** of this verb can be represented as

(10)   HIT, x, y

The PAS is an abstraction from the information contained in the **Lexical-Conceptual Structure (LCS)** of a word. A complete LCS of *to hit* would include that it denotes a movement in which an object is moved towards another one, and makes contact with that object with considerable force. This information is essential for a proper semantic interpretation, but we focus here on those aspects that have direct relevance for the syntactic behaviour of verbs, which are represented at the level of PAS.

The arguments of PAS are represented as variables such as x and y, which will receive a particular value in each concrete sentence. In the sentence *John hit the ball*, the value of $x = John$, and the value of $y = the ball$. We can also add labels for particular semantic roles to these variables, for instance Agent and Patient. The notion Agent refers to the entity that is in control of the event expressed by the verb. The Patient is involved in the event, but is not in control. Such semantic roles (also called **thematic roles**) are generalizations about the roles of participants in events denoted by verbs. Our grammar of English now has to state that these two arguments are normally expressed by the grammatical subject and the grammatical object of the clause respectively. This relationship between the PAS of a verb and its syntactic realization can be expressed as in (11) by linking the grammatical functions 'subject' (SUBJ) and 'object' (OBJ) to the arguments of PAS. The verb *to hit* is specified here as appearing with both a subject and an object. This means that it is a transitive verb.

(11) HIT, x_{AGENT}, $y_{PATIENT}$ Predicate Argument Structure
      | |
      SUBJ   OBJ   grammatical function frame

The two arguments of *to hit* are the core arguments that always have to be expressed. Most predicates require one or two arguments. There are also verbs with three arguments, that have an indirect object expressing a third argument, such as *to give*, as in *John gave his sister a book* in which *his sister* has the semantic role of Goal (or Recipient). The number of arguments a verb requires to be expressed is referred to as its syntactic valency.

In addition to the core arguments, there might be other entities involved in specifying the event of hitting such as the instrument and the location, as in *John hit his enemy in the back with a stick*. These latter specifications are always optional, and such participants in the event are usually called **adjuncts**. This enables us to reserve the term 'argument' for the core arguments.

The relationship between the two levels of PAS and grammatical functions is often predictable, by so-called **linking rules**. The following linking rule is relevant for *to hit*. If there are two arguments, then the argument that expresses the Agent of the action will be expressed as the grammatical subject, and the other argument as the grammatical object. If there is only one argument, the default linking rule applies: we have to do with an intransitive verb, and this argument will be linked to the grammatical function of subject.

Word order is one of the means to indicate which particular grammatical function is performed by a noun phrase. Linguists classify languages in terms of the order in which grammatical functions are expressed: SVO

(Subject–Verb–Object), SOV (Subject–Object–Verb), etc. That is, we need these grammatical functions for syntactic purposes. They also play a role in a proper account of **elliptical constructions**, as in

(12)   John hit his enemy, and (he) left

In this sentence, the subject of the second clause may be omitted. Here, we interpret the person who left as *John*, not as *his enemy*. It is crucially the subject position that can be gapped, and hence we must be able to refer to grammatical functions such as Subject in our account of ellipsis.

In many languages, morphology is used to mark grammatical functions, either through head marking or through dependent marking. Subject–Verb agreement, for instance, marks the grammatical function Subject by expressing some of the properties of the subject NP on the verbal head. This marking may be used by the language user in order to identify the subject of the clause. Case marking is a form of dependent marking which signals the grammatical function of an NP in a clause.

In Indo-European languages with morphological case systems the distinction between grammatical subject and grammatical object is marked by means of the opposition between nominative and accusative case. If there is only one argument (the case of intransitive clauses), it is case-marked as a nominative. When there are two arguments, the subject is marked as nominative and the object as accusative. This system is called the **Nominative-Accusative system**. An alternative case-marking system is the **Absolutive-Ergative system** used in, among others, many Australian languages. Usually, the symbols S, A, and O are used for the characterization of these two systems (Dixon 1994: 6):

(13)   S = intransitive subject, A = transitive subject, O = transitive object

A stands for the subject of transitive sentences. It may be defined as follows: '[T]hat role which is likely to be most relevant to the success of the activity will be identified as A' (Dixon 1994: 7). S is the subject in intransitive sentences, and O stands for the object in transitive sentences. (Instead of O the symbol P (for Patient) is also used.) These two systems for marking the grammatical functions can now be characterized as in (14). In the Nominative-Accusative system A and S receive the same case marking, whereas in the Absolutive-Ergative system this applies to O and S. The following examples from German (15) and Dyirbal (16) illustrate the two different systems of case marking (Dixon 1994: 10).

(14) PAS	PREDICATE, x	PREDICATE, x	y
	|	|	|
Grammatical function	S	A	O
	|	|	|
Nominative-Accusative system	NOM	NOM	ACC
Absolutive-Ergative system	ABS	ERG	ABS

(15) Der   Mann   lach-t
the.MASC.NOM.SG   man.MASC.NOM.SG   laugh-PRES.3SG
"The man (S) laughs"
Der   Mann   kauf-t   ein
the.MASC.NOM.SG   man.MASC.NOM.SG   buy-PRES.3SG.   a.NEUT.SG.ACC
Buch
book.NEUT.SG.ACC
"The man (A) buys a book (O)"

(16) ŋuma   nanaga-nʸu
father.ABS   return-NONFUT
"Father (S) returned"
yabu   ŋuma-ŋgu   bura-n
mother.ABS   father.ERG   see-NONFUT
"Father (A) saw mother (O)"

In some cases it is not only the case marking that is ergative in nature, but also the syntax, as can be seen in the construction of elliptical sentences. In ellipsis, the second of two identical NPs in coordinated clauses is omitted, as illustrated in (17) for English:

(17) John (A) saw his wife (O) and—(S) rejoiced (gapping of *John* under identity of A and S)

In a language with ergative syntax such as Dyirbal, the subjects of intransitive systems pattern with O, not with A:

(18) ŋuma   banaga-nʸu   yabu-ŋgu   bura-n
father.ABS   return-NONFUT   mother-ERG   see-NONFUT
"Father (S) returned and mother (A) saw him (O)"

There is no overt O in the second clause with the transitive verb *bura* "to see", and the required O is taken to be identical to the S of the first clause. That is, the S of an intransitive clause and the O of a transitive clause appear to behave as instances of the same grammatical function.

Things can be even more complicated, due to the phenomenon of **split ergativity**. In Dyirbal the morphological nominative-accusative case-marking system is used for the morphological marking of first and second person NPs; for all other NPs, the absolutive-ergative system is used. The syntax of Dyirbal is consistently ergative, however, as shown by the fact that in sentence (19), with nominative-accusative marking, it is the object of the first clause that controls the gapped subject in the second clause (Dixon 1994: 15):

(19) n^yurra   ŋana-n   bura-n   banaga-n^yu
      you.all.NOM   we.all-ACC   see-NONFUT   return-NONFUT
      "You all (A) saw us (O) and (we) (S) returned"

In sentence (19) the omitted subject (S) of "returned" is interpreted as "we", that is, as being identical to the O of the preceding clause. This shows that ergative morphology and ergative syntax are not the same, and not necessarily linked: a language may have (partially) nominative-accusative morphology, but absolutive-ergative syntax.

8.3 Morphology and syntactic valency

The relation between the level of PAS and the level of grammatical functions can be changed by morphological operations. The best known and widely studied example of such a change is **passivization**. In this operation, the Agent of the predicate is **demoted** to the status of an adjunct. The remaining argument, if any, will then receive the status of S, and receive nominative case in a nominative-accusative system. The following Greenlandic Eskimo sentences (from Fortescue 1984: 265) illustrate this process for an ergative language:

(20) a. inuit   nanuq   taku-aat
          people.ERG.PL   polar.bear.ABS.SG   see-3PL.3SG.IND
          "The people saw the polar bear"
      b. nanuq   (inun-nit)   taku-niquar-puq
          polar.bear.ABS.SG   people-ABL.PL   see-PASS-3SG.IND
          "The polar bear was seen (by the people)"

In the second sentence, the passive suffix has the effect of making the original subject optional. It can be added as an adjunct, marked with ablative case, whereas in the active sentence it is marked with ergative case. Note also that whereas in (20a) the person–number properties of both the plural Agent and the singular Patient are marked on the verb, in (20b) it is only the properties of the singular Patient that are marked on the verbal form. This is to be expected given the non-argument status of the Agent in sentence (20b).

In present-day Romance and Germanic languages, there is no synthetic passive form of verbs; instead, a periphrastic construction is used, consisting of a passive auxiliary and a participle. In French, the verb *être* "to be" functions as passive auxiliary, and the Agent can be expressed in a *par*-phrase:

(21) Je suis   insult-é   par Jean
     I   be.1SG.PRES insult-PAST.PTCP.MASC.SG by   Jean
     "I am insulted by Jean"

As stated above, passivization is an operation that affects the mapping between PAS and the grammatical function level. It is not an operation on the semantic level (LCS or PAS) since it does not change meaning, only the form in which meaning is expressed. This is also proven by the fact that the demoted Agent of the verbal predicate is semantically still available, for instance as a controller. Notice the contrast in the following two English sentences:

(22) a. The boat was sunk to collect the insurance money
      b. *The boat sank to collect the insurance money

In (22a), a passive sentence, the demoted Agent is still there semantically, as the implicit subject of the verb *collect* in the embedded infinitival clause. In (22b), the intransitive, non-passive verb *sink* is used, and hence there is no Agent involved at all. Consequently, an appropriate controller of the subject of *collect* is not available in sentence (22b), and hence it is ungrammatical.

The essence of passivization is the demotion of the Agent argument, not the promotion of the Patient argument. The promotion of the Patient to the status of grammatical subject can be seen as the effect of the default linking rule: when there is only one argument, it will be expressed as the grammatical subject. In conformity with this statement, Dutch and German exhibit passivization of intransitive verbs, the so-called impersonal passive, illustrated by the following example from Dutch:

(23) Er   werd   enthousiast   gedanst
      there AUX.PASS.PAST.IMPF   enthusiastically   dance.PAST.PTCP
      "There was enthusiastic dancing"

In this sentence, the Agent is no longer mentioned explicitly, and since the verb *dansen* "to dance" is intransitive, there is no other argument that can be linked to the subject position. Since Dutch clauses with finite verbs always require the presence of a subject, the subject position is filled with a dummy word, the word *er*.

The different patterns of linking arguments to grammatical functions are also referred to as different **voices** (**active voice** *versus* **passive voice**). Voices express semantic relations between the subject and the action described by the verb. Another example of voice is the **middle** voice. The grammarians of Sanskrit and Greek speak of the middle voice as a distinct verbal form, just as we may have different aspectual forms of a verb. In this case, the use of the middle voice instead of the active voice does not mean that the mapping of semantic roles on grammatical functions is different, but the middle voice marker changes the status of the subject with respect to the denoted action. Here is an example from Sanskrit (Klaiman 1991: 24, transcription simplified):

(**24**)   a.   Devadattah   katam   karoti
               Devadatta.NOM   mat.ACC   make.SG
               "Devadatta makes a mat"
         b.   Devadattah   katam   krute
               Devadatta-NOM   mat.ACC   make.SG
               "Devadatta makes himself a mat"

As this example shows, the middle voice indicates that the subject is also the beneficiary of the action expressed by the verb.

The term voice is also used for alternative markings of the pragmatic role fulfilled by the noun phrases in a clause. The following example is from the Mayan language Ixil (Ayres 1983, cited in Klaiman 1991: 34).

(**25**)   a.   A-k'oni   in   ta'n   uula
               2SG.ERG-shoot   1SG.ABS   with   sling
               "You shot me with a sling"
         b.   Uula   a-k'oni-b'e   in
               sling   2SG.ERG-shoot-INDEX   1SG.ABS
               "With a sling you shot me"

The index-suffix on the verb marks the promotion of the instrument to sentence-initial position, with the instrumental preposition omitted. Thus, focus is put on the instrument with which the shooting took place.

Instead of the Agent, the O can also be demoted. This is the **anti-passive** construction, found in particular in languages with an absolutive-ergative system. In this construction, the O can be omitted, or appear with instrumental case. Hence, you get an intransitive sentence. An example from Greenlandic Eskimo is the following (Fortescue 1984: 86):

(26) a. inuit   tuqup-pai
     people.ABS.PL   kill-3SG.3PL.INDIC
     "He killed the people"
   b. inun-nik   tuqut-si-vuq
     people.INSTR   kill-ANTIPASS-3SG.INDIC
     "He killed people"

Sentence (26a) exhibits the normal case marking; in (26b) we have an intransitive sentence, with the word for "people" marked with an instrumental case. The effect of the anti-passive is to 'despecify' the direct object of the transitive verb, if expressed at all. Hence, (26) does not refer to specific people that were killed. Note also that the person–number properties of "people" are no longer marked on the verb.

Instead of demoting an argument, you may also promote it. This is done in the **applicative** construction that is found in many African and Austronesian languages. For instance, an instrumental or locative NP can be promoted to the status of O as the effect of adding an applicative affix to the verb, as in example (27) from the Atlantic language Wolof. In other cases, an additional beneficiary argument is created, as in (28), from the Mexican language Classical Nahuatl (Comrie 1985: 318):

(27) a. Mungi   lekk   ag   kuddu
     PRES.3SG eat   with   spoon
     "He is eating with a spoon"
   b. Mungi   lekk-e   kuddu
     PRES.3SG   eat-APPL   spoon
     "He is eating with a spoon"

(28) Ni-c-no-pāqui-lia
     I-it-myself-wash-APPL
     "I wash it for myself"

In sum, verbs may carry morphological markings that determine how their arguments must be expressed on the level of syntactic structure. The syntactic valency of verbs may thus be affected by morphology.

Another way of changing transitive verbs into intransitive ones is noun incorporation. What happens mostly in noun incorporation is that an argument of the verb is not expressed by a separate NP, but as part of a verbal compound. The verbal compound then functions as an intransitive verb. The following example, a one-word-sentence, comes from the Amerindian language Tuscarora; the verbal compound of the form N + V is *khw-əti* (Mithun 1999: 45):

(29) w-e-khw-əti-ʔ
FACTUAL-FEM.AGENT-food-make-PERF
"she meal-made = she cooked"

In Tuscarora, verbs with incorporated nouns co-occur with verbs with independent noun phrases. The difference is that the verb with incorporated noun denotes an institutionalized action, whereas the independent noun phrases have referential potential. In the case of incorporation, the argument usually receives a non-referential and non-individuated interpretation. This functional difference is nicely illustrated by the fact that in Tuscarora you can have constructions of the type *She bread-made corn*, with both an incorporated noun and an independent NP, meaning "She made corn-bread" (Mithun 1999: 46).

What is the precise nature of noun incorporation? Suppose we could coin the verbal compound *wood-chop* in English (we can form the compound *wood-chopping*, with a deverbal noun as head, but Germanic languages tend to avoid verbal compounds). The verbal head *chop* is a transitive predicate with two arguments. The non-head constituent *wood* will be linked to the y-argument of *chop*. Put differently, the noun *wood* binds the y-argument of *chop*, that is, it functions as the value of the y-variable. So this argument cannot be expressed any more by an independent NP in the relevant clause. Hence, the only argument left for independent syntactic expression in a sentence is the x-argument. This implies that such verbal compounds are intransitive. What we see here, then, is that the semantic interpretation of a complex verb may lead to a syntactic valency that is different from that of its verbal head. Thus, unlike operations such as passivization, noun incorporation does not affect the interface between syntax and semantics directly. The intransitivization effect is the result of the semantics of a particular word-formation process, in combination with general principles concerning the relation between the Predicate Argument Structure of a word and its syntactic expression.

The phenomenon of noun incorporation has led some linguists to propose that some kinds of word-formation can be accounted for by syntactic operations. In such a syntactic approach, the incorporated noun is represented as an independent NP at the underlying syntactic level. The noun is then adjoined to the V, resulting in a verbal compound. For instance, the fictive English verbal compound *to bed-buy* would be derived as follows (with some simplification of the syntactic structure). This is represented in Figure 8.1.

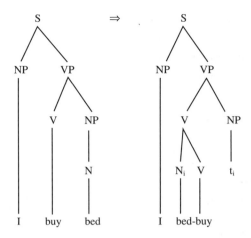

Fig. 8.1 Syntactic derivation of noun–verb compounds

The noun *bed* originates in the object position of the VP, which is then vacated; the empty position is indicated by *t* (for *trace*), and is co-indexed with the moved N. Through this co-indexation, the incorporated N will be interpreted semantically as the object of the verb. Thus, in this analysis (defended by Baker 1988, 1996, for the Amerindian language Mohawk), the intransitivization effect of this kind of noun incorporation is the effect of a syntactic operation. The main challenge for this syntactic approach to word-formation is providing a proper account of the semantic differences between verbs with independent NPs and verbs with incorporated nouns mentioned above.

The same debate as to the choice of a morphological or a syntactic analysis of word-formation plays a role in the analysis of **causatives**. Causative verbs are verbs in which the A has the role of the causer of an event in which one or two entities play a role. The classic example of a simplex causative verb in English is *to kill*, with the meaning "cause to die". More precisely, the semantic structure of this predicate can be represented as follows:

(30)   CAUSE (x, (DIE, y))

This is a semantic representation of the fact that sentences with causative verbs denote complex events, in this example the causation of the event of someone dying.

Many languages have causative affixes that turn non-causative verbs into causative ones. The semantic effect is the addition of a predicate CAUSE, and an additional argument, the causer. Hence, causativization has the effect of increasing the valency of words. This applies to adjectives, nouns and verbs. The following examples are from Diyari, an Australian language (Austin 1981: 168), and from Turkish (Comrie 1985: 323), respectively.

(31)   muka "sleep" (noun) > muka-ŋanka "to put to sleep"
       kidi "clever" (adj.) > kidi-ŋanka "to teach = to make clever"

(32)   Ali   Hasan-i   öl-dür-dü
       Ali   Hasan-DO   die-CAUS-PAST
       "Ali killed Hasan"

       müdür   mektub-u   imzala-di
       director letter-DO   sign-past
       "The director signed a letter"

       dişçi   mektub-u   müdür-e   imzala-t-ti
       dentist   letter-DO   director-IO   sign-CAUS-PAST
       "The dentist made the director sign a letter"

The last Turkish example shows how the addition of a causative suffix increases the valency of a verb. Thus, it is an example of a valency-increasing operation. We should realize, however, that causativization is a morphological process that primarily affects the semantic properties of a predicate, and hence the level of PAS. At the level of PAS, a CAUSER argument is added to the PAS of the input word. This will then affect its syntactic valency through the linking rules that map arguments onto the grammatical function frame of a verb. Therefore, although passive formation and causative formation both affect syntactic valency, the nature of these operations is different.

A syntactic approach to causativization assumes that the causative suffix functions as a verb with a complement that denotes the caused event. The syntactic structure of the first Turkish sentence in (32) above might be represented (in a somewhat simplified form and ignoring the past tense suffix) as in Figure 8.2. This syntactic structure nicely expresses that a sentence with a causative verb denotes a complex event. Since the causative verb is a bound morpheme, it cannot surface as a word of its own, and must be combined with a verbal stem. Hence, the verb of the embedded clause is moved to the higher clause, and attached through adjunction to the left of the causative suffix that functions as the verb of the main clause. This change of structure should also affect case assignment since the subject of the embedded clause *Hasan* will now have to be case-marked as object. This kind of syntactic analysis of causatives is argued for in Baker (1988, 1996).

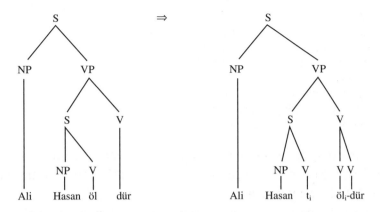

Fig. 8.2 A syntactic account of causative verbs

8.4 Periphrasis and constructional idioms

The notion 'periphrasis' is used primarily in the analysis of inflectional paradigms: for some cells of a paradigm, there is no specific morphological form available. Instead, a word combination has to be used, that is, an analytic form. Examples are the use of auxiliaries + participles of main verbs for the expression of perfect tense and the passive voice. In a number of languages, progressive aspect is expressed by a periphrastic form of the verb 'to be' + prepositional phrase, as illustrated by the following examples from Dutch:

(33) Jan   is   [[aan]$_P$ [[het]$_{Det}$ [fiets-en]$_N$]$_{NP}$]$_{PP}$
      John   is   at   the   cycle-INF
      "John is cycling"

(34) Jan   is   de   aardappels aan   het   schillen
      John   is   the   potatoes   at   the   peel-INF
      "John is peeling the potatoes"

The unity of this *aan het V-inf*-construction as the periphrastic progressive form of the verb is quite clear in sentence (34): the direct object *de aardappels* "the potatoes" is not located right before the verb, as is normally the case for objects in Dutch embedded clauses. Instead, the object precedes the word sequence *aan het* "at the" that signals the progressive aspect. Progressive aspect may also be expressed by using postural verbs such as "to sit" and "to stand" in coordination with a main verb, as illustrated here for Afrikaans and for West-Flemish, a dialect of Dutch:

(35)   *Afrikaans*
       Piet   staan   'n   glas   water   en   drink
       Pete   stands   a   glass   water   and   drink
       "Pete is drinking a glass of water"
       West Flemish
       Zij   zat   kousen   en   stoppen
       she   sat   stockings   and   mend-INF
       "She was mending stockings"

Note that it only the postural verb in the West Flemish sentence that has a finite form, the main verb appears in the infinitive (in Afrikaans there is no formal difference between infinitive and finite forms).

Such constructions with a periphrastic function are constructional idioms. Recall that constructional idioms are multi-word expressions that are idiomatic in nature but not completely fixed because some positions are variable. For instance, we may speak of the Dutch constructional idiom *aan het V-inf*, a sequence of word positions of which the first two are fixed, but the third one is a variable position, which may be filled by the infinitival form of any verb that denotes an activity. Hence, this is a productive pattern.

Many languages have preverb + verb combinations that function similarly to prefixed verbs. The notion **preverb** refers to words that appear before verbs, and form a close unit with that verb. Quite often, these phrasal constructions function as alternatives to prefixed verbs. This is the case for particle verbs in Germanic languages, and preverb + verb combinations in Hungarian. As shown in section 8.1, particle verbs have a phrasal status. The preverbs contribute to the aspectual properties of the verbal predicate, and may also influence its syntactic valency. For instance, the Dutch particle *af* expresses a result, and turns the intransitive verb *werken* "to work" into a resultative (hence telic and transitive) predicate, as in:

(36)   Bettelou   werkte   haar   opdrachten   af
       Bettelou   worked   her   assignments   PARTICLE
       "Bettelou finished her assignments"

That is, Dutch has a constructional idiom *af V* with the meaning "to finish V-ing" which may be specified in the lexicon. The meaning contribution of the particle *af* is specified as part of the meaning of the constructional idiom in which it occurs. The presence of the variable *V* indicates that new particle verbs of this form can be formed. Particle verbs are therefore lexical units, but not words in the morphological sense.

Analytic causative constructions are also instantiations of constructional idioms. In Germanic and Romance languages, the causative meaning is often not expressed by an affix, but by a separate causative verb such as *laten* "to let" in Dutch and *fare* "to do" in Italian. The combination of the causative and the main verb functions as a unit, and the recipient is marked by a preposition, *aan* in Dutch, and *a* in Italian:

(37) *Dutch*
      Ik   liet   het   boek   aan   mijn   collega   zien
      I   let   the   book   to   my   colleague   see-INF
      "I showed the book to my colleague"

      Italian
      Ho   fatto   vedere   il   libro   a-l   mia   collega
      have.1SG   make-PTCP   see.INF   the   book   to-DEF   my   colleague
      "I showed the book to my colleague"

The unitary nature of *laat zien* and *ho fatto vedere* manifests itself in the fact that they select a recipient argument marked by a preposition, whereas neither the causative verb nor the main verb select a recipient themselves.

Another type of constructional idiom that is functionally similar to complex verbs is that of **serial verbs**, found in many African, Austronesian, and Papua languages. The following examples are from São-Tomense, a Portuguese-based creole spoken on the island of São-Tomé in the Gulf of Guinea. Characteristics of such constructions are that the two (or more) verbs denote a single event, that there is only one overt subject, and one tense marker (Hagemeijer 2001: 416):

(38) Bisu   vwa   subli
      bird   fly.PAST   go.up
      "The bird flew upwards"

      Zon   toma   mantchin   kota   po
      Zon   take.PAST   machete   cut   tree
      "Zon cut the tree with the machete"

In sum, languages may have syntactic, analytic alternatives to the morphological expression of meaning. These syntactic alternatives may have the status of lexical units and may exhibit special syntactic behaviour.

Summary

The relation between morphology and syntax must be dealt with from a number of perspectives. One is the demarcation of the two: when is a multi-morphemic sequence a word, and when is it a phrase? The criterion of Lexical Integrity is the most important one for a proper delimitation of morphology from syntax. Secondly, morphology and syntax interact in two directions: syntactic constructs may form parts of complex words, and syntax in its turn governs the use of morphological case marking on words. The third perspective is that of syntactic valency: morphological operations may affect the syntactic valency of words. Finally, languages may have analytic alternatives to the morphological expression of grammatical and semantic content. Productive types of word combination of this kind can be qualified as constructional idioms.

Questions

1. Consider the following sentences of English:
   a.   John is a truck driver, and he often sleeps in it
   b.   John is a truck driver, and an excellent one

   What makes sentence (a) more difficult to interpret than sentence (b)?

2. English has the compound *small claims court*, with a phrasal left constituent. Why can we not use the phrase *very small claims* as the left constituent of a compound with *court* as its head (**very small claims court*)?

3. Recently, a new English novel was advertised as *unputdownable*. Does this word-formation imply that *put down* is one word?

4. The following sentence from Bolivian Quechua shows the use of the accusative maker *-ta* (van de Kerke 1996: 26):

   mikhu-chi-y   wawa-ta
   eat-CAUS-IMP   child-ACC
   "Make that the child eats"

   Explain why the word for "child" carries an accusative marking although it is the Agent argument of eating.

5. Consider the following active sentence and its passive counterpart in Turkish (Kornfilt 1997: 324):

   Hasan   ders-ler-e   başla-dı
   Hasan   lesson-PL-DAT   begin-PAST
   "Hasan began the lessons"
   ders-ler-e   başla-n-dı
   lesson-PL-DAT   begin-PASS-PAST
   "The lessons were begun"

   a.   What does this case marking pattern imply for the lexical specification of the Turkish verb for *to begin*?
   b.   Why does this pair of sentences support the claim that passive is demotion of the Agent, and not promotion of the Patient?

6. Which kind of valency change can be observed by comparing the following two Turkish sentences (Kornfilt 1997):

Hassan   sürahi-yi   dolab-a   koy-du
Hassan   pitcher-ACC cupboard-DAT put-PAST
"Hassan put the pitcher into the cupboard"
Hassan-a   sürahi-yi   dolab-a   koy-dur-du-m
Hasan-DAT   pitcher-ACC cupboard-DAT put-CAUS-PAST-1SG
"I made Hasan put the pitcher into the cupboard"

7. Bolivian Quechua makes use of an assistive derivational morpheme -ysi with the meaning "to help", as illustrated by the following sentence (van de Kerke 1996: 28):

mamma-y-ta   wawqe-y-ta   maylla-ysi-ni
mother-1SG-ACC brother-1SG-ACC wash-ASSISTIVE-1SG
"I help my mother to wash my brother"

Explain why there are two nouns with accusative marking in this sentence.

8. Which kind of valency change is involved in the difference between the two following sentences from the Austronesian language Kambera (Klamer 1998: 201):

I   Ama   na-kei-ya$_j$ na   menja$_j$
ART father 3SG.NOM-buy-3SG.ACC   ART   table
"Father buys the table"
I   Ama   na-kei-ngga$_k$ na   menja$_j$
ART father 3SG.NOM-buy-1SG.DAT   ART   table
"Father buys the table for me"

(Identical subscripts indicate coreference of a pronominal marker on the verb and an NP.)

9. The following two Dutch passive sentences only differ in that the first sentence has a present imperfective interpretation and the second a present perfective one.

a. Jan   word-t   geslagen
   John   become-PRES.3SG   beat.PAST.PTCP
   "John is beaten"
b. Jan   is   geslagen
   John   be.PRES.3SG   beat.PAST.PTCP
   "John has been beaten"

Note that both finite verbs wordt and is are present imperfect tense forms of the verbs worden "to become" and zijn "to be" respectively. How might this unexpected interpretation of worden and zijn in combination with past participles be accounted for in the grammar of Dutch?

10. Consider the following sentence from Middle Dutch:

Dit liep   hi ende dede den coninc cont
This walked he and   did   the king   word
"He went and told this to the king"

In this sentence, the object *dit* of the verbal expression *dede cont* "did word" precedes the intransitive verb *liep* "walked". How might this extraordinary position of the object be explained?

Further reading

The issue of how to analyse the lexical conceptual structure of Verbs is discussed in Talmy (1985), and in a number of studies by Jackendoff (see Jackendoff 2002 for a synthesis). The relation between lexical semantics and argument structure is discussed in Dowty (1991). The distinction between LCS, PAS, and the level of grammatical functions, and its relevance for morphology is defended in Rappaport et al. (1993) and in Booij (1992). Valency change is dealt with in Dixon and Aikhenvald (2000). A typological survey of causatives is presented in Song (1996).

The language-independent criteria for categorizing an NP as a grammatical subject are presented in Keenan (1976). Song (2001) gives a good survey of case assignment systems in the languages of the world. Dixon (1994) is a detailed study and survey of ergativity phenomena. There is an interesting debate on the morphological versus the syntactic analysis of noun incorporation. The syntactic approach is defended in Baker (1988, 1996), the morphological approach in Mithun (1984, 1999).

The notion 'constructional idiom' is discussed in Jackendoff (2002) and Taylor (2002), its relevance for morphology is argued for in Booij (2002c). Preverbs are discussed in a number of articles in *YoM 2003*.

9

Morphology and semantics

9.1 Semantic interpretation of morphological structure

A basic idea of modern linguistics is that the relation between the meaning and form of a simplex word is arbitrary. There is no particular reason why a book should be denoted by the sound sequence [buk], as is the case for English, and we might therefore say that the word *book* is an arbitrary linguistic sign. If all linguistic signs were arbitrary, we would have to memorize many linguistic expressions, and language would not be a very flexible communication system. Happily enough, the arbitrariness in the form–meaning relation of linguistic expressions is reduced by their having a layered structure: sentences are not holistic signs, and can be divided into constituents and ultimately words (syntactic structure), and words in their turn may have internal structure themselves (complex words). Language is clearly a combinatorial system. The meaning of complex words is not completely arbitrary, but (at least partially) **motivated**. It is an obvious task for morphologists to investigate the regularities involved in assigning a particular meaning to a complex word.

The most general principle for the semantic interpretation of both morphological and syntactic structure is the **Compositionality Principle**:

(1) The meaning of a complex expression is a compositional function of that of its constituents, and the way they are combined.

For morphology, this implies that we can derive the meaning of a complex word on the basis of its internal structure.

Compositionality is an important, but fairly general principle, and the content of this compositional function requires more detailed specification. A first specification of this compositional function is that semantic scope reflects structural hierarchy. Consider the two following nouns from the Amerindian language Yup'ik (Mithun 1999: 43):

(2)   [yug-pag]-cuar   [yug-cuar]-pag
      person-big-little   person-little-big
      "little giant"   "big midget"

In the example on the left, the suffix *-cuar* "little" has been added to the stem after the suffix *-pag* "big". Hence, *-cuar* has semantic **scope** over *yug-pag*. This means that the meaning of *-cuar* does not modify the meaning of *yug* only, but the meaning of the whole stem *yug-pag*. In the right example, the inverse situation applies. Hence, there are semantic differences between these two words with the same set of morphemes which reflect differences in morphological structure. A similar observation can be made about the English adjective *unbelievable*. This adjective has the meaning "cannot be believed", and not the meaning "can be not believed". This reflects the fact that the structure of this adjective is as follows:

(3)   [un[[believ]$_V$able]$_A$]$_A$

That is, the prefix *un-* has scope over the stem *believable*.

In the case of compounds, it is the notion 'head' that we need for a proper semantic interpretation: the meaning of the non-head of a compound functions as a modifier of that of the head. This latter statement is a correspondence rule that specifies the interface between the formal structure of a compound and its semantic interpretation. Consider the following nominal compounds of Dutch:

(4)   graan-molen "corn mill"
      mosterd-molen "mustard mill"
      verf-molen "paint mill"
      water-molen "water mill"
      wind-molen "wind mill"

These five compounds all denote a particular kind of *molen* "mill". This shows that the structural notion 'head of a compound' that we need for formal reasons (such as the fact that the head determines the gender of the whole compound) is essential for the semantic interpretation of compounds as well. Headship induces the 'is a' relation: a *graanmolen* is a *molen*. The relationship between head and non-head can be circumscribed as 'has some relation to'. This is an intentionally vague semantic qualification. When we paraphrase these five compounds we get quite different circumscriptions of their meanings:

(5) graan-molen: mill that grinds corn
    mosterd-molen: mill that grinds mustard seeds for the production of mustard
    verf-molen: mill that grinds wood for the production of paint
    water-molen: (i) mill that is powered by water, (ii) mill that transports water
    wind-molen: mill that is powered by wind

The semantic paraphrase 'has some relation to' can be referred to as R. What we have to say for languages with right-headed compounds is that the compound structure AB correlates with the semantic structure R(B,A), that is, 'B has some relation to A'. The exact nature of this relation is not a matter of the grammar, but of **world knowledge** (also called **encyclopedic knowledge**) and, in some cases, knowledge of the context in which a compound is used. The compounds in (4–5) are all established compounds, which means that the specific interpretation of R has been fixed. For new compounds, the content of R can be inferred at the time of its being uttered on the basis of knowledge of the world and/or context. For instance, when I came across the English compound *umbrella organization* for the first time, I had no problem in understanding it, and I did not have to look it up in my English dictionary (which does not list it anyway). The interpretation is obviously "organization that functions like an umbrella". An important semantic component of words is their function, and in this example *umbrella* is a further specification of that function. In addition, this compound shows that language users are able to interpret metaphorical use of language. In metaphors, notions from one domain of knowledge are transferred to another domain. We know that an umbrella has a protective function, and can keep one or more persons protected against rain or sun under its screen. This knowledge is then transferred to the more abstract domain of organizational structure, leading to the interpretation that we have to do here with some organizational superstructure.

It is useful to distinguish between the notions **meaning** and **interpretation**. The meaning contribution of right-headed compound structures of the type AB is R(B,A), and this relationship then receives a specific interpretation for each individual compound, by means of interpretational mechanisms as those discussed above. These mechanisms are pragmatic in nature since they follow from the pragmatic principle of **cooperation** between speaker and hearer: try to come up with the most sensible interpretation possible so that we understand each other.

The high degree of abstractness (or **vagueness**) of the meaning contribution of compound structure makes compounding an extremely flexible device from a semantic point of view. This, in combination with its transparent morphological structure, undoubtedly contributes to its enormous productivity in many languages.

A similar profitable vagueness can be observed in two other word-formation processes, conversion and the derivation of relational adjectives. Consider the following cases of conversion in Dutch:

(6) *Noun*   *Verb*
     bier "beer"   bier "drink beer"
     kaas "cheese"   kaas "produce cheese"
     melk "milk"   melk "take milk from an animal"
     tafel "table"   tafel "dine"
     water "urine"   water "urinate"

These verbs all have the meaning "action that has some relationship R with the base-noun", but the exact nature of this relation varies from word to word. Clearly, the meaning of these words is compositionally determinable, but we need other, non-linguistic resources to come up with a specific interpretation of R. Once they have been coined, with a specific interpretation, that interpretation might become the conventionalized interpretation, often registered in dictionaries. Storage of the conventionalized interpretation is particularly a must for English verbs derived from proper nouns such as *to boycott, to hoover*, and *to xerox*. The proper noun *Boycott* as such does not give you a clue as to what a verb *to boycott* might mean. Hence, the meaning of these verbs is not computable on the basis of the meaning of their base nouns without further information on these proper names.

Abstractness of the meaning contribution of morphological structure is also the key to understanding the manifold interpretations of reduplicative structures such as plurality, iterativity, and intensity. Consider the following sentences from Afrikaans (Botha 1988: 92–3):

(7) a. Die kinders drink bottels-bottels limonade
       the children drink bottles-bottles lemonade
       "The children drink many bottles of lemonade"

b. Hij   lek-lek   oor   sy   droë   lippe
   he   lick-lick over his   dry   lips
   "He licks and relicks his dry lips"

The following rule accounts for the different interpretations of these reduplicative structures:

(8)   Interpret $\alpha_i\ \alpha_i$ as [A INCREASED] (where A represents the meaning of α and INCREASED represents an abstract semantic unit). (Botha 1988: 94)

This is a correspondence rule that relates a particular morphological form to its semantic structure. The abstract meaning INCREASED will then receive a more specific interpretation by means of **conceptualization rules** which define conceptual well-formedness. For instance, the following conceptualization rule may be assumed: if A has the meaning component COUNTABLE THING, the property INCREASED must receive a numerical interpretation. This is the case in sentence (7a). In example (7b), it is a verb that is reduplicated. Verbs denote events with the measurable property of duration. Hence, with verbs the notion INCREASED should be interpreted as INCREASE OF TIME, another example of a conceptualization rule. However, licking one's lips is a bounded event. Hence, the only sensible interpretation here is an iterative one: repeated licking must be involved. This rule of iterative interpretation of bounded events is a third example of a conceptualization rule. Such rules thus do not specify the interface between formal structure and semantic interpretation, but further develop the semantic interpretation.

This analysis of the interpretation of complex words shows that meaning assignment is a dynamic and flexible process. This is also the case for the interpretation of complex adjectives. Many kinds of denominal adjectives function as relational adjectives (cf. section 4.1). Relational adjectives denote the existence of a relation between the noun that they modify and some other entity evoked by that adjective. They are distinguished from **qualifying adjectives** that denote a quality of the noun they modify. Consider the following examples from English:

(9)   the Americ-an flag
   a person-al computer
   a spous-al hire

The meaning contributions of the different denominal suffixes involved are all the same: "related to base noun". Thus, they relate the base noun of the adjective to the head noun that these adjectives modify in a phrase. *An*

American flag does not denote a flag that is American in nature, but the flag of America. Due to this relational nature of such adjectives, they cannot be used in predicative position (except when contrast is involved, as in (10b), nor can they be modified, unlike qualitative adjectives (10c):

(10)   a. *The flag is American/*a very American flag
        b. That flag is not Américan but Canádian.
        c. That flag is blue/a very blue flag

The same applies to the other two examples in (9): a personal computer is a computer meant for use by individual persons, not a computer that is personal in nature. A *spousal hire* denotes the situation in which the employer not only hires a person, but also her or his spouse.

By adding a modifier, relational adjectives can be forced to be interpreted as qualifying adjectives. If I call someone *a very American lady*, I invoke all the prototypical qualities of American ladies (wearing shorts in summer, speaking loudly and with a lot of gestures, etc.). This kind of interpretational shift is thus a case of type coercion: modifiers require qualifying adjectives as their adjectival heads, and hence, in such cases denominal adjectives are interpreted as qualifying adjectives. This is another demonstration of the dynamics and flexibility of meaning assignment to complex words.

Relational adjectives play an important though not exclusive role in what have been called **bracketing paradoxes**. For instance, a *moral philosopher* is not a philosopher who is moral, but someone who deals with moral philosophy. Hence, there seems to be a mismatch between the formal structure of this phrase, and its semantic interpretation:

(11)   syntax: [[moral]$_A$ [philosopher]$_N$]$_{NP}$
        semantics: [[moral philosophy]er]

The same observation applies to phrases such as *nuclear physicist, criminal lawyer, small farmer*, and *first violinist*. On second thought, however, there is no bracketing paradox involved. The same kind of interpretation occurs when there is no possibility of bracketing the phrase differently at the semantic level, as shown by the following examples with underived nouns:

(12)   a good athlete, an old friend

A *good athlete* is not necessarily a good person, but someone who is good as an athlete. Similarly, an *old friend* is not necessarily old, but someone the friendship with whom is old. In these cases, this interpretation cannot be attributed to a difference in bracketing between the formal and the semantic structure. What we need therefore is a semantic principle that tells us how to interpret such phrases, both those with denominal relational adjectives and those with simplex adjectives. The general idea is that an attributive adjective, whether a qualifying adjective or a relational adjective, may modify only part of the semantic structure of the head noun. The phrase *old friend* can mean "a friend who is old". In that case, *old* only says something of what we may call the PERSON component of the meaning of *friend*. If we interpret this phrase as "someone who has been a friend for a long time", the adjective mentions a property of another meaning component, the FUNCTION component "friendship". Denominal relational adjectives have the specific property that the entity invoked by their base noun, for instance *crime* in the case of *criminal*, functions as an argument of the FUNCTION component of the meaning of *lawyer*. This FUNCTION may be circumscribed as "giving advice on legal matters concerning x". In the phrase *criminal lawyer* the x will then be taken to stand for "crime".

How does the interpretation of morphological structure proceed in those cases in which the morphological operation involved does not consist of concatenation, but of operations such as vowel change. How do we deal with the interpretation of the past tense form *saw* of *to see*, in which there is no separate past tense morpheme? A possible answer is that such operations are triggered by the presence of morphosyntactic features such as [+past] or an abstract grammatical morpheme PAST. Such features or morphemes will then be linked to a semantic property PAST at the semantic level. The linking rules will also specify the scope of PAST. The semantic scope of this property is not just the verb itself, but the whole event described, as represented in a semi-formal way in (13):

(13)   Indriaas saw the accident ⇔ PAST [SEE, Indriaas, the accident]

Thus, it is specified that the event of Indriaas seeing the accident took place before the moment of speaking.

In sum, the Compositionality Principle is the main principle of interface between formal (morphological and syntactic) structure and semantic structure. This general principle requires further specifications of the sort discussed above, in order to do justice to the complexities of this interface. In addition, there are conceptualization rules pertaining to the semantic level only that further enrich semantic structure.

9.2 Semantics and syntactic valency

The relation between morphology and syntactic valency has already been broached in section 8.3. However, it also needs attention in a chapter on morphology and semantics because the syntactic valency of a complex word is (at least partially) determined by its semantic properties.

As observed in section 1.3, one of the functions of morphology is to change the syntactic category of words with the effect that other syntactic uses are made possible. A cross-linguistically very common form is that of **action nominalization**, in which verbal constructions are deverbalized, and acquire a noun-like behaviour. There are degrees of **deverbalization** as the following examples of deverbal nominalization in English show (Malouf 2000: 93):

(14) a. Chris was shocked that Pat illegally destroyed the evidence
     b. Chris was shocked by Pat having illegally destroyed the evidence
     c. Chris was shocked by Pat's having illegally destroyed the evidence
     d. Chris was shocked by Pat's illegal destroying of the evidence
     e. Chris was shocked by Pat's illegal destruction of the evidence

In (14b–d) we see the **gerundive nominals** *having destroyed* and *destroying*, and in (14e) the deverbal **action noun** *destruction*. In the sentences (14b–e), these deverbal nouns are used as the heads of a noun phrase. This can be concluded from the fact that they occur in a PP with the preposition *by*. Yet, they show some verb-like behaviour as well. This is most clearly the case with the gerundive nominals that co-occur with the adverb *illegally*, which is impossible to use with the derived noun *destruction*. Selecting adverbial forms as modifiers is a distinguishing property of verbs and adjectives, whereas nouns select adjectives as modifiers. Furthermore, in (14b, c), the object of the verb *destroy*, the phrase *the evidence*, appears as a bare NP, without a preposition. This is of course a prototypical property of verbs rather than of nouns. In (14e), the complement-NP of *destruction* has to be preceded by a preposition, the default preposition *of*.

It will be clear then that such nominalization patterns pose quite an analytical challenge to linguists, and raise the issue whether categories such as V and N can always be sharply distinguished. This is why deverbal nominalizations have been qualified as belonging to the set of **mixed categories** (also called **transcategorial constructions**). Other examples of such mixed categories are verbal participles. As we saw in section 5.1 for

German, they behave as adjectives with respect to inflection, and as verbs with respect to the kind of phrases with which they can combine.

These observations suggest that the function of morphology might be that of category change only, without any particular semantic effect. The (partial) preservation of the syntactic valency of the base of such complex words is referred to as **inheritance**. Deverbal nouns in -*ion* differ from gerundive nominals in exhibiting a lesser degree of inheritance of verbal properties, as we saw above. In deverbal nominalization of this type, the deverbal noun inherits the Predicate Argument Structure of its base verb, but the syntactic expression of the arguments is different from that of the base verb. They must be expressed in an *of*-PP, or in the prenominal possessive form with '*s*. Moreover, the syntactic expression of the inherited arguments of such deverbal nouns seems to be optional; compare:

(15)   a. Pat's destruction of the evidence
       b. the destruction of the evidence
       c. Pat's destruction
       d. the destruction

In (15c), *Pat* is interpreted as the Patient of *destruction*, not as Agent, unless there is some specific context in which objects can be omitted.

Action nouns can further develop from simple event nouns into **result nouns** denoting the result of the action. In the latter interpretation they no longer denote an event with participants, and hence do not allow for Agent phrases. When such nouns are interpreted as result nouns, they can be pluralized. Therefore, such plural deverbal nouns exclude the use of Agent phrases:

(16)   Extensive collections of shells (*by Indriaas)
       These expressions (*by my father) are old-fashioned

In sum, when there are differences in syntactic valency between verbs and their corresponding deverbal nouns, these differences can be seen as reflecting differences in their semantic structure. This shows once more the strong dependence of syntactic valency on the semantic properties of words.

The issue of inheritance of syntactic valency also crops up in the analysis of compounds of the following type:

(17)   coffee-maker, pasta-eater, story-teller, truck-driver

In these compounds headed by a deverbal agent noun, the left constituent is interpreted preferably as the Patient of the action denoted by the

verbal base of the head noun. How are we going to account for that interpretation? We cannot consider these words to be derived by means of the
suffix *-er* from verbal compounds of the N + V type, since this is not a
productive type of compounding in English: compounds such as *to coffee-
make* or *to pasta-eat* cannot be formed. Hence, a word such as *coffee-maker*
must be considered a case of N + N compounding, with the head noun
being a deverbal noun.

There are two ways of accounting for the Patient interpretation of the
left constituent. The default one is to simply assume that the Patient interpretation is a filling-in of the general relation *R* that exists between the two
parts of a compound. For *maker,* the most sensible interpretation of the
relation with *coffee* is that *coffee* is a specification of what is made. The
other analytical option is to assume that deverbal nouns keep the Predicate
Argument Structure of their verbal base. The semantic structure of *maker*
will then be as follows, with the PAS of its verbal base incorporated:

(18)   x [MAKE, x_{AGENT}, $y_{PATIENT}$]

This semantic structure is a slightly more formal representation of the
informal description of the meaning of *maker* as "one who makes something". The semantic effect of the *-er*-suffix is that it **binds** the x-argument
of the verbal base. This means that this argument cannot be expressed
any more. Hence, only the y-argument is left to be expressed by a nominal,
either as the left constituent of a compound, or as an NP that is preceded
by the default preposition *of.* Both the compound *coffee-maker* and the
phrase *maker of coffee are* well-formed expressions.

A possible argument for the second analytical option based on facts
of Dutch is that this language has a number of compounds of which
the deverbal head only occurs in compounds or with a PP-complement
(Booij 1988):

(19)   a. ijs-bereider/bereider van ijs "ice maker/maker of ice"
        b. bevel-hebber "lit. command haver, commander"
        c. woord-voerder "lit. word carrier, spokesman"

The nouns *bereider* and *voerder* do not occur outside these contexts, and the
deverbal noun *hebber* does occur as a noun by itself, but only in the idiosyncratic interpretation "greedy person". The verbs involved (*bereiden* "to
prepare", *hebben* "to have", and *voeren* "to carry" are obligatorily transitive
verbs, with two arguments. If argument structure is inherited by deverbal

nouns in *-er*, it is predicted that the second argument must be expressed, either morphologically or syntactically, as in (19a). The verb *hebben* "to have" is also obligatorily transitive. In the lexicalized compound *bevelhebber* the *x*-argument is bound by *-er*, and the *y*-argument by *bevel* "command". There is an alternative analysis, however, for words such as *bevelhebber* and *woordvoerder*. They might have been derived directly from the Dutch lexical units *bevel hebben* "to command" and *woord voeren* "to speak". In that case, we do need the nouns *hebber* and *voerder* as building blocks of these words. In short, there is no established analysis of such facts.

The inheritance of syntactic valency as analysed here is the effect of preservation of argument structure of the base words. There is, however, also a kind of inheritance of a more syntactic nature, with little or no semantics involved. Verbs may select a specific preposition for the complement they occur with, a prepositional object. This also applies to a variety of adjectives. This choice of preposition is an idiosyncrasy that has to be encoded in the lexicon, and this choice is taken over by the derived word, as illustrated in (20):

(20) to long for   longing for
     to compare to   comparable to
     to hope for   hope for
     to trust in   trust in
     divide by   divisible by
     averse to   averseness to
     curious about   curiosity about
     susceptible to   susceptibility to

This implies that in these cases there is a transfer of specific syntactic subcategorization information from the base word to its derivative.

The relation between the semantics of a word-formation process and its effect on syntactic valency is also at stake in two other English word-formation processes, the coining of deverbal adjectives ending in *-able*, and middle verbs:

(21) do-able "can be done"
     drink-able "can be drunk, fit for drinking"
     read-able "can be read, pleasant to read"
     wash-able "can be washed"

(22) This book reads easily
     These products sell well
     This chicken broils excellently

Both processes serve to create words that do not denote events but stative properties. In this respect they are quite unlike the passive construction, which does denote events. Since these types of word do not denote events, they cannot occur with an Agent phrase. The only argument that is expressed is the Patient-argument of the base verb. This argument is stated to have the property that it can participate in the kind of event denoted by the base verb. Thus, sentences like the following are ungrammatical:

(23)   *This tea is drinkable by Mary
       *This book reads easily by John

The semantic structure of these adjectives and verbs implies that there is no Agent to express, not even in a *by*-phrase, because there is no Agent-participant in the Lexical Conceptual Structure of these words, and hence they are intransitive predicates.

You may have noticed that my gloss of *drinkable* is somewhat imprecise. If we say of a wine that it is drinkable, we mean that it is a good wine to drink. What we observe here, is a more general pragmatic Non-Redundancy Constraint involved in the interpretation of words. It seems superfluous to say of wine that is drinkable, meaning that it can be drunk. Of course it can! Therefore, if someone nevertheless states that it is drinkable, we infer that this must mean it is good wine to drink, otherwise the information would be superfluous. We assume that speakers try to be informative, after all, and to provide relevant information. For the same reason, it seems odd to say that a book can be read. Thus, adjectives such as *drinkable* and *readable* receive an interpretation of positive evaluation. The same holds for middle verbs. In their concrete use in sentences, middle verbs are always accompanied by an evaluative adverb such as *well* or *easily*.

This pragmatic principle may also explain why denominal adjectives in *-ed* such as *eyed* do not occur on their own, but in compounds only:

(24)   ?eyed   blue-eyed
       ?faced   red-faced
       ?fisted   two-fisted
       ?handed   two-handed
       ?handed   right-handed

The adjectives in the left column of (24) are morphologically well-formed. However, they violate the pragmatic Non-Redundancy Constraint. It is expected that human beings have a face, and hence it does not seem to make much sense from a pragmatic point of view to say *My husband is faced*.

Hence the use of such adjectives is infelicitous (indicated here by the question mark) unless they are embedded in a compound. Yet, this might not be the whole story. If a man has a lot of hair we prefer to call him *a hairy man*, and *a haired man* sounds odd although it makes sense from the pragmatic point of view.

The crucial role of the semantics in determining the syntactic valency of derived verbs can be illustrated by the formation of Dutch verbs by means of the prefix *be-*. Morphology may be used to form obligatorily transitive verbs from verbs that are intransitive or optionally transitive. In Dutch, the prefix *be-* is used for this purpose as shown in (25). These examples show that, whatever the syntactic valency of the input verb, the syntactic valency of the output verb is always that of an obligatorily transitive verb. The Lexical Conceptual Structure of deverbal *be*-verbs can be circumscribed as follows: '*x* completely affects *y* by executing the action expressed by the base verb'. This means that the Predicate Argument Structure of such verbs always comprises two arguments. Moreover, the resulting verbs are always telic verbs because the endpoint of the action is implied: the *y*-argument is completely affected, and thus the end of the action is implied.

(25)	*Type of input verb*	*Output verb*
	intransitive	
	loop "to walk"	iets beloop "to walk on something"
	klim "to climb"	iets beklim "to climb on something"
	with prepositional object	
	aan iets twijfel "to doubt about something"	iets betwijfel "to doubt something"
	met iemand vecht "to fight with somebody"	iemand bevecht "to fight somebody"
	with direct object	
	iets schilder "to paint something"	iets beschilder "to cover something with paint"
	iets plak "to glue something"	iets beplak (met iets) "to cover something (with something)"
	with direct and prepositional object	
	iets van iemand roof "to rob someone from something"	iemand beroof (van iets) "to rob somebody (from something)"
	iets in iets plant "to plant something in something"	iers beplant (met iets) "to plant something (with something)"

Source: Booij 2002a: 192.

We can now predict the syntactic valency of *be*-verbs on the basis of the following rule: 'if a telic verb has a Patient-argument, this argument must always be expressed syntactically'. This regularity is an example of a correspondence rule that specifies the interface between syntax and semantics. Thus, the fact that these *be*-verbs are obligatorily transitive is fully predictable.

In sum, the effects of morphological operations on the syntactic valency of input words are primarily the effects of the semantic changes brought about by these operations. If the semantic changes are minimal, the differences in syntactic valency between base word and derived word will also be minimal.

9.3 Polysemy

Consider the following list of English deverbal nouns in *-er*, subdivided into a number of semantic categories:

(26) Agent   baker, writer
      Impersonal Agent   mower, pointer
      Instrument   atomizer, blotter
      Experiencer   feeler, hearer
      Action   breather, disclaimer
      Locative   diner, sleeper

Clearly, it is not the case that the suffix *-er* is used only to derive agent nouns. So should we assume a number of different suffixes *-er*, each with a meaning of their own? Well, there is certainly more than one suffix *-er* in English: there is also the comparative suffix *-er*, with a completely different meaning. That is, there are at least two homophonous suffixes *-er*. In order to interpret the variation in meaning for the deverbal suffix *-er*, another notion is more appropriate, that of **polysemy**. We speak of polysemy when a morpheme or a word has more than one meaning, but with some systematic relation between these different meanings. Consider the following meanings for the word *head*:

(27) 1. The top part of the body in humans and some other higher animals;
      2. Person (as in *dinner at 20 dollars a head*);
      3. Leader

Actually, there are many more meanings for *head*, but these three suffice for our purposes. Meaning 1 is the primary meaning of this word. Meaning 2 can be considered to be derived from this primary meaning through the semantic mechanism of **metonymy** in which a word is interpreted as denoting something that is associated with the object that it literally denotes. In this example, the word *head* is used to denote the person who is the owner of the head. In the third meaning, we speak of **metaphorical use**: just as a head in its literal sense governs the body to which it belongs, a human being may govern an institution of some sort (which can also be called a 'body'). Thus, these three different meanings of *head* can be related systematically in terms of general mechanisms of semantic interpretation, and we consider this a case of polysemy.

There are also systematic explanations for what one might call the polysemy of the suffix *-er*. To begin with, the subject argument of the underlying verb may be a human agent (*baker*), a non-human, impersonal one (*pointer*) or an experiencer (*hearer*). Hence, the different interpretations correlate with the different semantic roles of the subject arguments of the base verbs. In the case of *sleeper* something else is at stake. Here, the location (or space) of the action of sleeping is denoted. This interpretation can be understood by means of the notion **domain shift**: one may go from one semantic domain to another, related one, and thus derive new interpretations. An example of such a cross-linguistically valid domain shift chain is:

(28) PERSON > OBJECT > ACTIVITY > SPACE > TIME > QUALITY (Heine *et al.* 1991: 48)

In this chain, one might go from left to right, from one domain to the next. For instance, the English word *reader*, which is a word for a person, can also be shifted to the domain of OBJECT, and be interpreted as a kind of patient: "collection of reading material". Similarly, the word *diner* that can denote a person who dines can also denote a space where one dines, a (specific American type of) restaurant. The possibility of such domain shifts also explains the activity name *disclaimer* and the space or location name *sleeper*.

These kinds of domain shifts are examples of metaphorical and metonymical extensions. Metaphorical operations conceptualize domains of cognition in terms of other, usually less abstract domains. The shift from PERSON to INSTRUMENT is an example of domain shift that one often finds in natural languages. This chain can be seen as a metaphorical one: the notion AGENT is transferred to the domain of inanimate material things that are conceived of as agents that perform a particular task. A locative interpretation (as in *diner*) looks more like metonymy: the name for the agent is transferred to the location of the action denoted by the base verb.

In (29) deverbal nouns of Hungarian (Comric and Thompson 1985: 355) and Dutch (Booij 1986) illustrate that these domain shifts occur cross-linguistically. This is what should be the case since such interpretational chains are cognitive in nature, and hence applicable to different languages. Note, moreover, that quite a number of such nouns have more than one interpretation. The Dutch agent noun *sender* can be interpreted as an agent noun denoting a human being, but also as a radio or tv channel, or an instrument for transmitting signals. If the instrument interpretation is the established one, as is the case for Dutch *opener* (an instrument to open cans or bottles), the (human) agent interpretation can always be activated and used, as in *De opener van deze expositie* "The opener of this exhibition". The American English word *diner* for a certain type of restaurant can still be used for someone who dines. This means that we do not have to assume a list of different meanings for these deverbal suffixes. It is the individual complex words with these suffixes that show this semantic variation, and this variation follows from independently established principles of semantic interpretation.

(29) *Hungarian (deverbal suffix -ölö)*
   Agent   ir-ó "writer"
   Instrument   hegyez-ö "pencil sharpener"
   Location   társalg-ó "parlor"
   Dutch (deverbal suffix -er)
   Agent   schrijv-er "writer" < schrijf "to write"
   Instrument   maai-er "mower" < maai "to mow"
   Event   miss-er "failure" < miss "to miss"
   Patient   bijsluit-er "instruction" < bijsluit "to enclose (with medication)"

The variation in interpretation for different words of the same morphological type is also quite spectacular in the case of diminutives. Starting from the basic meaning SMALL, one may get to quite a number of interpretational types. Consider the following examples of denominal diminutive nouns in Dutch that serve to illustrate the wide variety of meaning contributions associated with the diminutive suffix. Note that some of these diminutive nouns are themselves polysemous:

(30)   kind "child"   kind-je "small child, darling"
       broek "trousers"   broek-je "pants"
       Geert "boy's name"   Geert-je "girl's name"
       bier "beer"   bier-tje "glass of beer"
       man "man"   mann-e-tje "small man, little boy, unofficial worker"
       auto "car"   autoo-tje "small, inexpensive car, toy car"

Cross-linguistically, the basic meanings of diminutives are those of "child" or "small", two closely related meanings that relate to size. The meaning component "child" extends into notions such as affection, sympathy, and pet, that is, there is often a meaning component of endearment involved. The notion "small" may also be associated with contempt, as when one refers to a small and cheap car as an *autootje*. This second cluster of meanings might be subsumed under the notion 'attitude' or 'evaluation'. Thus, diminutive morphology belongs to the semantic category of evaluative morphology. The use of diminutive morphology for the creation of female names probably reflects the idea that women are physically smaller than men. The different meanings of the diminutive can be related by conceiving of its semantics as a **radial category**. A radial category has one or more core meanings from which the other meanings derive through semantic extension mechanisms such as metaphor. The structure in Figure 9.1 is a reduced version of what Jurafsky (1996: 542) considers as the universal structure of the semantic category 'diminutive'. The Dutch examples given above are instantiations of the different semantic categories in this scheme. In Figure 9.1 related core meanings are given in bold. The diminutive noun *biertje* in (30) is an example of the partitive use of the diminutive, it denotes a part of a container with beer. The extensions on the bottom line of this scheme are typically pragmatic in nature: since small children tend to evoke affection, these feelings can be transferred to other categories and situations.

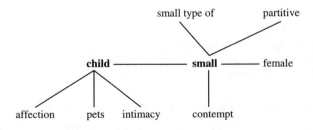

Fig. 9.1 The radial semantic structure of diminutives

In many cases the use of a diminutive suffix has a strong pragmatic rationale, instead of just qualifying something as small. Therefore, Dressler and Barberesi (1994) interpret the evaluative nature of the diminutive by considering the pragmatic feature [non-serious] as its basic meaning. It is often used in 'motherese', the language addressed to small children, as in the following example from Viennese German (Dressler and Barberesi 1994: 106).

(31) Gut-i   gut-i   bist   doch   g'scheit-i   g'scheit-i
      good-DIM   good-DIM are   PARTICLE clever-DIM   clever-DIM
      "Good-y good-y, you are a nice little clever child"

The following observation by Wierzbicka (1991: 55), cited by Dressler and Barbaresi (1994), on the use of the diminutive suffix in English is also very relevant for grasping the role of diminutives:

(32) 'Thus calling mosquitoes *mozzies*, the speaker is good-humouredly dismissing the problem: he thinks of *mozzies* as small (but not endearing), and expects that the addressee would share this attitude'.

This is the kind of euphemistic use of the diminutive that also occurs when a Dutch speaker asks: *Hebt U nog een minuutje voor me* "Do you have a minute-DIM for me?". You can be pretty sure that the conversation will take more than a minute.

Another pragmatic role for morphology is the use of **honorifics** that express different degrees of politeness, and may also reflect the position in the social hierarchy of speaker and addressee. In Japanese, for instance, the predicate of a subject receives a special honorific form if the speaker addresses a socially superior person. A relatively simple example of the politeness use of the honorific suffix -*masi* in Japanese is given in (33) (Harada 1976: 502):

(33) a. Ame   ga   hut-ta
          rain SUBJ   fall-PAST
          "It rained"
      b. Ame   ga   huri-masi-ta
          rain SUBJ   fall-HONOR-PAST
          "It rained" (polite speech)

These examples show that the interpretation and use of complex words is not only a matter of cognitive principles and mechanisms, but also has a pragmatic dimension.

A particular interpretation of a complex word may be the established one, as is often the case. This is referred to as lexicalization. It does not mean necessarily that such a word has become irregular, or that other interpretations are now impossible (recall the example of *diner*), but simply that a particular interpretation of a word has become part of the lexical norm of the language community involved. Advertisements make use of this. For instance, in an advertisement for convertible cars the Dutch adjective *dak-loos* "lit. roof-less, homeless" was used in the sentence *Wij willen U graag dakloos maken* "We would like to make you homeless/roofless", in which the literal interpretation "roof-less" is reactivated, thus playing with the contrast between poor, homeless people, and people who can afford to buy a convertible type of car.

Summary

The semantic interpretation of complex words is governed by the general principle of compositionality. Correspondence rules specify relationships between formal structure and semantic interpretation of complex words. The semantic scope of morpho-syntactic properties may be larger than the word on which they are marked, as is the case for tense and mood properties. The semantic interpretation of a word may be further enriched by conceptualization rules.

Pragmatic principles, knowledge of the world and of the context in which a word is used, must also be invoked to arrive at a proper interpretation and use of complex words.

The semantic interpretation of complex words and the semantic effects of morphological operations may have implications for the syntactic valency of complex words, since the syntactic valency of a word reflects its semantic properties.

Polysemy of affixes and of individual complex words is a pervasive phenomenon in the realm of complex words. It is the effect of semantic extension mechanisms such as metaphor and metonymy, and can be understood more generally in terms of domain shift chains.

The meaning contribution of a particular affix may be strongly pragmatic in nature, as is the case for diminutives and honorifics.

Questions

1. Specify the semantic relationship between the two constituents of the following English compounds: *horse doctor, tree doctor, voodoo doctor, hospital doctor*.

2. Identify for each of the following complex words which semantic extension mechanism is involved in their interpretation: *beehive, bottleneck, convention, cliffhanger, holder, opposition, printer*.

3. Which meaning component of the head noun is modified by the preceding adjective in the following NPs: *a rural policeman, a Martian expedition, an early riser, an individual decision*?

4. Consider the following cases of adjective reduplication in Malagasy (Keenan and Polinsky 1998: 571):

   fotsy "white"   fotsyfotsy "whitish"
   maimbo "stinky"   maimbomaimbo "somewhat stinky"
   hafa "different"   hafahafa "somewhat different"
   lo "rotten"   lolo "somewhat rotten"

   What conclusion can be drawn from these data as to the universality of correspondence rule (8)?

5. In the following sentence with a deverbal noun in *-ion* the use of a prepositional *by*-phrase leads to ungrammaticality:

   John was the selection of/*by the committee

   Why does the use of *by* lead to ungrammaticality?

6. Consider the following Turkish noun phrase (Kornfilt 1997: 225):

   Türk-ler-in   Istanbul-u   feth-i
   Turk-PL-GEN   Istanbul-ACC   conquest-3SG
   "The Turks' conquest of Istanbul"

   How might it be explained that the noun *Istanbul* receives accusative case here from a (deverbal) noun?

7. Dutch has a compound *parkeergarage* "lit. parking garage, multi-storey/ underground car park". To what extent is this compound a violation of the Non-Redundancy Constraint, given the following range of meanings of the Dutch word *garage*: "garage, service-station"?

8. Specify the semantic scope of the suffix *-ible* in the following sentence:
   This number is divisible by three

9. The following English deverbal nouns in *-ing* are all polysemous. Determine for each of them how their different meanings relate to each other: *blessing, crossing, drawing, dwelling, opening*.

10. Some languages allow for double diminutives in which the root of the word is followed by two diminutive suffixes, as in Polish *kot-eč-ek* "cat-DIM-DIM, dear pussy", and Afrikaans *huis-ie-tjie* "house-DIM-DIM, dear little house".

Explain why it is not so odd from the semantic point of view to use two diminutive suffixes in one word.

Further reading

Conceptualization rules are discussed in Jackendoff (1983, 2002). The interpretation of English conversion verbs is discussed in Clark and Clark (1979) and Aronoff (1980).

The semantic resolution of the bracketing paradox issue is dealt with in more detail in Spencer (1988) and Beard (1991).

A survey of phenomena of inheritance and nominalizations, and discussions of their proper analysis is found in Comrie and Thompson (1985), Hoekstra (1986), Grimshaw (1990), and Koptjevskaja-Tamm (1993). The analysis of verbal compounds is discussed in Selkirk (1982), Botha (1984), Hoeksema (1985), and Booij (1988).

The Non-Redundancy Constraint is discussed in Ackerman and Goldberg (1996), and Goldberg and Ackerman (2001).

Cruse (2000) deals with polysemy in general. The polysemy of English and Dutch -er-nouns is discussed in Booij (1986) and in Booij and Lieber (2004).

Part V

Morphology and Mind

10

Morphology and psycholinguistics

10.1 Morphology and mind

The previous chapters provided an introduction to morphological phenomena, and discussed how these phenomena should be accounted for in the grammar of natural languages. In this chapter, we will see how morphological knowledge (knowledge of complex words and of morphological rules) is represented in the human mind and how it is used in language processing. This is an important topic because the mental representation of morphological knowledge is a battle ground for different theories about the nature of linguistic rules, as we will see below. A related topic is the balance between storage and computation. Knowledge in a particular domain of human cognition always comprises both storage of information and the ability to compute new information. For instance, when we want to use the word *books*, we have two ways to do this: either we retrieve this plural form of *book* from our lexical memory, or we create it on line, by adding the plural suffix *-s* to the stem *book*. What determines the choice between these two routes? Empirical research of such questions may thus help us to get a better understanding of the nature of human cognitive capacities. Morphology may therefore be qualified as a window on the human mind.

In this chapter the empirical domains of psycholinguistic research will be reviewed: the mental lexicon ('the dictionary in your head'), the acquisition of morphological knowledge, and the role of this knowledge in language perception and production. In the next chapter, on morphological change, we will see that language change also provides information about the mental representation of morphological knowledge.

10.2 The mental lexicon

It is quite clear that the lexical knowledge that one has of one's native language does not have the format of a dictionary. First, the number of lexical entries in a good dictionary is much higher than that in our individual mental list of words. There are many words that most speakers do not know. You can compute the size of your own vocabulary by checking, on the basis of a representative sample of words from a good dictionary of your native language, how many of the words in that sample you know. Such a sample may be construed in a number of ways, for example by taking the first word of each page of that dictionary. This will give you a percentage p of known words. If the dictionary contains n words, the size of your mental lexicon is p times n. Adult speakers of English with a higher education might know up to 50,000 word types, and sometimes more, but it is certainly a smaller set than the whole English vocabulary, which comprises hundreds of thousands of words. This estimate concerns the passive vocabulary, the number of words that you understand. The active vocabulary, the set of words one uses in language production is much smaller.

A dictionary is conservative by nature, and hence it will contain words from the past that nobody uses any more. Each new edition of a printed dictionary will contain new entries, but will also have deleted a number of words from the previous edition that have become obsolete. Notwithstanding this kind of updating, your mental lexicon will always be ahead of the dictionary, and contains a substantial number of words that are not listed in dictionaries. New words (**neologisms**) are coined continuously, and dictionaries always lag behind. Moreover, the editors of dictionaries use a threshold for the listing of words: a new word must have a certain degree of permanence in the language use of more than one speaker before it gets an entry in a dictionary. Language users do not have such a threshold for their mental lexicon.

A second difference between a dictionary and the mental lexicon is that words in the mental lexicon bear a number of relationships to each other. Words with similar meanings or similar phonological forms appear to be related in the mental lexicon, as can be concluded from speech errors. For instance, someone who wanted to talk about the sympathy of a musical conductor used the word *symphony* instead of *sympathy*. The similarity in form between these two words, and the semantic relatedness of *symphony* and *conductor* must have played a role in this speech error. In a dictionary, on the other hand, semantic relations between words are usually not expressed directly. Thus, we may conceive of the mental lexicon as a multi-dimensional web of words, with all kinds of connections between those words: semantic similarities, phonological similarities, and morphological relationships. In a dictionary, on the other hand, words have one type of relationship only, that of alphabetical ordering. This ordering is based on the degree of orthographical similarity between words.

A third difference between a dictionary and a mental lexicon is that the latter also stores information about the frequency with which you come across a word. Linguists may compute the frequency of words on the basis of large corpora of actual language use. Frequency counts indicate how many tokens are found for each word type in a particular corpus. For instance, function words such as determiners have a relatively high frequency, and the probability that the next word that you come across when reading an English text is the word *the* is much higher than that it is the word *ubiquitous*. Within the set of English adjectives, the word *nice* is used far more frequently than the word *opaque*.

At first sight, this kind of frequency information may be seen as external to the human mind and without relevance for the mental representations of words. Language users do not have a specific frequency number for each word in their mental lexicon, as if you are continuously counting tokens of words when using language. However, speakers are able to estimate the relative frequencies of words based on their continuous exposure to language use. When you ask an English speaker if *nice* is less or more frequent than *ubiquitous*, he/she is certainly able to come up with the right answer. Moreover, a word with a relatively high frequency of occurrence is more easily recognized and retrieved than a word with a relatively low frequency. A possible psycholinguistic interpretation of this latter frequency effect is to assume that frequency of exposure to a word correlates with the **activation level** of that word in the mental lexicon. A word with a higher activation level is activated faster in language processing.

The standard way of finding out about such frequency effects is that of psychological experimentation, for instance by means of a **lexical decision** task. The participants in such an experiment may be asked to determine if a sequence of letters shown on a screen is a word of their language. There are two buttons, one for yes and one for no, and the time interval between the letter sequence appearing on the screen and one of the buttons being pushed, the **response latency**, is measured in milliseconds. The prediction then is that the higher the frequency of a word as determined by the experimenter on the basis of a corpus, the shorter the time it takes to come to a decision. This effect has been found time and again, and it is very robust indeed. It is referred to as the **frequency effect**.

A related effect is the **cumulative frequency** effect. If, for instance, the singular form of a noun is highly frequent, this will also have a frequency effect on its plural form, even when that plural form itself is not particularly frequent: the token frequencies of related inflectional word forms contribute to the activation level of each of them. This is called the **base frequency** effect. Another example is the **cumulative root frequency** effect: the summed frequencies of all words with the same root also appear to affect response latencies of individual complex words containing that root.

An example of the calculation of these frequencies for the English verb *to calculate* is given in Table 10.1. These counts are based on the CELEX

Table 10.1. *Frequency data for* calculate

Inflected forms	Token frequency	Family members	Base frequency
calculate	108	calculate	574
calculated	340	calculable	4
calculates	21	calculation	343
calculating	105	calculator	89
		calculus	50
		incalculable	26
		incalculably	1
		miscalculate	5
		miscalculation	25

Source: De Jong *et al.* 2000: 329.

database, which contains token frequency counts for Dutch, English, and German words (Baayen *et al.* 1995). The base frequency of *calculate* is the summed token frequencies of its four inflectional forms, 574. The cumulative root frequency of *calculate* is the sum of the frequencies of all the words in its family, 1117.

The standard psychological interpretation of the base frequency effect and the cumulative frequency effect is that of **activation spreading**. Activation can be spread from one word or word form to a related one in the mental lexicon, thus raising the activation levels of related words. Therefore, the response latencies of words of the same family in lexical decision tasks will be affected by their forming part of that family.

Recently, it has been discovered that response latencies for simplex words are also affected by the **family size** of these words, that is, the number of morphologically related word types. The larger the family size, the faster lexical decisions on simplex words will be made. In the case of *calculate*, the family size is eight, since there are eight morphologically related word types. This effect on response latencies is called the family size effect (Schreuder and Baayen 1997).

It takes a number of years to build up your mental lexicon, and during your whole life you will continue adding and losing words. It does not suffice just to memorize the simplex words of your native language, and either decompose (in case of perception) or construct (in case of production) complex words on the spot. First, complex words have to be memorized if they have an unpredictable property, for instance an idiosyncratic meaning aspect. Secondly, even though a complex word is completely regular, it has to be memorized if it is the conventional name for a particular thing. The device we call a *typewriter* in English could also have been called a *writing machine*. Both words have transparent semantic interpretations, and are formed according to the English rule of nominal compounding. We have to remember that it is the first word that is the conventional name for this device, and therefore it must be stored in lexical memory. Moreover, we have to memorize that it cannot be used as a synonym for *typist*.

There is also a psychological reason why we store regular complex words. There are two ways in which linguistic information can be accessed, either through computation or through storage. If we come across a complex word that we have to recognize and interpret correctly (the task of **word recognition**) there are two ways of reaching our goal. If we use computation, we first decompose the complex word into its constituent morphemes, and then retrieve the meaning of these morphemes from the entries in our mental lexicon. In the storage scenario, the complex word as such is stored in our mental lexicon, and word recognition is performed by matching the perceived word with its corresponding entry in our mental lexicon. The first scenario is the only possible one for complex words that we never came across before. For words that we already know, there are two routes: retrieval from memory or computation. Our human memory has such a vast capacity that there is no reason to assume that our lexical memory is redundancy-free. That is, we have the capacity to store information that might also be computed. The advantage of using the retrieval-from-memory route is its speed: it will take less processing time than the computing route, in particular when the stored word has a high frequency of occurrence, and thus a high level of activation. Hence, an important part of psycholinguistic research is finding out about the proper balance between storage and computation in morphology.

A clear proof of this point is that some of the regular plural forms of Dutch and Italian nouns have been found to be stored. Inflection is typically associated with rules. Dictionaries quite often do not give the regular plural forms of nouns because they can be formed by the language user who knows the relevant inflectional rules. Yet, there are frequency effects for plural nouns: plural nouns with a high frequency of occurrence are recognized faster in lexical decision tasks than plural nouns with a low frequency of occurrence, even if the words do not differ in their base frequency. This difference in activation level shows that these high frequency regular forms must be stored in the lexicon (Baayen, Burani, and Schreuder 1997; Baayen, Dijkstra, and Schreuder 1997). Yet, speakers also know the rule for plural nouns, since they can make plural forms that they never came across before.

10.3 Acquisition of morphology

How does a child acquire the morphological system, the set of morphological rules of his or her mother tongue? Morphological rules have to be discovered on the basis of words that are formed according to these rules. Therefore, the first stage in the acquisition of morphology is the acquisition of individual complex words. Based on this knowledge, the child will be able to use morphologically complex words correctly without making use of morphological knowledge, by retrieving them from memory. Next, (s)he may discover certain recurring properties of, for instance, plural nouns in English, and conclude that they are formed by adding the ending -*s* (with the allomorphs [s], [z], and [ɪz]) to the stem. So the child is able to apply the rule for English plural nouns to new cases, and create plural nouns that (s)he has never heard before.

In cases where rules have exceptions, a further refinement is in order, and three stages have to be distinguished. These three stages of morphological acquisition have been argued for in a classic paper by Berko (1958). In the first stage, children learn a number of, for instance, past tense forms of English verbs by rote. Hence their production of past tense forms of both regular and irregular verbs (*asked, went*) is correct. In the second stage, children acquiring English have discovered the rule for past tense forms, but will also apply the rule to the class of irregular verbs. Hence, they will produce the correct form *asked*, but the incorrect form *goed* instead of the correct *went*, a case of **overgeneralization**. In the third stage, both the rule and the set of exceptions have been acquired, and thus children will produce *asked* and *went*. So the learning process has the shape of a U-curve: the number of correct past tense verbs in stage I decreases in stage II, and increases again in stage III. This learning curve has been found for many languages. In Romance languages, with a number of different conjugations for verbs, it is the default conjugation that is overgeneralized. In French, for instance, the conjugation of verbs in -*er* is the conjugation with the highest type frequency and the default one. It is that conjugation that verbs might incorrectly be assigned to in stage II.

Overgeneralization in certain stages of language acquisition nicely reveals that discovering the regularities is part and parcel of language acquisition. Another example is the way in which Dutch children treat the plural of loan words from English such as *flat* and *tram*. Adult speakers of Northern Dutch use the English plural forms *flats* and *trams*. These are irregular forms since normally the Dutch plural suffix -*s* is not used after monosyllabic consonant-final nouns. Children, however, may use the plural forms *flatten* and *trammen*. These are the regular forms, since Dutch monosyllabic nouns that end in a consonant take -*en* as their plural ending. Children may use these regular forms because their mental lexicon does not yet contain the irregular plural forms *flats* and *trams*.

One may wonder why the stored form *went* does not block the creation of *goed* in the second stage, where overgeneralization applies. After all, this form is kept in memory at an early age due to its high frequency, and it may therefore be expected to block the creation of *goed*. It is probably the case that children in that stage of acquisition consider *went* as a verb of its own, and not as a (suppletive) form of *to go*. This is supported by the fact that some children create the past tense form *wented*.

The persistence of irregular or non-default word forms in a language has to do with their high frequency of use. Many of the stem-alternating or irregular verbs of the Germanic languages have a high frequency of use. Hence, these forms are entrenched very strongly in lexical memory, and will therefore not be replaced with the competing regular suffixed past tense forms. Frequency also plays a role in the preservation of suppletion. Words that have suppletive forms, such as the adjective *bad* with the suppletive form *worse*, are often words with a high frequency of use.

In languages with case marking, children will use case-marked word forms from very early on because it is words in their surface forms (not stems) that form the basis of acquisition. For nouns, the nominative form is usually the default case form, used in all syntactic contexts. Children can discover the role of case marking in syntactic contexts at a very early age. For example, Russian children already use accusative nouns after transitive verbs before the age of 2 (Clark and Berman 2004).

In the domain of word-formation children discover the building principles for complex words quite soon. We know this because they are able to coin new words themselves at a very early age. Children coin words for concepts for which there are already established words. For adults, established words have priority above new coinings, in accordance with the principle of conventionality that gives priority to established words, and thus blocks the creation of new words that are synonymous to existing ones. Children are less hampered in their word-formation creativity by this principle because their mental lexicon does not yet contain that many words, and still has many lexical gaps. For instance, my daughter Suzanne created the Dutch compound *oorlogsman* "war man" with the meaning "soldier" instead of using the established word *soldaat* "soldier". An English example is the use of the compound *sky car* instead of the established compound *aeroplane*. This behaviour is thus parallel to the case of overgeneralization with the past tense form *goed*. These observations show that children do not just memorize the complex words they are exposed to, but are able to discover the structural principles behind those complex words. The development of this ability in children is also manifested in the creation of new compounds for complex concepts without corresponding established words in their native language, such as *lion book* "book about lions", *baby-bottle* "bottle the child had used as a baby", and *hole-sack* "sack with holes in it" (Clark 1993: 117).

Compounding is acquired relatively early because it complies with two principles, those of transparency and simplicity. The meaning of compounds can be related very easily to those of its constituent words, and hence their meaning is transparent. Moreover, the form of the constituent elements is not really changed when they are part of compounds, and thus conforms to the requirement of simplicity (Clark 1993). This stands in contrast to word pairs like *magic–magician* where the base word *magic*, with initial stress, has a different phonological shape when it is part of *magician*: stress on the second syllable instead of the first, and a different root-final consonant. It is therefore harder to discover the morphological structure of *magician*. The principles of transparency and simplicity are also obeyed in conversion. Consider the following coinages by children of 2–3 years old: (Clark 1993: 117):

(1) to flag "to wave with a flag"
     to fire "to light (a candle)"
     to bell "to ring"
     to gun "to shoot"
     to dust "to get dust on"

The meaning of these verbs can be easily determined on the basis of the meaning of the base noun. They denote activities in which the base noun plays a role, and which can be further identified on the basis of the context in which these verbs are used. Hence, their meanings are transparent. In conversion, the forms of the words remain the same. Thus, noun–verb conversion complies with the requirements of transparency and simplicity.

A third factor involved in the acquisition of morphology by children is that of productivity. In English both compounding and conversion are very productive. This is reflected by the fact that children acquire and use these types of word-formation at an early age. In French, on the other hand, compounding and conversion are not productive, and derivation is used instead. Thus children acquiring French will use suffixation earlier and on a larger scale than children acquiring English. In Germanic languages, productive affixes such as deverbal *-er* for the coinage of agent and instrument nouns (in English, German, and Dutch) are acquired earlier than less productive ones.

Two morphological processes in the same language may be both transparent, and yet differ in productivity in adults. That is, transparency is a necessary condition for productivity, but not a sufficient one. For instance, the English suffixes -*ness* and -*th* differ in that new de-adjectival nouns in -*th* are almost never created. Yet, both types of de-adjectival nouns conform to the principles of transparency and simplicity. Clearly, children have to discover these differences in productivity. They have to know the morphological preferences of the language community when they are going to make new words.

Since children discover morphological processes on the basis of the words they are exposed to, they must be able to compare and analyse words, and assign them morphological structure if possible. This is clear from word forms like *goed*, as discussed above. Moreover, children appear to analyse words consciously, and ask questions like: *Does cornflakes have corn in it?* (Clark 1993: 40). This analytic activity also manifests itself in what we may call folk etymology: children may come up with a motivation for a particular word that is incorrect. An example from Dutch is that a child interpreted the name of the province of *Friesland* as meaning "land where it is always freezing" (Dutch has a verb *vries* "to freeze" that has nothing to do with the first constituent of the compound *Friesland*).

10.4 Sources of evidence

How can we determine how morphological information is represented in the mind? There are two main sources of evidence: experimental and naturalistic data. Psychologists use experiments, and in the realm of morphology lexical decision tasks are the most widely used way of probing into the mental representation of morphology. Lexical decision tasks are often used in combination with **priming**, the prior presentation of another word. This means that the subject who has to make a lexical decision first receives some other information.

An example of priming is the following: if one has to decide if *calculation* is a word of English, the response latency will be reduced if, before this task is performed, the same word *calculation* is presented to the eye or the ear of the subject, a case of identity priming. This effect suggests that the word *calculation* receives a higher level of activation by previous access to the same word. Other ways of priming are phonological priming (the prime word is phonologically similar to the target word), and semantic priming (with a semantically similar word as the prime). In the case of the target word *calculation*, the words *calcium* and *computation* may function as phonological and semantic primes. If these primes reduce response latencies for the target word, one can conclude that words in the mental lexicon are connected to words that are either phonologically or semantically similar. In morphological priming, a word that is morphologically related to the target word is used as a prime. For instance, *calculate* will function as a prime for *calculation*. As this example shows, it may be that the latter kind of priming is in fact a combination of phonological and semantic priming, and not an independent phenomenon.

Naturalistic data are the second source of evidence for theories of morphology in the mind. These are data concerning the actual behaviour of language users. When we observe that children coin new words or word forms that they have not come across before, this forms naturalistic data that may be interpreted as evidence for the children's having acquired morphological rules. The same applies to the language use of adults. We can conclude that a morphological pattern has the status of productive rule if new instantiations of that pattern are found in the actual language use of native speakers.

Speech errors (which can also be elicited in experiments) are another instance of naturalistic data. Consider the following slip of the tongue (Aitchison 2004):

(2)   Take the freezes out of the steaker (take the steaks out of the freezer)

In this sentence, the roots *freeze* and *steak* have been exchanged erroneously. This speech error shows, first of all, that the correct allomorph of the English plural ending can be computed by rule: the plural suffix for *steak* is [s], whereas that for *freeze* is [ız], because the stem ends in /z. Secondly, this exchange of roots bears on the issue of the lexical representation of morphological structure. The word *freezer* is a complex word that is presumably stored as such in the mental lexicon, given its specific conventional meaning (a storage device in which things are kept frozen in order to keep them), and its frequency. Yet, as this speech error shows, its internal morphological structure is still accessible. Therefore, we conclude that complex words can be stored in lexical memory with their morphological structure still present.

A similar example from Dutch is the following speech error:

(3) Met excuses voor het verbind-en van de verbrek-ing (het verbrek-en van de
     verbind-ing)
     "With apologies for the connect-INF of the interrupt-ion"

Crucially, in both (2) and (3) it is morphological units that are exchanged, and not phonological units such as syllables. The word *freezer*, for instance, consists of the syllables (free)$_\sigma$ and (zer)$_\sigma$, but it is the sequence of sounds *freez*, a morphological unit, that is exchanged. In example (3) the morphological units *-en* and *-ing* are exchanged. This exchange cannot be a matter of syllables since the syllable division of the target words is as follows: *ver.bre.ken, ver.bin.ding*. If we exchanged syllables, we would get the words *verbinken* and *verbreding*.

A last source of naturalistic data to be mentioned here is that of language pathology. The language behaviour of people with a language deficit, such as aphasia, may throw light on the mental representation of morphology. Aphasia is a language impairment resulting from damage to the brain, in most cases due to a cardiovascular accident. Aphasics that suffer from **agrammatism** (the inability to use rules), usually referred to as Broca aphasics, may not be able to produce correct plural forms of nouns, except for nouns with a high frequency plural form such as the word *eyes* (Aitchison 2004). This is evidence for the position that high-frequency plural nouns are retrieved from lexical memory, whereas low-frequency plural forms are computed on the spot, and may not be stored. In an investigation of three German aphasic patients with agrammatism it was found that their syntactic abilities were severely impaired, whereas their ability to use inflectional morphology was still intact (de Bleser and Bayer 1988). This fact can be interpreted as evidence for the position that syntactic rules belong to a different module of the grammar than the rules of inflectional morphology.

10.5 Models of morphological knowledge

The observed ability of native speakers to coin new words or word forms is the basic argument for assuming that morphological knowledge encompasses more than storage of the complex words that language users are exposed to. There must be mechanisms in the mind that enable us to extend the set of complex words in a language. For languages with a rich system of inflectional morphology such as Turkish, where each word may have hundreds or thousands of forms, it would even be quite absurd to assume that all these forms are memorized as such. The memory load for such languages can be reduced considerably by making use of rules. A possible model is that language users acquire morphological rules by constructing abstract rules or templates on the basis of their lexical knowledge. However, there are also morphological patterns that are not productive, but can still be called patterns. The stock example is the set of English past tense verb forms. Regular past tense forms are created by suffixing *-ed* to the stem. On the other hand there are a number of stem-changing verbs where the past tense form and the past participle are marked by having a different vowel than the present tense form. For instance, we have an *-ing/k -ang/k -ung/k* pattern for verbs such as the following:

(4)   ring, sing, spring, drink, shrink, sink, stink

The class of verbs with this kind of vowel alternation will normally not be extended. Yet, it is clear that native speakers of English are able to recognize the abstract pattern involved. It has been observed that some speakers tend to also inflect the verb *to bring* according to this pattern, resulting in the forms *brang* and *brung*. If people are asked to make the past tense forms of non-existing verbs with a similar phonological make-up as the words in (4), such as *spling*, they tend to come up with either *splang* or *splung*. Moreover, verbs that were once regular have changed into irregular ones, such as the English verb *to dive* (with the past tense form *dove* instead of *dived* in American English).

These facts have led a number of linguists to defend a **dual system** model of morphological knowledge (cf. Pinker 1999). The past tense and participial forms of regular English verbs are not stored in lexical memory, but always created by rule. The irregular forms, on the other hand, are stored in memory. These stored irregular forms are linked to each other in an associative way, and thus the language user will be able to discover similarity patterns such as *-ing/k -ang/k -ung/k* for the set of verbs in (4). This explains why the pattern may be extended incidentally to similar verbs such as *to bring*.

The dual system theory has also been defended based on a type of evidence that has not been mentioned yet: neurological evidence. Jaeger *et al.* (1996) have argued that regular and irregular verbs in English are processed by different neural systems. The processing location can be determined by PET-scans. PET stands for Positron Emission Tomography. The assumption underlying this technique is that changes in brain activity during the performance of a task are associated with changes in blood flow in the different regions of the brain. Blood flow can be made visible by injecting a participant's veins with a radioactive fluid. Thus, the blood flow can be traced through differences in radioactivity in the different parts of the brain: the more blood flow, the more radioactivity. This radioactivity is caused by the emission of positrons. Participants had to read or speak past tense forms (regular and irregular ones). Jaeger *et al.* (1996) found that regular forms are processed faster than irregular forms, and also that the irregular past task activated significantly larger areas of the brain than the regular past task.

The dual system theory in the form presented above thus correlates the distinction between regular and irregular morphology with the distinction between computation and storage: regular forms are computed on the spot, whereas irregular forms are stored. This theory predicts that frequency effects (differences in frequency correlating with differences in processing speed) will only be found for irregular forms, and not for regular forms, although the latter have a high frequency of use. Some linguists have claimed this prediction to be correct (for instance, Clahsen 1999 for German verb forms).

A problem for this theory is that in a number of studies frequency effects have been found for regular inflectional forms as well. These findings do not necessarily contradict the idea of an opposition between rules versus associative patterns, but imply that a correct model has to allow for the storage of regular inflectional forms of relatively high frequency besides storage of irregular forms. Remember that there is no logical contradiction between a process being regular and productive, and the storage of some of its outputs: our mental lexicon is not redundancy-free. Even if one accepts the storage of regular forms, the dual route theory might be maintained. The crucial property of regular forms is not that they cannot be stored, but that they can be computed if necessary, unlike the irregular forms

The dual system theory raises the question of how to distinguish between rules and associative patterns. The crucial difference between these two notions is that rules make use of variables, whereas associative patterns refer to specific properties of the words involved, for instance their specific phonological make-up. That is, unlike associative patterns, rules also apply to types of input that the language user has not been exposed to. This reasoning can be illustrated by a study of Modern Hebrew by Berent *et al.* (2002). As we saw in Chapter 2, Hebrew makes use of abstract consonantal patterns to define the triconsonantal roots that form the basis of Hebrew morphology. A general constraint on these triconsonantal roots is that the first two cannot be identical, but the last two can. For instance, roots with the pattern *smm* are well formed, unlike roots of the form *ssm*. If you do not believe in abstract rules, you may claim that this generalization is of a statistical nature, a strong tendency that native speakers may discover on the basis of frequent exposure to words with such roots. Speakers of Hebrew were asked to evaluate the acceptability of non-existing roots in which either the first two or the last two are identical. The crucial finding of Berent *et al.* (2002) is that native speakers only accept roots of the second type (the last two consonants identical), even with foreign consonants such as the English phoneme /θ/, but systematically reject roots where the first two consonants are identical. In other words, speakers are able to make systematic judgements although they have never been exposed before to consonantal roots with this foreign phoneme. Berent *et al.* (2002) therefore argue that this constraint on identical consonants is not a statistical generalization about the set of existing roots, but a real abstract constraint, a constraint with a variable for "consonant".

The dual system approach to morphological knowledge stands in opposition to a class of theories with the common denominator that they are **single system** theories. These theories might be called rule-less theories because they do not make a rigid distinction between rules on the one hand, and (lexical) representations on the other. The most influential single system theory is the **connectionist** approach, applied to the domain of English past tense forms in a famous study by Rumelhart and McClelland (1986). This approach uses the model of the **neural network** to represent English speakers' knowledge of past tense forms. Neural networks model how the brain encodes information. Information is encoded by means of connections of varying strength between neurons. Such models may also be used to model linguistic knowledge, although there is no logical necessity that the architecture of knowledge systems mirrors the way in which that knowledge is neurologically encoded directly. The basic idea of the connectionist approach is that morphological knowledge is conceived of as a pattern associator memory, a set of associations between pieces of linguistic information. The strength of these associations varies with the number of times that one has been exposed to the relevant information. In the connectionist modelling of English past tense formation, the memory contains present tense and past tense forms of words, or, more precisely, their different phonological components (these tense forms are not represented as units themselves). These components are associated to each other. For instance, the phonological components of the input *walk* are associated to that of the output *walked*. This set of associations has a morphological label, for instance [past tense]. The set of associations between the phonological features of the sounds in the sequence *alk* and those in the sequence *alked* under the label [past tense] will also hold for the pair *talk–talked*. Similarly, there will be a network of associations of considerable strength between the phonological constituents of *ing* and *ang* that accounts for the past tense forms of *to sing* and the other verbs listed in (4).

A small part of such a pattern of associations is represented in Figure 10.1. Each line is an association line between pieces of information. Each input unit and each output units consists of a linear sequence of three pieces of information. A piece of information is either a phonological feature or a bracket. The left and right brackets [ ] indicate the beginning and the end of a word. Each input unit thus specifies a subsequence of three segments (including the word boundaries) of words. For instance, the present tense verb *swim* corresponds to the input unit 'high nasal]' since it ends in a sequence of a [high] vowel and a [nasal] consonant followed by a right bracket. Therefore, association line 1 applies to *swim–swam*. Indeed, *swam* ends in a [back] vowel followed by a [nasal] consonant and a right bracket. Association line 2 holds for the pair *ban–banned*. Association line 3 holds for words with a word-initial cluster of two consonants, and hence relates the word pairs *swim–swam, sleep–slept*, and *bleep–bleeped*. Association line 4 applies to *sleep–slept*, and also to *bleep–bleeped*: the stem forms of these words end in a [high] vowel plus a stop consonant, and the past

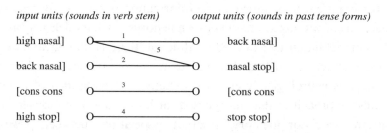

Fig. 10.1 Some association patterns for English past tense forms (after Pinker 1999: 105)

tense forms end in two stops. The second output unit, 'nasal stop]' is also associated with the first input unit (association line 5) because there are pairs such as *trim–trimmed*: the past tense form *trimmed* ends in a nasal stop sequence.

The association patterns and their strengths are developed by training the model: it will be offered a corpus of present and past tense forms. The more frequent a particular association of pieces of information is, the stronger that association will become. Once the model has been exposed to a sufficiently large number of data, it will also predict the past tense forms of verbs that did not belong to its "training space". Most verbs exhibit the pattern *x–x+ed* for present and past tense. Yet, the high token frequency of the past tense forms of irregular verbs results in great strength of the associations between the phonological features sequences of *ing/k* and *ang/ k* in the domain [past tense] for the irregular English verbs. If the input *sing* is fed into the network, the input units that correspond with parts of the phonetic string of *sing* will be switched on. These input units then activate the output units with which they have strong associations. This will have the effect that for the verb *to sing* the past tense form that is computed by the model will be *sang* rather than *singed*. The verb *trim*, with different initial segments, will activate a different set of strong input–output associations, and thus produce the past tense form *trimmed*.

A second type of rule-less approach is the model proposed by Bybee (1988, 1995, 2001). In her model, unlike what is claimed in the connectionist approach, individual inflectional forms of words are listed in the lexicon. This also applies to past tense verb forms, both regular and irregular ones. The regularities in the formal relationship between present tense and past tense forms are captured by abstract **schemas** that can be constructed on the basis of sets of words. For instance, the lexical representation of the past tense forms *played, spilled, spoiled, banned,* and *rammed* will be linked as in Figure 10.2. The correlation between the phonological and semantic

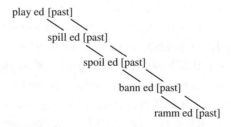

Fig. 10.2 Schema for English past tense forms (Bybee 2001: 23)

properties of these forms results in a morphological schema in which -*ed* is connected to [past]. The basic point is that one may represent the relevant generalization without necessarily extracting it as an abstract rule or template independent from the individual words involved.

A third single system approach without rules is the analogy-based model. To be sure, analogy has been recognized as a source of new complex forms in all kinds of morphological models. In the case of analogy, a new word is formed on the basis of a related existing word, without an abstract morphological template being involved. For instance, the coinage of the English word *seascape* is based on the word *landscape* (a borrowing from Dutch), according to the following pattern of analogy:

(6) land : sea = landscape : *seascape*

A similar example is the coinage of the word *zweisam* "being with some-body else" in analogy to *einsam* "being alone" by the German philosopher Martin Buber. In these cases it is an individual complex word that forms the basis for the new word, and this kind of analogical word-formation has an incidental character.

In recent theorizing, analogical models have been extended to larger sets of data. These **exemplar-based models** presuppose that individual complex words are stored in the lexicon. These words are exemplars of a particular category, for instance of the noun–noun-compound category. There are no abstract patterns or rules that define that category. New words are coined in analogy to the set of stored words. An example of this kind of model-ling concerns the selection of a linking element in Dutch nominal com-pounds. Many of these compounds have *s* or *en* as a linking element between the two parts of the compounds; other compounds have no link-ing element at all (represented here as ø). It is hard to come up with a rule that predicts with absolute certainty which linking element should be chosen for a new compound, and there is sometimes variation among native speakers. Yet, there are tendencies that can be related to the distri-bution of linking elements in existing Dutch compounds. The preferences of native speakers for a particular linking element in a new compound can be predicted on the basis of its degrees of similarity to existing compounds. This implies that there is no rule that predicts the insertion of a linking element on the basis of properties of the two constituents. Instead, a paradigmatic approach is chosen in which the relation to other existing compounds plays a crucial role, and preferences can be predicted.

Consider the following data concerning linking elements in Dutch NN-compounds:

(7) schaap-s-kooi "sheepfold"
     schaap-s-vlees "mutton"
     schaap-ø-herder "shepherd"
     schap-en-poot "sheep's leg"
     schap-en-vacht "sheep's fleece"
     schap-en-bout "leg of mutton"
     koei-en-oog "cow's eye"
     paard-en-oog "horse's eye"
     pauw-en-oog "peacock's eye"
     varken-s-oog "pig's eye"

(the variation *schaap/schap* is only a matter of orthography). Given these data, we might wonder which is the appropriate linking element for the compound *schaap-?-oog* "sheep's eye" (the question mark indicates the position of the linking element). It is clear that the left constituent *schaap* allows for all three linking elements, but *en* is the most frequent one. Moreover, most constituents *oog* as heads of compounds are preceded by the linking element *en*. Hence, the most probable linking element is *en*. It appears that speakers tend to choose that linking element that is most common among the existing compounds with that initial constituent. For instance, the choice of the linking element *s* for a new compound *leven?* *therapie* "life therapy" appears to be predictable on the basis of the existing compounds with *leven* as their first constituent, such as *leven-s-vorm* "life form" and *leven-s-probleem* "life problem" (Krott *et al.* 2001). The second constituent may play a role as well, as is illustrated here by *oog* that is usually though not always preceded by *en*.

This survey of different models of morphological knowledge, and the debate about these models illustrates that morphological phenomena play an important role in the debate on the nature of linguistic knowledge. Morphology is an important window on the mental representation of natural language and the human mind.

10.6 Morphological processing

The insight that complex words are often stored as such in the lexicon raises the question of how they are processed. There are two ways in which a complex word can be processed, the direct route, and the indirect route.

When perception of complex words is involved, the direct route means that we do not first parse the complex word, but go directly to its representation in the lexicon, in order to access its meaning. The indirect route means that a complex word is parsed into constituent morphemes, and that its meaning is computed after we have gained access to its constituent morphemes and their meanings.

There are data that might be interpreted as showing that language users try to parse words into morphological sub-constituents. For instance, when speakers of Dutch are confronted with non-words in a lexical decision task, it takes more time to make the correct decision when that word begins with a syllable that could have been a prefix, compared to words where this does not apply. Consider the following three non-words:

(8)   aderibag, afgeblar, afbegepakt

The first word does not contain a potential prefix of Dutch, the second word begins with two prefixes (*af-*, *ge-*), and the third word begins with three prefixes (*af-*, *be-*, *ge-*). Correlating with this difference, the last non-word has been found to have the longest response latency, as is expected if language users try to strip prefixes from words that are not in their lexicon.

The existence of two routes has led to the assumption of morphological race models. In such models, both routes will be used for word recognition, and compete with each other. If the word is not stored in lexical memory, the indirect route is the only one that will lead to recognition, on the basis of parsing. If the word is stored, the direct route will be faster than the indirect route if the stored complex word has a high frequency, that is, a high level of activation. For a complex word with a low frequency, on the other hand, parsing is the obvious route. Both routes are followed, and one of them will turn out to be the fastest, depending on the level of activation of the complex word.

The parsing of complex words is also affected by **relative frequency**: the frequency of the complex word compared to that of its base word. If the complex word has a lower frequency than the base word, this will make parsing of that complex word easier and more efficient than direct retrieval. If the inverse situation obtains, direct access to the complex word will be the most efficient route (Hay 2001). For instance, the English word *dazzlement* will be parsed because its frequency is much lower than that of its base *dazzle*, whereas *government* will be accessed as a whole because the frequency of this word is higher than that of its verbal base *govern*. Note that the meaning of *government* is not completely compositional, unlike that of *dazzlement*. There is also a relation to productivity: the more complex words with a certain affix will be parsed, the more productive the corresponding word-formation process will be, because parsing the affix will increase its activation level (Hay and Baayen 2002).

The morphological race model can also be used as a model of word production. It helps us to understand why it is irregular forms of high frequency that are maintained in a language, whereas low-frequency irregular forms disappear more easily. Suppose we have to make the past tense form of *to go*. We can go directly to the lexicon, where the word *went* will be retrieved. Because *went* is a high-frequency form, this route will be faster than the indirect route where the past tense form has to be created by rule, resulting in the incorrect *goed*. The race model thus accounts for the blocking effect of high-frequency words on synonymous words that are computed by rule.

Summary

Children acquire the morphological system of their mother tongue on the basis of exposure to complex words. At a relatively early age, they acquire and use the competence to create new words themselves. Word-formation processes that obey the constraints of transparency and simplicity are acquired first. Children also coin a high number of new words because their creativity is not yet hampered by the conventional lexicon.

There are a number of ways in which we can find out how morphological knowledge is represented in the mind and used in language processing: by studying naturalistic data (corpora of language use, speech errors, effects of language impairment, etc.) and experimental data (lexical decision tasks, production tasks, etc.). Morphology is a battlefield for competing models of linguistic knowledge, and for discussion on the nature of linguistic rules.

The frequency of words in actual language use correlates with their activation level in the mental lexicon. Statistical and probabilistic data are therefore relevant for adequate models of morphological knowledge.

Questions

1. The list of differences between a dictionary and the mental lexicon in section 10.1 is not exhaustive. What other differences can you mention?

2. The following compounds coined by children have been observed by Elbers (1988): *car-milk* "gasoline", *moon-nuts* "cashew nuts". Why would children coin these words instead of using the existing words for these concepts?

3. Consider the data in the table concerning the frequency of words with the prefix *un-* and their bases in the CELEX database.

   Which of these *un*-words do you expect to be processed via the direct route? To what extent does this correlate with your intuitions about the semantic transparency of these words?

	Frequency	Base frequency
uncanny	89	20
unleash	65	16
unscrew	44	187
unaffected	54	169
unobtrusive	42	17
uncouth	34	2
unkind	72	390

   Source: Hay 2001: 1047.

4. The following cases of noun–verb conversion occurred in the speech of my children (native speakers of Dutch) at the age of 2 to 4 (none of these verbs are used by adult speakers):

noun	verb
au "ouch"	au "to hurt"
telefoon "telephone"	telefoon "to telephone"
drop "liquorice"	drop "to eat liquorice"
viltstift "felt pen"	viltstift "to use a felt pen"

   How does this kind of word-formation relate to the principles of transparency, simplicity, and conventionality that Clark (1993) identifies as playing a role in morphological acquisition?

5. Although *to ride* is a verb with the irregular past tense from *rode*, the past tense of *to joyride* is *joyrided*. Try to explain this. How can this observation be used to defend a rule-based approach to morphology?

6. Consider the following speech errors

   The speaker received a standing ovulation (ovation)
   His initiatives were engraved on the cigarette case (initials)
   A visual circle (vicious)

   What conclusion can be drawn from these speech errors about how words are related in the mental lexicon?

7. Consider the data in the table concerning reaction times (in milliseconds) for a number of Italian nouns. Sometimes the singular form has the shortest reaction time, in other cases the plural form. How can this be explained?

Singular form		Plural form		Gloss
albero	583	alberi	542	tree
capello	578	capelli	522	hair
dente	527	denti	503	tooth
piede	528	piedi	494	foot
soldato	548	soldati	549	soldier
naso	523	nasi	556	nose
piazza	534	piazze	522	square
sorella	569	sorelle	534	sister

Source: Baayen, Burani, and Schreuder 1997: 30.

8. One form of speech errors is blending two words. The following blends can be found in Fromkin (1973) and are cited as evidence for production models in Levelt (1989):

   The competition is a little stougher [stiffer/tougher]
   Irvie is quite clear [close/near]
   At the end of today's lection [lecture/lesson]

   What kind of relationship between words in the mental lexicon must be the basis for this kind of speech error?

9. Consider the following speech error in which two verbs have been exchanged: . . . *that I'd hear one if I knew it* instead of the correct . . . *that I'd know one if I heard it*. In Janssen *et al.* (2002) this observation is used to argue that in language production first lexemes (such as KNOW and HEAR) in their abstract form are selected before selection of the actual morphological forms takes place. Why does this speech error support the assumption of these two stages in language production?

10. In the course of the history of Dutch, a number of Dutch verbs with a stem vowel *ij* [ɛi] changed from regular verbs, with a suffixed past tense form, to ablauting verbs, with a past tense vowel *ee* [e:]. This applies to, for instance, the Dutch verbs *prijzen* "to praise" and *lijken* "to resemble", with the past tense stems *prees* and *leek* respectively (see Table 6.6 for a survey of Dutch ablauting verbs). Note that the English counterparts of these verbs are regular. Other examples of such verbs that changed from weak to strong are *schrijven* "to write", *belijden* "to confess", and *zwijgen* "to keep silent". The class of *ij-ee* verbs comprises about a quarter of all ablauting verbs of Dutch. What does this change tell us about the psychological reality of the vowel alternation patterns of irregular verbs?

Further reading

A textbook completely devoted to the mental lexicon is Aitchison (1987). Clark (1993) presents an analysis and survey of studies on the acquisition of morphology, in particular word-formation. The importance of speech errors as linguistic evidence is shown in Fromkin (1973) and Cutler (1982).

An extensive discussion on the issue of storage versus computation in relation to regular and irregular morphology can be found in Pinker (1999) for English, and in Clahsen (1999) for German. Both defend a rule-based approach to morphology (with association patterns for irregular verbs only), and Pinker argues in detail against the connectionist model. The 'variable' criterion for calling something a rule can be found in Marcus (2001), and in Berent et al. (2002). Clahsen (1999) is followed by a number of invited critical comments.

Evidence for the lexical storage of inflected forms is given in Baayen, Burani, and Schreuder (1997) and in Baayen et al. (2002). A broader discussion of the issue of storage and computation for different domains of grammar can be found in Nooteboom et al. (2002). Gürel (1999) argues that even for a language with rich agglutinative morphology such as Turkish, frequent words are accessed as whole words rather than through decomposition.

Morphological race models are proposed in Frauenfelder and Schreuder (1992), Baayen (1993), and Schreuder and Baayen (1997). The role of morphology in language production is discussed in Levelt (1989); Janssen et al. (2002) deals with inflectional forms in language production.

A survey of the role of probabilistic data in morphology is presented in Baayen (2003).

11

Morphology and language change

11.1 The historical perspective

Speakers are able to use their native language without any knowledge of its history. Therefore, the historical perspective on language seems to be superfluous when we want to understand how language works. In this chapter it will be shown that this is not true: language change is a relevant empirical domain for linguists who want to develop an adequate account of language systems and their use.

First, we may want to know how the morphology of a language got the properties that it has. Why do Germanic languages obey the Right-hand Head Rule? And why did Dutch develop a system of linking elements between the constituents of compounds. Such questions can only be answered by looking at the history of languages.

A second reason for studying language change is that it provides another window on the human mind. Patterns of language change tell us how language users interpret the language data on the basis of which they develop their linguistic competence. Thus, they provide evidence about what goes on in the minds of language users, in addition to what psycholinguistic data can tell us.

In order to understand morphological change, it is useful to first give some attention to the nature of language change (section 11.2). We are then ready to understand how morphological systems could develop (section 11.3) and how these systems and the complex words they create can change (sections 11.4 and 11.5).

11.2 The nature of language change

The opening lines of Geoffrey Chaucer's famous *Canterbury Tales* clearly show that English has changed in the course of time:

(1) When that Aprill with his shoures soote
     "When that April with his showers sweet"
     The droghte of March hath perced to the roote
     "The drought of March has pierced to the root"
     And bathed every veyne in swich licour
     "And bathed every vine in such liquid"
     Of which vertu engendred is the flour;
     "Of which virtue engendered is the flower"

Middle English as used in these lines is different from Modern English, and we might need some guidance in decoding these lines. If we assume that it is still the same language, English, we have to conclude that languages can change. But why do they?

The statement that languages change is in fact metaphorical in nature. It presupposes that we conceive of a language as an organism that grows, changes, and sometimes dies. This way of speaking suggests that languages have a mode of existence outside their users. This is true to a certain extent, as we will see below, but a language primarily exists in the minds of its speakers. That is why we say that a language has died when its last speaker has died, as has, alas, happened often in recent years. So it is speakers that change their language while using it in language perception and production.

Why do language users change their language? In fact, 'change' is not always the appropriate word for what is going on. When a language acquires new words through the activities of its users, it would be better to speak of construction or innovation of language. What does change when new words or new meanings of words get established is the lexical norm of that language, not the system behind it. The main reason for changing the lexical norm of a language is that language users need expressions for new concepts, or new things. One way of meeting this need is extending the meaning of existing words. For instance, the word *mouse* acquired a new meaning as a navigation device for computers. Alternatively, we may coin new denoting expressions, either phrases or words. The phrase *hard disk* has been introduced into English to denote a memory device for computers. The word *anti-virus-program* is a complex word that fills a lexical gap in the same domain of language use. Lexical gaps can also be filled through borrowings. Dutch, for example, has borrowed many words from English recently. The word *printer* is a good example: even though Dutch has the word *drukker* for "printer" (interpreted as a human agent), it uses the English word *printer* for a printing device. On the other hand, German uses *Drucker* for both the human agent and the printing device. Speakers of languages may differ in their attitudes towards borrowing. If they try to avoid it, they are called **purists**.

The change of the lexical norm consists of two steps. The first step is that an individual language user coins a new lexical unit (a word or a phrase), borrows one from another language, or gives an existing word a new interpretation. The following step is that this innovation is accepted by other language users, and is also used by them. This is also why dictionary makers will not simply list in their dictionary each new word they come across in a corpus of language use. It must have been used by different users on different occasions before it is evidence for a change of the supra-individual lexical norm. So we see that the kind of language change we may call **lexical innovation** arises because language users need to express new concepts. Maybe we should not call it language change, but language construction.

Although language is primarily located in each individual language user, 'norm' as introduced here implies that it also has a derivative form of existence at the supra-individual level, just like many other non-material objects such as norms, knowledge, religions, and philosophical ideas. Norms are things we can share with other people. Sharing our language with other people is part and parcel of being a language user. This paradox of language being simultaneously individual and social in nature has been stressed by Ferdinand de Saussure (Saussure 1916), and is therefore called the **Saussurean paradox**.

The study of language change therefore has a psychological and a social dimension. It will arise in the mind of one or more individual language users, but must find its way in the language community before the new use of a language form is actuated as a language change.

A second source of linguistic innovation besides changing the lexical norm is **reanalysis**. Language users cannot grasp the system behind a language in a direct fashion. The only evidence they have are outputs of the system, concrete cases of language use. This opens up the possibility that a language user reconstructs the system underlying the perceived outputs in a slightly different way than previous users. Some linguists have therefore hypothesized that **imperfect learning** by children is the driving force behind language change. Children have to reconstruct the rule system on the basis of what they hear, and might thus come up with a slightly different system than the system of adult speakers that underlies these outputs. A morphological example is the potential regularization of past tense formation of the irregular verbs of English discussed in Chapter 10. Children might start using *goed* and *bringed* instead of *went* and *brought*. This kind of change is impeded by the effect of conventionality: children appear to adjust themselves quite readily to the adult system with its exceptions. Moreover, adult speakers may also change their language through reanalysis, since they are continuously interpreting the outputs that they perceive. In sum, language users may be involved in language change at different stages of their lives.

The types of change discussed so far are examples of **internal change**, caused by the internal dynamics of language usage and by its transfer to the next generation of language users. Language change may also be effected by external causes, in particular **language contact**. This is called **external change**. Language contact may lead to borrowing of words from other languages. Most Germanic languages borrowed many words from French, for some centuries the dominant European language in the realm of culture, science, and diplomacy. English was influenced much earlier and more strongly by French due to the Norman conquest of 1066.

Borrowing from French had its impact on the morphology of Germanic languages. In Dutch, for instance, quite a number of affixes of French origin are used productively in combination with non-native stems, and sometimes even with native stems (as in *flauw-iteit* "silly joke" derived from the native adjective *flauw* "silly"). These non-native affixes also occur in complex words that have no counterpart in French, a clear indication that they have become affixes of the borrowing language. That is, these affixes might have entered the language as parts of borrowed words, but are recognized as morphological building blocks of these words. An example of this kind of borrowing in English is the de-adjectival suffix -*ity*, like Dutch -*iteit* the counterpart of French -*ité*. Once English had a number of adapted loan words of the type *X-ity*, this pattern could be extended to other adjectives, resulting in new nouns of this type.

Borrowing of inflectional forms may also take place. English has Greek and Latin plurals, such as *criteria, schemata, musea*, and *data*. These learned plurals came to be replaced with regular plurals such as *schemas* and *museums* (*musea* is no longer used in English). They are not always felt as plural forms—witness the increasing tendency to use *data* as a subject NP with a singular verbal form (*The data is reliable, Much data was lost*). In Dutch, with the same borrowed plural form *musea*, one often comes across the plural form *musea-s*, which indicates that the stored form *musea* is no longer felt as an unambiguous plural form. Similarly, one often hears *data-s* as the plural of *datum* "date" instead of *data* or *datums*.

Lack or rarity of morphology is considered by some linguists to be typical for pidgin and creole languages. **Pidgin languages** arise when, in a situation of language contact, there is no common language. This situation obtained, for instance, on plantations in the Americas with African slaves: the slaves did not speak English or Spanish, while the plantation owners did not speak the languages of the slaves. **Creole languages** are pidgin languages that have come to be used as a first language by a new generation of language users. From recent research it has become clear, however, that both pidgins and creoles do have morphology, both inflection and word-formation (derivation, compounding, reduplication). For instance, Haitian Creole borrowed many complex words from French, which resulted in this language having productive derivational morphology (Lefebvre 2003).

Language contact as a source of loss of inflectional morphology can be observed in the development of Afrikaans. In South Africa, Dutch came into contact with Portuguese, Malay, and local African languages, and thus Afrikaans exhibits the language contact effects that are typical for pidginization and creolization. Compared to its mother language Dutch, Afrikaans has an extremely simple kind of inflectional morphology, with a present tense form that is identical to the stem, without person and number marking, and a periphrastic form for the non-present tense. Likewise, the strong inflectional erosion of English during an earlier episode in history may also be the effect of language contact, namely that between the original population of England and the Viking invaders.

A pervasive type of morphological change is the erosion of inflectional systems in the Germanic and Romance languages, referred to as **deflection**. English has the poorest inflectional system of all. Most Germanic languages have lost their case system (German and Icelandic are exceptions), and the three-gender system, again preserved in German and Icelandic, has been reduced to two genders in Dutch and most North Germanic languages, whereas English has lost gender in full NPs completely. This kind of long-term change over a number of centuries has been dubbed **drift** by the American linguist Sapir.

It is no coincidence that case and gender are the morphological categories that are subject to erosion. For instance, the distinction between nominative and accusative case is a matter of contextual inflection, required by syntactic context. This stands in opposition to inherent inflection such as number inflection for nouns, which expresses a semantic distinction. The role of contextual inflection can be taken over by other means of expression such as the use of prepositions or postpositions and word order. Similarly, gender is a category that manifests itself in agreement patterns, and thus plays a role in contextual inflection only. Thus, although we cannot predict when and how languages change, it is possible to identify linguistic factors that constrain and shape language change, such as the distinction between inherent and contextual inflection.

Whatever the cause of language change, it is remarkable that language users seem to cooperate in achieving a particular result such as the loss of a language's case system. In order to understand this, we might invoke the **invisible hand theory** originally devised by Adam Smith in his *The Wealth of Nations* to explain how the economic market seems to behave as a rational person, as if led by an invisible hand. Each individual action is a contribution to a result that has not been planned by individuals. If there are too many cars on the road you have to use your brake from time to time, and all drivers will do so. Quite soon, you will thus get stuck in a traffic jam, although none of the individual drivers had the aim of creating it. In the same way, the acts of individual language users may have unforeseen effects.

Language change is obviously not restricted to the morphological system of languages. The quotation above from Chaucer, when compared to its modern English glosses, also shows phonological, syntactic, and semantic changes. Phonological change is exemplified by the loss of the final vowel of *roote* that has become *root* in Modern English. The word order noun–adjective in *shoures soote* corresponds with the Modern English word order adjective–noun: *sweet showers*. An example of semantic change is that the present-day meaning of *liquor* is no longer "liquid", but denotes alcoholic liquids only. For obvious reasons, this chapter will focus on morphological change.

11.3 Historical sources of morphology

Morphological systems not only erode, they may also arise. An example is the emergence of nominal compounding in Germanic languages that arose from noun phrases of the type

(2) [N-GEN N]$_{NP}$

In this type of noun phrase, the pre-nominal noun with genitive case functions as a modifier of the head noun. Such noun phrases were reinterpreted as compound nouns. This emergence of Germanic compound structure is still reflected by the fact that sometimes an old case ending appears at the end of the first constituent. These case endings might be reanalysed as allomorphic extensions of the first constituent, or as linking elements. This also applies to case endings such as the genitive case endings *-s* and *-en* of Middle Dutch. Hence, we see transitions of the following kind:

(3) (des)   her-en   huis >   her-en-huis
     (the-GEN) lord-GEN   house.NOM   lord-LINKING ELEMENT-house "mansion"
     (des)   konink-s   krone >   koning-s-kroon
     (the-GEN) king-GEN   crown.NOM   king-LINKING ELEMENT-crown
                                        "royal crown"

These changes thus led to the emergence of a system of compounding with internal linking elements.

Univerbation, the reinterpretation of phrases as words, does not necesarily lead to language change. Consider the following examples of univerbation:

(4) Old High German *hiu tagu* "this day-INSTR" > Modern High German *heute* "today"
     Latin *ad ipsum* "to itself-ACC" > Italian *adesso* "now"
     French *peut être* "can be" > French *peut-être* "perhaps"

These changes imply the addition of lexemes to the lexicon, but do not affect the morphological system. That also applies to the following conjunctions of Dutch:

(5) door-dat "due to", om-dat "because", op-dat "in order to"

Such words arose from univerbation of a preposition with the first word of a clausal complement, the complementizer *dat* "that":

(6) Rebecca   viel   [[om]$_P$ [dat ze niets zag]$_S$]$_{PP}$
      "Rebecca fell   for [that she nothing saw]$_S$"   *reanalysed as*:
      Rebecca   viel   [omdat ze niets zag]$_S$
      Rebecca   fell   [because she nothing saw]$_S$
      "Rebecca fell because she saw nothing"

Although this kind of univerbation did not lead to new morphological rules, there is an important lesson that we can draw from these historical facts: when a word is multi-morphemic, this does not necessarily imply that it has been created by a morphological process. So the Dutch complementizers in (5) are not the products of compounding (combining prepositions with complementizers), and we can thus maintain the regularity that word-formation processes create words of lexical categories, that is, content words only.

Univerbation did lead to a morphological rule in the case of Latin phrases such as *clara mente* "with a clear mind, ABL". After univerbation and semantic reinterpretation of this phrase, words such as *claramente* "in a clear manner" served as models for new de-adjectival words in -*mente*. Thus, -*mente* became a productive suffix in Romance languages. This example illustrates that two mechanisms are involved in morphological change of this type: reanalysis and analogy. The first step is reanalysis: the existing word combination is given another structural interpretation. The second step, which affects the morphological system, is the extension of the class of words in -*mente* through analogy. The first step pertains to the syntagmatic axis of language structure, the second step to its paradigmatic axis. The compounds in (3) also show that univerbation can lead to a morphological change, the emergence of nominal compounding. The univerbated phrases were reinterpreted as compounds, and new compounds were created directly on the model of the univerbated ones, without having passed a phrasal stage.

An example of a productive prefix that derives from a syntactic construction is the Frisian prefix *witte-* "very" that is a reduced form of the word sequence *wa wit hoe* "who knows how". This word sequence forms a clause in combination with an adjective, as in *Wa wit hoe fier* "Who knows how far". This prefix is used productively in modern Frisian, as in the following words (Dyk 1988).

(7)   witte-fier "very far"
      witte-heech "very high"
      witte-lang "very long"
      witte-djip "very deep"

The specific meaning of the original word sequence underlying *witte-* has changed into the more general meaning "very".

The emergence of this prefix illustrates that frequency plays a role in grammaticalization, which has also been defined as 'the process by which a frequently used sequence of words or morphemes become automated as a single processing unit' (Bybee 2003: 603). The word sequence *wa wit hoe* expressing the meaning "high degree" is a clear example of such an automated, single processing unit. It is well known that high frequency triggers phonological reduction: the speaker can afford to be sloppy in the pronunciation of a unit if that unit is easily retrievable for the hearer due to its high frequency. Reduction will then lead to simpler phonological forms. The reduced form *witte* [wɪtə] has the phonological shape of a trochee. Recall that a trochee is a foot that consists of two syllables, of which the first carries stress. In Germanic languages, the second syllable of a trochee prefers to have schwa as its vowel. As we saw in section 7.2, Germanic prefixes tend to be prosodic words of their own. An optimal prosodic word consists minimally of a trochaic foot. Thus, the phonological reduction of the clause *wa wit hoe* led to a prefix *witte-* with an optimal prosodic form.

Morphological processes not only arise through **desyntactization**, as was the case for compounding, but also through **dephonologization**. A famous case is that of umlaut in German. This originally phonological rule had the effect of fronting back vowels of stems when followed by a /i/ or /j/ in the next syllable. In Early Old High German the declension for the word *gast* "guest" was as in (8). In later Old High German the instrumental form changed into *gastiu*, thus creating a systematic correlation between the

(8)

	SG	PL
NOM	gast	gesti
GEN	gastes	gestio
DAT	gaste	gestim
ACC	gast	gesti
INST	gestiu	

Source: Wurzel 1980: 448

opposition SINGULAR : PLURAL and the opposition back vowel : front vowel. This kind of change in which formal differences within the same (sub)paradigm are removed is called **paradigmatic levelling**. In Middle High German, the case ending vowel reduced to schwa, resulting in the following paradigm (the separate instrumental case had disappeared). When the

(9)	SG	PL
NOM	gast	geste
GEN	gastes	geste
DAT	gaste	gesten
ACC	gast	geste

Source: Wurzel 1980: 448.

syllables with these sounds were reduced to syllables with schwa, the conditioning environment for the vowel change (the presence of a high vowel or glide) was destroyed. Yet, the contrast between back and front vowels was maintained, and this vowel alternation thus obtained the function of marking the plural, as in modern German *Gast–Gäste* [gɑst–gɛstə] (with the diaraesis still representing the umlaut in the orthography). In this example, the plural is also marked by the ending *-e*, but in other cases the plural is expressed by umlaut only, as in:

(10)   Apfel–Äpfel "apple(s)"
       Kloster–Klöster "convent(s)"
       Mutter–Mütter "mother(s)"
       Vater–Väter "father(s)"

Umlaut may co-occur with the overt plural suffixes *-e* and *-er*, and also occurs in complex words with certain derivational suffixes such as *-lich* (as in *Vater* "father"–*väterlich* "fatherly").

   Umlaut might be analysed in two ways. One possibility is claiming that umlaut has completely morphologized. This means that it has become simi-lar to ablaut in that it expresses a morphological property (plural) by means of vowel change. This analysis implies that the property plural is sometimes marked doubly, through vowel alternation and suffixation with *-e*, as in *Gast–Gäst-e* "guest SG/PL". The other option is interpreting umlaut as a case of stem allomorphy triggered by particular morphological categories such as PLURAL and words with the adjectival suffix *-lich*. In that analysis, the property PLURAL is also marked twice in *Gäste*, through stem allomorphy and suffixation.

This umlaut system has been preserved remarkably well in modern German, whereas it has almost completely disappeared in English, with a few alternations such as *foot–feet* and *goose–geese* being the only remnants.

It is interesting to see how the reduction of allomorphy in a paradigm (that is, paradigmatic levelling) applies, and which allomorph is kept. In singular–plural pairs of nouns, it is usually the stem-form of the singular that is kept. However, if the plural form is more frequent than the singular form, it is the plural stem-form that may win. In Frisian there is an allomorphy pattern called **breaking**. An unbroken (falling) diphthong in the singular stem alternates with a broken (rising) diphthong in the plural stem. The pattern of paradigmatic levelling in (11) has been found in Frisians (Tiersma 1982: 834):

(11)   *Conservative dialect*   *Innovative dialect*
    a. hoer [huər]–hworren [hworən]   hoer [huər]–hoeren [huərən] "whore"
        koal [koəl]–kwallen [kwɑlən]   koal [koəl]–koalen [koələn] "coal"
        poel [puəl]–pwollen [pwolən]   poel [puəl]–poelen [puələn] "pool"
    b. earm [iərm]–jermen [jɛrmən]   jerm [jɛrm]–jermen [jɛrmən] "arm"
        toarn [toərn]–twarnen [twɑrnən] twar [twɑrn]–twarnen [twɑrnən]
                                                                           "thorn"
        trien [triən]–trjinnen [trjɪnən] trjin [trjɪn]–trjinnen [trjɪnən] "tear"

In (11a), the singular forms are more frequent than the plural forms, hence levelling goes into the direction of the singular form. In (11b), on the other hand, the plurals are used more often than the singulars because they denote entities that come in a pair (arms), or in groups (thorns, tears). This led to levelling in the direction of the plural allomorph. The levelling of Frisian breaking is thus a case of **bidirectional levelling**.

An important source of morphology is the phenomenon of grammaticalization. This phenomenon is usually defined as follows:

(12)   '[G]rammaticalization is [. . .] that subset of linguistic changes through which a lexical item in certain uses becomes a grammatical item, or through which a grammatical item becomes more grammatical' (Hopper and Closs Traugott 1993: 2).

An example of the change from lexical to grammatical item is the development of verbs into auxiliaries. In English the verb *to have* not only functions as a main verb, with the meaning "to possess", but also as an auxiliary in perfect tense forms. The verb *can* has lost its status as lexical verb completely, and functions as a modal auxiliary only. In these examples grammaticalization does not create morphology. This does happen if a (lexical or grammatical) morpheme becomes an affix. Dutch has a productive prefix *door-* exemplified in (13):

(13)   door-boor "to drill through completely"
door-ploeg "to through plough, to plough completely"
door-zien "to through-see, to grasp"

This prefix arose through reinterpretation of the directional postposition *door* "through". For instance, the rise of the verb *doorboor* can be pictured as follows:

(14)   [[de muur]$_{NP}$ [door]$_P$]$_{PP}$ [boor]$_V$ > [de muur]$_{NP}$ [door[boor]$_V$]$_V$
the wall   through   drill
"pierce the wall"

This is another example of reanalysis: a structural interpretation is assigned to a sequence of words that differs from the original one. The second ingredient is again analogy: the reanalysed pattern must be extended to other cases in which the original structure does not play a role. This is indeed the case here: *door-* has become a productive prefix in Dutch.

Grammaticalization often goes together with the semantic development of **bleaching**: the meaning of the grammaticalized element becomes more abstract. The meaning of the Frisian prefix *witte-* discussed above is a clear illustration of bleaching. In the case of *door-*, its originally concrete spatial or locative meaning has developed into a more abstract aspectual one. It indicates the completeness of the action performed: the object is completely affected.

A classic example of the development of a suffix out of a word is the past tense suffix in Indo-European. In many Indo-European languages it contains a dental or alveolar consonant (hence it is called the **dental preterite**). This dental preterite developed from the proto-Indo-European verb for *do* which already had this dental consonant. In Romance languages, some of the inflectional endings in verbal paradigms arose from grammaticalization of the Latin verb *habere* "to have". This is the case for French future forms that arose from a periphrastic Latin form, as illustrated in (15) (Hopper and Closs Trangott 1993: 10):

(15)   cantare habemus > (nous) chanter-ons "we will sing"

The ending *-ons* which derives from *habemus* combines with a stem form which is identical to the infinitive form *chanter*, the French counterpart of the Latin infinitive form *cantare*. The choice of stem form thus reflects the history of the future inflectional form.

A lexical morpheme can also grammaticalize when it forms part of a complex word. The non-head constituents of compounds, which function as modifiers, often develop into prefixes with a more general interpretation. Examples are the Dutch lexical morphemes *bloed* "blood" and *kut* "cunt": the first has developed into a general intensifying prefix, the second into a general prefix of negative evaluation:

(16)   a.   bloed-heet "lit. blood-hot, very hot"
            bloed-mooi "lit. blood-beautiful, very beautiful"
            bloed-link "lit. blood-dangerous, very dangerous"
       b.   kut-wijf "lit. cunt-wife, nasty woman"
            kut-auto "lit. cunt-car, bad car"
            kut-smoes "lit. cunt-excuse, bad excuse"

The same can happen to the heads of compounds. The Dutch suffixes discussed in section 7.2 that were qualified as non-cohering derive historically from lexical morphemes. For instance, the non-cohering suffix *-baar* derives from the verb stem *baar* "to carry", and the same applies to the English counterpart *-able* which still has *able* as a lexical correlate. English suffixes such as *-dom* and *-hood* as in *freedom* and *childhood* derive from nouns. That is, words containing these morphemes used to be compounds, but their head nouns have been reanalysed as suffixes since they do not occur any more as words on their own.

The new life of the morpheme *-baar* as a suffix was enhanced by another type of reanalysis. As we have seen, affixes may impose constraints on the word class of their bases. Originally, the lexical morpheme *baar* combined with nouns, as in German *frucht-bar*, Dutch *vrucht-baar* "fertile", both originally compounds meaning "fruit-carrying". In some words in *-baar*, the first constituent could be reinterpreted as a verb, as in *strijd-baar* "militant". The base word *strijd* is both a noun "fight" and a verb "to fight". Subsequently, *-baar* could be reinterpreted as a suffix that takes verbal bases, and it is in this use that it has become productive in Dutch and German.

The distinction between affix and lexical morpheme tends to be blurred in the case of cliticization, because both affixes and clitics require a host word to combine with. In Finnish and Hungarian, some case endings arose from cliticized postpositions. This ambiguity of cliticized morphemes also explains why in a number of Germanic languages the genitive case ending *-s* of nouns in pre-nominal position could be reinterpreted as a phrasal affix, that is a clitic. This latter, reverse development is called **degrammatic-alization** since a suffix has developed into a grammatically independent possessor marker. This is the case for *s* in phrases such as *the king of England's hat*.

The phenomenon of degrammaticalization has raised the question whether grammaticalization is subject to the condition of **unidirectionality**. Is there only one irreversible direction of change in grammaticalization, from lexical to grammatical, and from grammatical to more grammatical morphemes, or can a grammatical morpheme become less grammatical, or even lexical as well? This depends on one's definition of grammaticalization. If unidirectionality is one of its defining properties, changes into the opposite direction simply require another descriptive term, for instance degrammaticalization. The reinterpretation of the English genitive case morpheme *-s* as a clitic is a restricted form of degrammaticalization. It is a restricted case because the suffix does not end up as a full lexical word. In Early Modern English it has also been interpreted as the weak form of the possessive pronoun *his*, that is, as a full word. Thus, Shakespeare writes *the count his galleys* "the count's galleys" (Greg Stump, personal communication). This change is related to the fact that English lost its case system (except for pronouns), and this made a reanalysis of the genitive suffix *-s* necessary. There appears to be consensus that degrammaticalization is restricted in nature, whereas grammaticalization is a pervasive phenomenon in natural languages.

11.4 Changes in morphological rules

Erosion of inflectional morphology has taken place in most Germanic and Romance languages. This means that some inflectional rules have disappeared from the grammar of those languages. Dutch, for instance, has lost its morphological cases. The case system has only survived in a number of fixed expressions, as illustrated by the following examples, prepositional phrases in origin. The prepositions in these phrases govern a particular case. Some of these frozen expressions are considered as words, others are still spelt as phrases. The case endings are in italics:

(17)   te-gelijk*er*-tijd "at the same time, simultaneously"
　　　met di*en* verstande "with that understanding"
　　　in di*er* voege "in such a manner"

An interesting case of change in inflectional morphology is that of adjectival inflection in Afrikaans. In Dutch, adjectives in attributive position are inflected according to the following rule: 'add the suffix -e [ə] to the adjectival stem unless the NP in which it occurs carries the features [indefinite], [neuter], and [singular]'. Thus we get the following contrasts for NPs with attributive adjectives (*paard* "horse" is neuter, *koe* "cow" is non-neuter):

(18) een groot-ø paard "a big horse"   een grot-e koe "a big cow"
      het grot-e paard "the big horse"   de grot-e koe "the big cow"
      (de) grot-e paarden "(the) big horses"   (de) grot-e koeien "(the) big cows"

(The variation *groot/grot* is due to spelling conventions.) The dependence of the absence of the inflectional schwa on three different features is quite a complex system, witness the fact that many non-native speakers of Dutch never learn to master it properly and always add -e to the prenominal adjective. No wonder this system broke down in Afrikaans, a creolized variant of Dutch. In the new system that developed, the adjectives are divided into two classes: either they always carry the inflectional schwa in attributive position, or they never do. The adjectives that do take the schwa are morphologically complex adjectives, and simplex adjectives that exhibit stem allomorphy. For instance, the adjective *sag* "soft" has the stem allomorph *sagt*, as shown in the inflected form *sagte*. Hence, it will have the form *sagte* in attributive position, whereas *sag* is used in predicative position. What we can learn from these facts is that relics of a previous stage of the language, "historical junk" in the words of Lass (1990), might be kept, and even re-used in a different way.

Afrikaans exhibits another kind of rule change, rule simplification. Both in Dutch and in Afrikaans, there are two competing plural suffixes: -s and -en /ən/. The choice between these two suffixes is governed by a prosodic constraint: -s is selected after an unstressed syllable, -en after a stressed one. The effect of this selection principle is that a plural noun always ends in a trochee. In Dutch, this prosodic principle is overruled in some types of complex words. For instance, de-adjectival nouns in -e /ə/ always select the plural ending -en /ən/ (with concomitant prevocalic schwa-deletion), although -s would also be in line with the prosodic constraint. In Afrikaans, this morphological factor is ignored, and the plural suffix for complex nouns is selected in the same way as for simplex nouns. Thus -s is selected for words ending in the suffix -e (Van Marle 1978: 147):

(19) | *noun* | *Dutch plural* | *Afrikaans plural* |
|---|---|---|
| blank-e "white person" | blank-e-n | blank-e-s |
| geleerd-e "scholar" | geleerd-e-n | geleerd-e-s |
| gevangen-e "prisoner" | gevangen-e-n | gevangen-e-s |

In the realm of derivational morphology two types of change are prominent. First, rules may change as to their productivity. Dutch has two suffixes for deriving deverbal adjectives, -*baar* "-able" and -*(e)lijk* "-able". In Middle Dutch the suffix -*elijk* was still productive. However, in the standard variety of Modern Dutch it can no longer be used to coin new adjectives, unlike its competitor -*baar*. Thus, we see that affixes can lose their productivity. Another example of a now unproductive suffix is the Dutch suffix -*el* that we find in nouns such as in (20).

(20) | *base* | *derived noun* |
|---|---|
| drup "drop" | drupp-el "drop" |
| eik "oak" | eik-el "acorn" |
| ijs "ice" | ijz-el "freezing rain" |

This suffix derives from an Indo-European suffix -*l* that indicated descent, and hence also diminution. Why has it become unproductive? An inspection of Dutch nouns in -*el* will reveal that for most of them there is no base noun. This applies for example to the following nouns:

(21) korrel "grain, granule", kruimel "crumble", kwartel "quail", pukkel "pimple", sleutel "key", stempel "stamp", vezel "fibre", wezel "weasel"

Consequently, these nouns will not be parsed into morphological sub-constituents, and thus the suffix -*el* will have an extremely low activation level. That is, these words have lost their morphological structure.

A second observation on these nouns is that their semantics tend to vary: they do not belong to one clear semantic category. Consequently, most speakers of Dutch do not consider words in -*el* as complex. These observations support the view that the abstract patterns we call word-formation rules depend for their existence on the formal and semantic transparency of the complex words over which they generalize. The existence of transparent complex words is necessary for a word-formation pattern to remain productive.

Another type of possible change in derivational rules is a change in the category of the base words to which they apply. Very productive rules tend to extend their domain of application to new categories. The productive diminutive suffix -*tje* of Dutch, for instance, is no longer restricted to the domain of nouns, but also attaches to adjectives, verbs, and adverbs:

(22) strijk "to stroke"   strijk-je "small string orchestra"
      blond "blond"   blond-je "blond girl"
      uit "out"   uit-je "outing"

Category change of the inputs of a word-formation rule may occur as the result of reinterpretation, as happened in the case of the suffix -*baar*, as discussed above.

The vicissitudes of the French suffix -*age* also illustrate category change (Fleischmann 1977). This suffix derives from the Greek–Latin adjectival suffix -*āticus*. The neuter forms of these adjectives could be used as nouns, as in *viāticum* "money for a journey". In addition, -*age* was reinterpreted as being nominal on the basis of the elliptical use of phrases. For example, the French noun *fromage* "cheese" derives from the phrase *cāseu fōrmāticu* "cheese made in a mould" (with the adjective *fōrmāticu* "moulded"), and thus changed its status from adjective to noun. Thus, -*age* could be interpreted as a nominalizing suffix. In Medieval French, this nominalizing -*age* attached to nouns, as in *mouton-age* "tax on a lamb" and *hommage* "honour" (from *homme* "vassal"). This -*age* is also found in the French word *langage*, and its English counterpart *language*. In Modern French, this nominalizing suffix is no longer productive with nouns, but only with verbs, as in *lavage* "washing" from *laver* "to wash". This change of base category was probably brought about by reinterpretation. Some base words could be interpreted as either noun or verb. For instance, *aunage* "measuring by the ell" could be seen as derived from either the noun *aune* "ell", or the verb *auner* "to measure by the ell".

The suffix -*age* entered many European languages through borrowing of French words in -*age*. English has extended its use to native, Germanic nominal, and verbal stems, which shows its productivity in Modern English:

(23)   base N: foot-age, front-age, mile-age, shipp-age, wreck-age, yard-age
       base V: break-age, brew-age, cover-age, drain-age, leak-age, sew-age

The word *shortage* shows that -*age* has even been extended to adjectival bases. In Dutch we find both denominal and deverbal nouns in -*age*; as in English, it has also been attached to native stems, an indication of its productivity.

11.5 Changes in word structure

Complex words, once they are coined, may be subject to reanalysis and reduction. In reanalysis, words receive a different structural interpretation. A classical example is the reinterpretation of the word *hamburger*. This word, derived from the base noun *Hamburg*, and denoting a specific kind of food originating from that city, received the following structural reanalysis:

(24)   [[hamburg]er] > [[ham][burger]]

Reanalysis can only be observed when the reanalysed structure serves as a model for new words. In this case, many new words in *-burger* have been coined, such as *beefburger, cheeseburger, fishburger*, and the like. A similar pattern is the coinage of *turkeyfurter* on the model of *frankfurter*. The piece *burger* itself has been reinterpreted as a noun, witness the brand name *Burger King*. So in fact we cannot conclude that a new suffix *-burger* has developed in English. *Burger* is a new noun denoting a particular kind of fast food, and can be used as the head of nominal compounds.

Semantic reinterpretation may also lead to a new set of words. This has been the case for *-gate*, as used in *Watergate* (the name of an apartment building in Washington, DC, that was burglarized by order of President Nixon). The morpheme *-gate* received a new interpretation, "political scandal", thus leading to many new words such as *Monicagate* and *Irangate* (cf. question 4.4). This suffix also acquired the more general meaning of "scandal", as in *nipplegate*, a scandal in which the pop star Janet Jackson was involved. We may conclude that *-gate* has become a suffix because this specific meaning of *gate* is only available when it is combined with a noun. This suffix *-gate* has been borrowed massively in most European languages. For instance, a recent political scandal around the prospective bride *Mabel* of one of the Dutch princes is referred to as *Mabelgate*.

Reanalysis may also have the effect of a sequence of affixes becoming an affix. A morphological structure [[[x]A]B] can be reinterpreted as [[x]AB]. An example from Dutch is the suffix *-erij*, originally a combination of the suffixes *-er* and *-ij*:

(25)   *base*   *noun in -er*   *noun in -ij*
       bak "to bake"   bakk-er "baker"   bakk-er-ij "bakery" > bakk-erij

This suffix -*erij* is now productively attached to verbal bases without an intermediate noun in -*er* being necessary), and also to base nouns, which confirms that -*erij* has started a life of its own:

(26)   race "to race"   race-erij "racing"
       drogist "chemist"   drogist-erij "drugstore"

This phenomenon of two affixes becoming one is referred to as **affix telescoping**. It also occurred in French where *bijouterie* "jewellery" could be reinterpreted as *bijout-erie* (*bijou* "jewel" > *bijout-ier* "jeweller" > *bijout-er-ie* "jewellery"). This French telescoped suffix -*erie* was also borrowed in Middle Dutch, and it became -*erij* due to a regular sound change of diphthongization of /i/ to /ɛi/. Thus, the borrowed -*erij* enhanced the rise of a native suffix -*erij*.

A type of morphological change that concerns individual words is **systematization**. In Turkish, many nouns denoting persons end in the suffix -*cI* (the capital *I* stands for the set of high vowels, because the vowel of this suffix is subject to vowel harmony). This suffix may also be found attached to loan words from French such as the following (Lewis 1967: 60, cited in Van Marle 1978: 148):

(27)   şoför "chauffeur"   şoför-cü
       garson "waiter"   garson-cu

The addition of this suffix to loan words has the effect that all nouns denoting persons are denoted in a uniform way. That is why this morphological change is qualified as systematization. This morphological pattern complies with a tendency in natural language that is called the one meaning—one form principle: each meaning should correspond with one form. That is, sameness of meaning implies sameness of form. Compliance with this principle is achieved in this case by adding a suffix that is strictly speaking superfluous, and hence a pleonastic addition. Thus, in this case, systematization leads to **overcharacterization**.

Such pleonastic affixation is also found with Dutch acronyms that denote certain professions or ranks. Quite often these acronyms are enriched with the suffix -*er* which creates such denominal names (as in *wetenschapper* "scientist" from *wetenschap* "science"):

(28)   UD (< Universitair Docent "university teacher") > UD-er
       KVV (< Kort Verband Vrijwilliger "short-term volunteer") > KVV-er

For the same reason, some complex words of Dutch ending in schwa were adapted, with replacement of -e by -er, and personal names were extended with -er, as in:

(29)   a. herd-e "shepherd" > herd-er, scutte "shooter, rifleman" > schutt-er,
        schenke "cupbearer" > schenk-er;
       b. Dominic-aan "Dominican" > Dominic-an-er, Farizee "Pharisee" >
        Farizee-er

An example of affix substitution from child language that is also a case of systematization is the replacement of -ig by -baar in the Dutch adjective door-zicht-ig "lit. through-see-able, transparent", leading to door-zicht-baar. It is the suffix -baar that normally expresses the meaning "-able", and hence this adaptation by my daughter Suzanne at the age of 2 is also a case of systematization.

Reduction of word-internal structure takes place when a complex word is no longer semantically transparent. In that case, it may lose its morphological structure and change phonologically into the direction of the canonical phonological form of simplex words. The Dutch word aardappel "potato" is originally a compound made from the lexemes aard "earth" and appel "apple". However, it is not felt as a kind of apple, and hence became opaque. This reinterpretation is reflected by the way this word is parsed into syllables. Whereas each lexical constituent of a compound is an independent domain of syllabification, the word aardappel is now parsed as a simplex word:

(30)   compound $[[aard]_N[appel]_N]_N$ $(aard)_\omega(ap.pel)_\omega$ [a:rtɑpəl]   reanalysed as
       simplex word $[aardappel]_N$ $(aar.dap.pel)_\omega$ [a:rdɑpəl]

The different patterns of syllabification (indicated by the dots) which reflect the loss of morphological structure have an effect on the phonetic form of this word. In Dutch, syllable-final obstruents are devoiced. Hence, the phonetic form [a:rdɑpəl] with a [d] betrays the loss of morphological structure.

A second example is the Dutch adverb natuurlijk "of course" that derives from the denominal adjective natuur-lijk "natural" (< natuur "nature"). In its adverbial use, there is no longer a clear semantic relation to its base noun natuur, and hence this frequently used adverb is pronounced as tuurlijk [ty:rlək] in casual speech. The latter phonetic form has the shape of a trochee, with the second syllable headed by a schwa, which is the optimal prosodic form of Dutch simplex words. The only marked aspect of this phonetic form is that the first syllable contains a long vowel followed by a consonant, whereas Dutch word-internal syllables prefer to be bimoraic (that is, they end either in a long vowel or in a short vowel + one consonant). This constraint is obeyed in the even more reduced form of *natuurlijk* that we also find in casual speech: [tylək]. When used as an adjective, however, the word *natuurlijk* has a transparent morphological structure, and cannot be reduced phonetically.

Prefixes may also lose their morphological status. This is quite clear in English borrowings from Latin such as *abortion* and *adoption*. These words contain the prefixes *ab-* and *ad-* respectively. In transparent complex words, a prefix boundary coincides with a syllable boundary. In these words, however, this is not case: the syllabifications are *a.bor.tion* and *a.dop.tion* respectively. The Dutch prefix *ge-*, as in *geloof* "to believe" is no longer productive as a verbal prefix. In Afrikaans, the verb *geloof* has become a simplex verb, *glo*, with deletion of the schwa (remember that Dutch simplex words prefer to begin with a syllable containing a full vowel, cf. section 7.2). This adaptation implies that in Afrikaans the past participle is *ge-glo*, whereas in Dutch it is *ge-loof-d*, the regular form for verbs with an initial unstressed prefix.

Summary

Word-formation processes lead to new words, and hence the morphological system of a language contributes to lexical innovation. The morphological system itself is also a potential target of change, with external factors and internal factors involved. Forms of external change are borrowing and simplification, both due to language contact. Borrowing of complex words may lead to enrichment of the morphological system, whereas simplification means reduction of its complexity. Internal causes of change are that each generation has to find out the rules behind the system (imperfect learning, which may also lead to simplification), and that language users analyse the outputs of the linguistic system, which may lead to reanalysis.

Morphology may develop in the course of history from syntactic constructions through univerbation and grammaticalization. In addition, phonologically conditioned allomorphy can be preserved after the loss of the conditioning phonological environment, and may be reinterpreted as marking morphological distinctions.

Complex words, once established, may undergo changes. They may get a different shape through systematization and overcharacterization. Complex words may lose their semantic transparency, and hence their morphological structure. This loss of structure can sometimes be inferred from the way in which they are syllabified, or from phonetic reduction, which makes them phonologically more similar to simplex words.

Questions

1. The existence of the English suffix -able is due to borrowing of French adjectives in -able. Nowadays, it can also be attached to native verbal stems (doable, readable). What evidence can you provide for this suffix behaving as a non-native suffix of English as well?

2. What is the relationship between bidirectional levelling and the findings on response latencies for the Italian nouns mentioned in question 10.7?

3. English has two plural forms for brother, brothers and the archaic brethren. These plural forms have different meanings in present-day English. Try to explain why these words have different meanings.

4. The English word shepherd [šɛpərd] derives historically from the compound sheep-herd. Give an account of the phonetic reduction that this compound underwent, and why this reduction could take place.

5. The Italian word for "tomato" is pomodoro (plural pomodori). Its original form is pomo d'oro "apple of gold". Why can't we assume this lexical unit is still phrasal in nature?

6. Try to find violations of the one meaning—one form principle in your native language.

7. The Latin word requiem is the ACC. SG form of the lexeme requies "rest", and is used in many languages to denote the Roman Catholic Mass for the Dead. How can it be explained that languages may apparently borrow cases of contextual inflection from other languages?

8. The Dutch compound scheidsrechter "referee" consists of the verbal stem scheid "to separate" and the noun rechter "judge". The linking element between the two constituents is s. Why can't we say that this s is a lexicalized genitive case ending, and why must it be seen as a stem extension or linking element?

9. Bakker (2003: 23) established the following hierarchy of preservation of inflectional marking on nouns in pidgin languages: number > case> gender. This means that marking for number is more common than for case, and marking for case is more common than for gender. How might this hierarchy of preservation be explained?

10. Compare the following two NPs with the same meaning from Old Swedish and Modern Swedish respectively (Norde 1997: 261):

Old Swedish:	en-s	man-s	synd
	one-GEN	man-GEN	sin
Modern Swedish:	en	man-s	synd
	one	man-s	sin
	"one man's sin"		

How can this change in the morphological marking of the possessor of the head noun be classified?

Further reading

The invisible hand theory of language change is proposed in Keller (1994). Aitchison (2003) points out that children play a less prominent role in language change than sometimes claimed.

The morphological erosion in pidgin and creole languages is discussed in McWhorter (1998). As argued in detail in a number of articles in Plag (2003a), the idea that pidgin and creole languages do not have morphology is incorrect.

A good survey of the phenomena and the theoretical debates concerning grammaticalization is found in Heine et al. (1991), Hopper and Closs Traugott (1993), Bybee et al. (1994), and Heine (2003). Heine and Kuteva (2002) is a reference work on grammaticalization phenomena in the languages of the world. Bybee (2003) stresses the role of frequency in grammaticalization. Bybee et al. (1994) and Closs Traugott (2003) argue that it is the reinterpretation of the whole construction of which a lexical word forms part that leads to grammaticalization of that lexical word. Good surveys and critical evaluations of grammaticalization theory are given in Newmeyer (1998) and Campbell (2001). Norde (1997, 2001) discusses degrammaticalization. The rise of verbal particles and prefixes in Germanic languages through reanalysis is discussed in more detail in van Kemenade and Los (2003) and in Blom and Booij (2003).

The remarkable persistence of paradigm irregularities in morphological change is discussed in Maiden (1992).

Answers to questions

Chapter 1. Morphology: basic notions

1. *Supposedly* has the not completely predictable meaning "most likely, presumably".

2. The pronunciation and meaning of *-able* as an affix are different from *able* as a word.

3. [[un[happi]$_A$]$_A$ness]$_N$,   [[contrast]$_N$ive]$_A$,   [[dis[connect]$_V$]$_V$ing]$_V$, [[contradict]$_V$ion]$_N$,   [[blue]$_A$[[eye]$_N$ed]$_A$]$_A$ or   [[[blue]$_A$[eye]$_N$]$_N$ed]$_A$, [[[connect]$_V$ive]$_A$ity]$_N$

4. *col-league* or *colleague, cord-ial, cor-rel-ate* or *cor-relate, electr-o-meter, e-long-at-ion, e-vapor-ate, etern-ity, eu-phem-ism* or *euphem-ism, habit-ual* or *habitu-al, happ-y* or *happy, mus-ic* or *music, negoti-able, per-form-ance* or *perform-ance, theo-logy* or *theo-log-y*.

5. Plural endings: *-oollee, -oota,* and *-eellee*; stem-forms: *raeedd-, uw-, eel-, -kob-, harr-,* -and *sang-*.

6. (i) There are corresponding simplex verbs *bid, get, give, go,* and *swear*. (ii) There is a recurrent element *for*. (iii) They have the same strong inflection as the corresponding simplex verbs.

7. All these words indicate that something comes out of something.

8. This is a case of analogical word-formation: mother : father = mother tongue: *father tongue*.

9. *Falloween*: an extended celebration or observance of Halloween, often beginning several weeks before the day; the retail season that extends from the beginning of fall through Halloween and Thanksgiving in the US (*fall + Halloween*). *Giraffiti*: graffiti painted at a high spot (*graffiti + giraffe*). *Metrosexual*: an urban male with a strong aesthetic sense who spends a great deal of time and money on his appearance and lifestyle (*metropole + heterosexual*). *Nicotini*: a nicotine-laced martini (*nicotine + martini*). *Pedlock*: the condition or state of being so crowded that people are unable to move easily in any direction (*pedestrian + gridlock*).

10. a blending (back + acronym)

Chapter 2. Morphological analysis

1. *disagreeable: dis-, -able*
   acceptability: ac-, cept, -able, -ity

ungrammaticality: un-, gram, -at, -ic, -al, -ity
discriminatory: dis-, crimin, -at, -ory
permafrost: perma-
fascination: fascin, -ation
protolanguage: proto-
versification: -ific-, -at, -ion
intolerance: in-, toler, -ance
unidirectionality: uni-, -ion, -al, -ity

2. a. The mid front vowels [œ] and [ɛ] become back vowels [ɔ] and [a] respectively before the suffixes *-al, -itude, -aire, -ité, -ifier, -in,* and *-iste.*

   b. This is a morphonological rule because its application is conditioned by the presence of specific suffixes.

3. a. [t], [d], [ɪd].

   b. Assume an underlying /d/ as the phonological form of the past tense suffix. The /d/ is devoiced and thus becomes a [t] if the stem ends in a voiceless consonant; the vowel [ɪ] is inserted before the /d/ if the stem ends in /d/ or /t/.

4. ki-tapin-a:-wa:w
   2PERS-sit-PL–2PERS
   "You (plural) sit"

5. Suffixation and vowel change.

6. a.
```
   a    a  a      a    a  a
   |    |  |      |    |  |
   CVCCVCV      CVCCVCV
   |  \/  |      |  || |
   b  k   l      t  lf n
```

   b.
```
   a    a  a
   |    |  |
   CVCCVCV
```

7. Plural suffix is *-i.* The last vowel of the stem is deleted in plural nouns with a stem ending in /r, n, m/. Stem-final /k/ is voiced before the plural suffix.

8. Past Active: infixation with *-um-;* Past Passive: infixation with *-in-;* Present Active: Partial Reduplication and infixation; Present Passive: Partial reduplication and infixation.

9. Copy the first (C)VC of the stem, and prefix this copy.

10. fam, giall, virtú, blu.

Chapter 3. Derivation

1. The verb *to joyride* is a conversion of the noun *joyride,* with the structure [[[*joy*]ₙ[[*ride*]ᵥ]ₙ]ₙ]ᵥ. Hence, the feature [+ablaut] of the verbal root *ride,* from

which the head noun *ride* of the nominal compound *joyride* is derived, cannot be percolated to the highest V node, because there are intervening N nodes that cannot carry such a feature.

2. The suffix *-able* can be attached to verbs of Germanic origin such as *do* and *read: doable, readable*.

3. The prefix *en-* appears to turn nouns and adjectives into verbs. Thus, it seems to determine the category of the prefixed word, and to function as head, although it is in left position. This is a problem for the Right-hand Head Rule, unless one assumes that the base nouns and adjectives have first been converted to verbs, and have subsequently been prefixed with *en-*.

4. One may assume that the prefix *in-* derives verbs from adjectives, and that such verbs are automatically assigned to the default conjugation, just like the converted nouns *dribblare* and *scioccare*. Hence, the appearance of the thematic vowel *-a-* is a predictable effect of the assignment to this conjugation, and not due to suffixation with *-a* as part of a parasynthetic word-formation process.

5. In these nouns there is no base noun with a gender specification that can be percolated to the dominating node.

6. This use of reduplication is not iconic, since we would then expect an intensified meaning for such reduplicated adjectives.

7. The prefix *de-* has a privative or a reversative meaning, and attaches to verbs and nouns. The prefix *dis-* mainly attaches to verbs, with reversative or privative meaning, and may also express negation. Of these two, the prefix *dis-* is the preferred one before vowel-initial stems. Both combine with non-native base words only. The prefix *in-* has a negative meaning and attaches to non-native adjectives only. The prefix *non-* attaches to adjectives and nouns, with negative meaning. It differs from *un-* in that it preserves the relational character of its adjectival base. The prefix *un-*, with the meaning 'not' can be attached to adjectives, verbs, and nouns, of both native and non-native origin.

8. a.   No, we might consider this suffix an adjectival suffix, that assigns the category A to the diminutive adjective.

   b.   This suffix cannot be attached to relational adjectives since it has a qualifying meaning.

9. The prefix *a-* appears before consonant-initial stems, the prefix *an-* before vowel-initial stems. Thus vowel hiatus (two vowels in adjacent position) is avoided.

10. This is a case of type coercion: *American* has to be interpreted as a qualifying adjective.

Chapter 4. Compounding

1. NN   computer desk
   AN   blackboard
   VN   pickpocket
   PN   underground
   AA   dark-blue
   NA   ice-cold
   VV   freeze-dry
   AV   blindfold
   NV   brainwash

   The heads of English compounds are N, A, or V. Prepositions only combine with N heads. Vs do not combine with A heads.

2. [[[re[create]$_V$]$_V$ion]$_N$[hall]$_N$]$_N$
   [[book]$_N$[[keep]$_V$ing]$_N$]$_N$
   [[truck]$_N$[[driv]$_V$er]$_N$]$_N$
   [[pick]$_V$[pocket]$_N$]$_N$
   [[under]$_P$[dog]$_N$]$_N$
   [[home]$_N$[[grown]$_V$]$_A$]$_A$

3. The left constituents function as heads of these compounds.

4. Although *gate* is a lexeme, it has a completely different meaning when used as part of these complex words. Hence, we might consider these words as cases of derivation with the affix *-gate*.

5. In (5b) the noun is incorporated. This results in a verb that denotes an institutionalized act, tree-chopping. The incorporated noun is non-referential, hence the object *in-kool* "my cornfield" is possible.

6. The first A + N combination is a compound, the second one a phrase.

7. In this compound neither of the constituents functions as the head, and therefore it is exocentric.

8. *bear jam*: a traffic jam in a park caused by motorists stopping to watch one or more bears;

   deprivation cuisine: food prepared in such a way that it is healthy, but bland;

   flash mob: a large group of people who gather in a usually predetermined location, perform some brief action, and then quickly disperse;

   information pollution: the contamination of a culture or of a person's life caused by exposure to excessive amounts of information or data;

   man breasts: excess fatty tissue that causes a man's chest to resemble a woman's breasts;

   office creeper: thief who walks into the workplace looking for pricey laptops and purses;

   salad dodger: an overweight person, a person who shuns healthy foods.

The following words are hard to interpret on the basis of the meanings of the constituent words: *bear jam, deprivation cuisine, flash mob, office creeper, salad dodger*.

9. Such coordinative compounds do not have a head.

10. This is a case of coordinative compounding by means of full reduplication. In addition, the first consonant of the second constituent is replaced with *sh*; this segment is added before a vowel-initial second stem.

Chapter 5. Inflection

1. This is an elliptical construction with the accusative case assigning verb omitted. It means "I wish you a good morning".

2. The synthetic form is used for monosyllabic adjectives (*big–bigger*), and bisyllabic adjectives with a final light syllable (*happy–happier*). In other cases the periphrastic form is used, as in *more excellent/*excellenter* and *more meaningful/*meaningfuller*.

3. This depends on your theory of inflection. In a realizational theory of morphology you do not have to, because there will be no rule that is triggered by the presence of the feature [infinitive].

4. These facts show that inflected nouns can form constituents of compounds, and hence feed word-formation.

5. The two suffixes in *anno-i-n* are cases of inherent inflection, whereas the other endings are cases of contextual inflection. The case markings on *vet-tä* and *koira-lle* are due to structural case assignment (government), the case marking on *kahde-lle* is an instance of agreement.

6. This is quite tricky because it means that suppletion will be applicable to all pairs of different lexemes with similar, related meanings (for instance *man – woman, bicycle – moped*), and hence the notion suppletion will lose much of its distinctive power.

7. The GEN.SG form is a case of cumulative exponence since the suffix *-e* expresses both GENITIVE and SINGULAR. This form is a case of extended exponence as well, since the vowel alternation and the alternation in the stem-final consonant also mark GEN.SG. The DAT.SG form is also a case of extended exponence, since the property cluster DAT.SG is expressed by both a vowel alternation and a consonant alternation.

8. In the British English lexicon, the word *police* must be specified as [+plural], in the American English lexicon as [-plural].

9. MASCULINE + FEMININE = MASCULINE.

10. Panini's Principle. The rule that suffixes *-eren* will be subject to a more specific condition since it has to refer to a diacritic feature, say [+eren], and hence takes precedence over the more general rule of *-en*-suffixation.

Chapter 6. Inflectional systems

1. The cut-off point for the threefold distinction is between animate and inanimate. Human beings and (larger) animals can be referred to with *he* and *she*, but for inanimate entities, only *it* can be used.

2. a.   Stem shapes for *käsi: käs* (nominative, comitative), *käde* (genitive, translative, abessive, inessive, elative, adessive, ablative, allative, instrumental), *kätt* (partitive), *käte* (essive, illative); for *tyttö: tyttö* (nominative, partitive, essive, illative, comitative), *tytö* (all other cases).

   b.   *tytön.*

3. a.   vyr-, broli-, arkli-

   b.   NOM.PL = VOC.PL

4. The notions periphrasis and suppletion. In the periphrastic forms both stems are different from that of the synthetic forms.

5. Past tense is used here for creating distance, hence indirectness, and thus politeness.

6. In plural forms, NOM = ACC = VOC.

7. The verbal infinitive can function as a neuter noun; hence, it will trigger gender, person, and number agreement between the subject and the predicate.

8. The numeral functions here as the head of the phrase since it imposes genitive or ablative case on the constituent *çocuk-lar* "children". Hence, the genitive or ablative case marking on *çocuk-lar* must be a case of dependent marking.

9. The presence of the time adverbial *morgen* "tomorrow" in the Dutch sentence already indicates that the event will take place in the future.

10. Coughing is a punctual event, and is only semantically compatible with progressive aspect if the event is repeated.

Chapter 7. The interface between morphology and phonology

1. This can be concluded from the syllabification of words with these suffixes, for instance: *rea.da.ble, wor.ker, wor.king.* Crucially, the word-internal syllable boundaries do not coincide with a morphological boundary.

2. These function words do not contain a full vowel, and hence no syllable that can bear stress. Thus, they cannot form a foot, and hence no prosodic word of their own, which is a requirement for lexical words. Therefore we can conclude that they must be function words.

3. The /n/ also occurs in other derived words from the same root, such as *Platonist* and *Platonism*. By considering the /n/ as part of the stem, we predict this systematic appearance before (non-native) suffixes.

4. We might explain this by assuming that the domain of this rule of assimilation is the phonological word. The prefix *in-* can be considered as a cohering prefix, and the prefix *non-* as a non-cohering prefix. Hence, the rule of assimilation will only apply to the prefix *in-* since it forms one phonological word with the stem, a domain in which the assimilation rule can apply.

5. This can be shown by making a tableau, for instance for the word *bak-er* with the morphological stem *bake*:

[[bak] er]	ALIGNMENT-LEFT	NO EMPTY ONSET	ALIGNMENT RIGHT
bak.er		*!	
☞ ba.ker			*

6. In this case, the compound constituent *beren* is deleted under identity with an independent noun *beren*. Therefore, these constituents are syntactically not identical, and cannot be gapped if this process is conditioned by syntactic identity. Hence, their identity must be identity on the prosodic level where they both form a prosodic word (*beren*).

7. This change follows from the requirement that a lexical word is minimally a prosodic word. Hence, each lexical word requires the presence of at least one full vowel. Thus, the letter *i* that stands for schwa in the suffix is reinterpreted as a full vowel [ɪ].

8. This rule will give the right result for *bréakfast tàble* because both constituents are disyllabic. As soon as a compound has longer constituents, wrong predictions are made. In *hístory tèacher*, with secondary stress on the syllable *tea*, this rule would assign stress to the last syllable of *history* instead of the first syllable of *teacher*. Therefore, the two parts *history* and *teacher* must form independent domains of stress assignment.

9. This suffix, or the vowel /e/ of this suffix, must be qualified as transparent: it does not affect vowel harmony, otherwise the dative suffix would be *-nek* in both words. The choice of the vowel is clearly determined by the vowels of the roots of these words.

10. The determiner *a* is selected before a consonant-initial word, the determiner *an* before a vowel-initial word. Since the English determiners form one phonological word with the following noun, the choice of *an*, as in *an arm*, with the syllabification *a.narm*, avoids violation of the No Empty Onset Constraint that would be violated in *a arm* with the syllabification *a.arm*. The choice of *a* before a consonant-initial word avoids a violation of the Open Syllable constraint: in *an book* with the syllabification *an.book* the first syllable is closed, unlike the first syllable in *a book* with the syllabification *a.book*.

Chapter 8. Morphology and syntax: demarcation and interaction

1. The intended referent of *it* in sentence (a) is *truck*. This latter word is here part of a compound, and thus the word *truck* is not directly accessible for rules of anaphora because of Lexical Integrity. In sentence (b), the pronoun *one* refers to the whole word *truck driver*, and hence we do not have to violate Lexical Integrity to establish the relevant anaphoric relation.

2. The phrase *small claims* embedded in a compound has a classificatory function: a *small claims court* is a court for a particular kind of claims, small claims. The phrase *small claims* has therefore a classificatory function. Hence the adjective *small* cannot be modified by *very*.

3. No, lexical units larger than one word can also feed word-formation.

4. The Causer argument of the causative verb is the highest argument, and will be assigned the grammatical function of subject (in imperative clauses, the subject is usually not expressed, but understood as the addressee). Hence, the Agent argument will receive the grammatical function of object, and therefore be marked with accusative case.

5. a.   The verb for "to begin" must be lexically specified as imposing dative case on its object, since the default case marking for objects is accusative.

   b.   In the passive sentence, the noun *dersler* 'lessons' is not case marked as a Subject, but keeps its dative case marking. Hence, it is not a Subject, unlike what we would expect if passivization were the promotion of Patient to the grammatical function of Subject.

6. This is a case of valency increase.

7. The addition of the assistive derivational morpheme creates a verb with three arguments, and hence there are two arguments that are non-subjects. Both "mother" and "brother" are marked with the appropriate case for non-subjects, the accusative case.

8. This is a case of applicative verb formation in which the beneficiary of the action is also expressed. Hence, it is an instance of valency increase.

9. The combinations of these verbs with past participles can be considered as the periphrastic fillers of passive cells of the verbal paradigm. The specific, non-compositional meaning of these word combinations will be assigned to these cells. You may also consider these combinations of the verbs *worden* and *zijn* with a past participle as constructional idioms. The passive meaning and the unexpected perfective interpretation of the imperfective forms of *zijn* + past participle will then be considered properties of these constructional idioms.

10. The two verbs in this sentence, *liep* and *dede cont*, apparently function as a verbal unit. We do not have two coordinated clauses here, but one clause with a coordinated verb cluster. The object *dit* "this" of *dede cont* thus

becomes an object of this multi-word unit, and therefore precedes this unit when it is fronted.

Chapter 9. Morphology and semantics

1. Doctor who treats horses; doctor (gardener) who treats trees; doctor who makes use of voodoo rituals; doctor employed in a hospital.

2. beehive: metaphor (place where many people come together)
   bottleneck: metaphor
   convention: metonymy (activity > set of people involved in the activity)
   cliffhanger: metaphor (end of television soap with situation of suspense)
   holder: metaphor or metonymy (person > instrument or location)
   opposition: metonymy (activity > people involved in the activity)
   printer: metaphor (person > impersonal agent > instrument)

3. rural policeman: the *location* of the police
   Martian expedition: the *goal* of the expedition
   early riser: the *time* of rising
   individual decision: the *agent* of deciding

4. The correspondence rule cannot be universal because in Malagasy the semantic interpretation of completely reduplicated forms is not "increased", but "decreased".

5. The use of *selection* as a predicate of *John* implies a result noun interpretation. Hence it cannot be combined with an agent phrase.

6. The deverbal noun inherits the case-assigning properties of its base verb.

7. This is no violation of the Non-Redundancy Constraint since the constituent *parkeer* makes the interpretation of the Dutch word *garage* unambiguous: as part of this compound, it cannot be interpreted as a service station.

8. The scope of this suffix which denotes "possibility of undergoing an action" is: *x divide by three*. It means: "for this number x, it is possible to divide x by three". Hence the scope is larger than just the verb *divide*.

9. blessing: action and result of action
   crossing: action and location of action
   drawing: action and result of action
   dwelling: action and location of action
   opening: action and result of action

10. This follows from the polysemy of diminutive suffixes. The first occurrence of a diminutive suffix in these words denotes the small size, the second occurrence signals endearment. Hence, these diminutive suffixes have different meanings, and can therefore be stacked up.

Chapter 10. Morphology and psycholinguistics

1. Dictionaries do not always specify the phonological form of a word (only the orthographical form). The mental lexicon will also contain individual associations with words based on individual, personal experience. For instance, in your personal lexical entry for *dog* you may have your own prototype of a dog, or an association with fear.

2. These children do not yet command the established, conventionalized words for these concepts.

3. The words with a relatively low base frequency: *uncanny*, *unleash*, *unobtrusive*, and *uncouth*. This correlates with a relative low degree of semantic transparency of these words.

4. These verbs obey the principles of simplicity (conversion is a simple formal operation) and transparency (meaning can be grasped easily). The principle of conventionality will have no impact due to the small size of the mental lexicon of children.

5. The verb *to joyride* is a conversion of the compound noun *joyride*, and hence has no irregular verb *to ride* as its head. Hence, the irregular past tense form *rode* is of no relevance here, and the regular rule of past tense formation will apply. If such a rule did not exist, we would expect the association between *ride* and *rode* to result in the past tense form *joyrode*.

6. Words that have identical word-initial phonological strings are associated in the mental lexicon. Hence, they might be exchanged.

7. This correlates with token frequency. One refers more often to more than one tree, hair, tooth, foot, and sister than to a singular tree, a singular hair, etc. Thus, the plural forms of the corresponding Italian nouns have a higher token frequency, and hence a shorter reaction time than the singular forms. In the case of "nose", speakers will more often refer to a singular nose than to noses. For *soldato* and *piazza* the pragmatic differences between the singular and the plural notions are minimal. Hence we do not find large differences in response latency for their singular and plural forms.

8. The basis for these errors must be the semantic relationship of (near) synonymy.

9. The past tense forms of the verbs involved differ in that it is made by vowel change in the case of *to know*, and by means of suffixation in the case of *to hear*. It is the abstract feature [past] that must have been transferred from *to hear* to *to know*, not the suffix -*d*. Otherwise we would have expected the form *knowed* in the *if*-clause.

10. This shows that patterns that hold for a more or less closed set of words only, are nevertheless recognizable as such for the language user.

Chapter 11. Morphology and language change

1. The non-native suffix -ity can be added to an adjective in -able, whereas -ity cannot be attached to native adjectives such as yellow (*yellowity).

2. If plural forms are used more frequently than singular forms, they will have a higher activation level than singular nouns, and paradigmatic levelling will also go in the direction of plural forms.

3. This is in accordance with the tendency in natural languages that a difference in form implies a difference in meaning.

4. The word shepherd has lost its semantic transparency, and has become a simplex word. Hence, its phonological form has developed into that of a simplex word (a phonological word consisting of one trochee). The second syllable does not bear stress any more, and its vowel has been reduced to schwa.

5. If this word were still phrasal, we would expect the plural form pomi d'oro. Thus, the plural form shows that this expression has become a simplex word.

6. Synonyms are violations of this principle.

7. The accusative form requiem is the first word of the opening line of the Mass for the Dead:

Requie-m   aetern-am   dona   eis   Domin-e
Rest.FEM-ACC.SG   eternal-FEM.ACC.SG. give-IMP.SG   them   Lord-VOC
"Give them eternal rest, o Lord"

This first word became the name of the whole Mass.

8. The first constituent of this word is a verbal stem, and hence it cannot have a genitive ending since verbs do not have case.

9. In most contexts, information about number of nouns is non-redundant. Gender has no clear semantic function, and can therefore be dispensed with easily. Case marking has a semantic function but can be dispensed with as well, because word order and prepositions may take over the role of marking grammatical functions.

10. This change is the same as that in which the English genitive suffix -s was involved: it became a clitic (phrasal affix). This is therefore a case of degrammaticalization.

References

BLM   Booij, G., Lehmann, Ch., and Mugdan, J. (eds.), *Morphology.*
         An International Handbook of Inflection and Word Formation
         (Berlin: De Gruyter), i (2000), ii (2004).
JL   *Journal of Linguistics*
Lg   *Language. Journal of the Linguistic Society of America.*
NLLT *Natural Language and Linguistic Theory*
YoM   *Yearbook of Morphology*, edited by Geert Booij and Jaap van Marle.
         Dordrecht: Foris (1988–90), Dordrecht: Kluwer Academic Publishers
         (1991–)

ACKERMAN, F., and GOLDBERG, A. (1996). 'Constraints on Adjectival Past
    Participles', in A. E. Goldberg (ed.), *Conceptual Structure, Discourse and*
    Language, 17–30. Stanford: CSLI.

AITCHISON, J. (1987). *Words in the Mind: An Introduction to the Mental Lexicon.*
    Oxford: Blackwell [2002, 3rd revised edition].

—— (2003). 'Psycholinguistic Perspectives on Language Change', in Joseph and
    Janda 2003: 736–43.

—— (2004). 'Speech Perception and Production', *BLM* ii, art. 163.

ANDERSON, S. R. (1985). 'Inflectional Morphology', in Shopen 1985: 150–201.

—— (1992). *A-Morphous Morphology*. Cambridge: Cambridge University Press.

ANDERSSON, E. (1994). 'Swedish', in König and van der Auwera 1994: 271–312.

ARONOFF, M. (1976). *Word Formation in Generative Grammar*. Cambridge,
    Mass.: MIT Press.

—— (1980). 'Contextuals', *Lg* 56: 744–58.

—— (1994). *Morphology by Itself: Stems and Inflectional Classes*. Cambridge
    Mass.: MIT Press.

—— and FUHRHOP, N. (2002). 'Restricting Suffix Combinations in German and
    English: Closing Suffixes and the Monosuffix Constraint', *NLLT* 20: 451–90.

AUSTIN, P. (1981). *A Grammar of Diyari, South Australia*. Cambridge: Cambridge
    University Press.

AYRES, G. (1983). 'The Antipassive "Voice" in Ixil', *International Journal of*
    American Linguistics 49: 20–45.

BAAYEN, R. H. (1992). 'Quantitative Aspects of Morphological Productivity',
    YoM 1991, 109–50.

—— (1993). 'On Frequency, Transparency, and Productivity', *YoM 1992*,
    181–208.

—— (2003). 'Probabilistic Approaches to Morphology', in R. Bod, J. Hay, and S. Jannedy (eds.), *Probabilistic Linguistics*, 229–87. Cambridge, Mass., and London: MIT Press.

—— PIEPENBROCK, R., and GULIKERS, L. (1995). *The CELEX Lexical Database*. Phildelphia: Linguistic Data Consortium, University of Philadelphia (CD-rom).

—— BURANI, C., and SCHREUDER, R. (1997). 'Effects of Semantic Markedness in the Processing of Regular Nominal Singulars and Plurals in Italian', *YoM 1996*, 13–34.

—— DIJKSTRA, T., and SCHREUDER, R. (1997). 'Singulars and Plurals in Dutch: Evidence for a Parallel Dual Route Model', *Journal of Memory and Language* 36: 94–117.

—— SCHREUDER, R., DE JONG, N. and KROTT, A. (2002). 'Dutch Inflection: The Rules that Prove the Exception', in Nooteboom *et al.* 2002: 61–92.

BAKER, M. (1988). *Incorporation: A Theory of Grammatical Function Changing*. Chicago and London: University of Chicago Press.

—— (1996). *The Polysynthesis Parameter*. New York and Oxford: Oxford University Press.

—— (2001). *The Atoms of Language*. New York: Basic Books.

BAKKER, P. (2003). 'Pidgin Inflectional Morphology and its Implications for Creole Morphology', *YoM 2003*, 3–35.

BARLOW, M., and FERGUSON, C. (eds.) (1988). *Agreement in Natural Language. Approaches, Theories, Descriptions*. Stanford, Calif.: CSLI.

BAUER, L. (2001). *Productivity*. Cambridge: Cambridge University Press.

BAUER, W. (1993). *Maori*. London and New York: Routledge.

BEARD, R. (1991). 'Decompositional Composition: The Semantics of Scope Ambiguities and "Bracketing Paradoxes" ', *NLLT* 9: 195–229.

BECKER, T. (1990*a*). *Analogie und morphologische Theorie*. Munich: Wilhelm Fink Verlag.

—— (1990*b*). 'Do Words Have Heads?', *Acta Linguistica Hungarica* 40: 5–17.

BERENT, I., MARCUS, G. F., SHIMRON, J., and GAFOS, A. I. (2002). 'The Scope of Linguistic Generalizations: Evidence from Hebrew Word Formation', *Cognition* 83: 113–39.

BERKO, J. (1958). 'The Child's Learning of English Morphology', *Word* 14: 150–77.

BHATIA, T. K. (1993). *Punjabi: A Cognitive-Descriptive Grammar*. London and New York: Routledge.

BLAKE, B. (1994). *Case*. Cambridge: Cambridge University Press.

BLESER, R. DE, and BAYER, J. (1988). 'On the Role of Inflectional Morphology in Agrammatism', in Hammond and Noonan 1988: 45–69.

BLOM, C., and BOOIJ, G. E. (2003). 'The Diachrony of Complex Predicates in

Dutch: A Case Study in Grammaticalization', *Acta Linguistica Hungarica* 50: 61–91.

BOOIJ, G. E. (1977). *Dutch Morphology: A Study of Word Formation in Generative Grammar*. Dordrecht: Foris.

—— (1985). 'Coordination Reduction in Complex Words: A Case for Prosodic Phonology', in H. van der Hulst and N. Smith (eds.) *Advances in Non-Linear Phonology*, 143–60. Dordrecht: Foris.

—— (1986). 'Form and Meaning in Morphology: The Case of Dutch "Agent" Nouns', *Linguistics* 24: 503–17.

—— (1988). 'The Relation between Inheritance and Argument Linking: Deverbal Nouns in Dutch', in Everaert *et al.* 1988: 57–74.

—— (1992). 'Morphology, Semantics, and Argument Structure', in I. Roca (ed.), *Thematic Structure: Its Role in Grammar*, 47–63. Berlin and New York: Foris.

—— (1994). 'Against Split Morphology', *YoM 1993*, 27–50.

—— (1996*a*). 'Inherent versus Contextual Inflection and the Split Morphology Hypothesis', *YoM 1995*, 1–16.

—— (1996*b*). 'Cliticization as Prosodic Integration: The Case of Dutch', *The Linguistic Review* 13: 219–42.

—— (1997*a*). 'Allomorphy and the Autonomy of Morphology', *Folia Linguistica* 31: 25–56.

—— (1997*b*). 'Autonomous Morphology and Paradigmatic Relations', *YoM 1997*, 35–54.

—— (1997*c*). 'Non-Derivational Phonology Meets Lexical Phonology', in I. Roca (ed.), *Constraints and Derivations in Phonology*, 261–88. Oxford: Clarendon Press.

—— (1998). 'Phonological Output Constraints in Morphology', in W. Kehrein and R. Wiese (eds.), *Phonology and Morphology of the Germanic Languages*, 143–63. Tübingen: Niemeyer.

—— (2000). 'The Phonology–Morphology Interface', in L. Cheng and R. Sybesma (eds.), *The First Glot International State-of-the-Article Book*, 287–306. Berlin: Mouton de Gruyter.

—— (2002*a*). *The Morphology of Dutch*. Oxford: Oxford University Press.

—— (2002*b*). 'Prosodic Restrictions on Stacking up Affixes', *YoM 2001*, 183–202.

—— (2002*c*). 'Constructional Idioms, Morphology, and the Dutch Lexicon', *Journal of Germanic Linguistics* 14: 301–27.

—— and LIEBER, R. (2004). 'On the Paradigmatic Nature of Affixal Semantics in English and Dutch', *Linguistics* 42: 327–57.

BORER, H. (1988). 'On the Morphological Parallelism between Compounds and Constructs', *YoM 1988*, 45–66.

BÖRJARS, K., VINCENT, N., and CHAPMAN, C. (1997). 'Paradigms, Periphrases, and Pronominal Inflection', *YoM 1996*, 155–80.

BOSCH, P. (1983). *Agreement and Anaphora: A Study of the Role of Pronouns in Syntax and Discourse*. New York: Academic Press.

BOTHA, R. P. (1984). *Morphological Mechanisms: Lexicalist Analyses of Synthetic Compounding*. Oxford: Pergamon Press.

—— (1988). *Form and Meaning in Word Formation: A Case Study of Afrikaans Reduplication*. Cambridge: Cambridge University Press.

BRESNAN, J., and MCHOMBO, S. (1995). 'The Lexical Integrity Principle: Evidence from Bantu', *NLLT* 13: 181–254.

BROSELOW, E. (2000). 'Transfixation', *BLM* i. 552–7.

BYBEE, J. L. (1985). *Morphology: A Study of the Relation between Meaning and Form*. Amsterdam: Benjamins.

—— (1988). 'Morphology as Lexical Organization', in Hammond and Noonan 1988: 119–42.

—— (1995). 'Regular Morphology and the Lexicon', *Language and Cognitive Processes* 10: 425–55.

—— (2001). *Phonology and Language Use*. Cambridge: Cambridge University Press.

—— (2003). 'Mechanisms of Change in Grammaticization: The Role of Frequency', in Joseph and Janda 2003: 602–23.

CAMERON-FAULKNER, T., and CARSTAIRS-MCCARTHY, A. (2000). 'Stem Alternants as Morphological Signata: Evidence from Blur Avoidance in Polish Nouns', *NLLT* 18: 813–35.

CAMPBELL, L. (2001). 'What's Wrong with Grammaticalization?', *Language Sciences* 23: 113–61.

CARSTAIRS, A. (1987). *Allomorphy in Inflexion*. London: Croom Helm.

—— (1988). 'Some Implications of Phonologically Conditioned Suppletion', *YoM 1988*, 67–94.

CARSTAIRS-MCCARTHY, A. (1992). *Current Morphology*. London and New York: Routledge.

—— (1993). 'Morphology without Word-Internal Constituents: A Review of Anderson (1992)', *YoM 1992*, 209–34.

—— (1994). 'Inflection Classes, Gender, and the Principle of Contrast', *Lg* 70: 737–88.

CHOMSKY, N., and HALLE, M. (1968). *The Sound Pattern of English*. New York: Harper & Row.

CHUNG, S., and TIMBERLAKE, A. (1985). 'Tense, Aspect, and Mood', in Shopen 1985: 202–58.

CLAHSEN, H. (1999). 'Lexical Entries and Rules of Language', *Behavorial and Brain Sciences* 22: 991–1060.

CLARK, E. V. (1993). *The Lexicon in Acquisition*. Cambridge: Cambridge University Press.

—— and BERMAN, R. A. (1984). 'Structure and Use in the Acquisition of Word Formation', *Lg* 60: 542–90.

CLARK and BERMAN (2004). 'Morphology in First Language Acquisition', *BLM* ii, art. 165.

—— and CLARK, H. H. (1979). 'When Nouns Surface as Verbs', *Lg* 55: 767–811.

CLOSS TRAUGOTT, E. (2003). 'Constructions in Grammaticalization', in Joseph and Janda 2003: 624–47.

COATES, R. (2000). 'Exponence', *BLM* i. 616–30.

COMRIE, B. (1976). *Aspect*. Cambridge: Cambridge University Press.

—— (1981). *Language Universals and Linguistic Typology*. Oxford: Blackwell.

—— (1984). *Tense*. Cambridge: Cambridge University Press.

—— (1985). 'Causative Verb Formation and Other Verb-Deriving Morphology', in Shopen 1985: 309–48.

—— (2001). 'Recipient Person Suppletion in the Verb "Give" ' (lecture handout, Berlin).

—— and THOMPSON, S. (1985). 'Nominalization', in Shopen 1985: 349–98.

CORBETT, G. (1991). *Gender*. Cambridge: Cambridge University Press.

—— (2000). *Number*. Cambridge: Cambridge University Press.

—— and FRASER, N. M. (1993). 'Network Morphology: a DATR Account of Russian Nominal Inflection', *JL* 29: 113–42.

COWAN, W., and RAKUŠAN, J. (1985). *Source Book for Linguistics*. Amsterdam and Philadelphia: Benjamins.

CROFT, W. (1990). *Typology and Universals*. Cambridge: Cambridge University Press.

CRUSE, A. (2000). *Meaning in Language: An Introduction to Semantics and Pragmatics*. Oxford: Oxford University Press.

CSATÓ, E. A., and JOHANSON. L. (1998). 'Turkish', in L. Johanson and E. A. Csató (eds.), *The Turkic Languages*, 203–35. London and New York: Routledge.

CUTLER, A. (ed.) (1982). *Slips of the Tongue and Language Production, Linguistics* 19, issue 7–8.

—— HAWKINS, J. A., and GILLEGAN, G. (1985). 'The Suffixing Preference: A Processing Explanation', *Linguistics* 23: 723–59.

CYSOUW, M. (2001). *The Paradigmatic Structure of Person Marking*. Ph.D. diss. University of Nijmegen [revised edn. Oxford: Oxford University Press, 2003].

DELL, F. and SELKIRK, E. O. (1978). 'On a Morphologically Governed Vowel Alternation in French', in S. J. Keyser (ed.), *Recent Transformational Studies in European Languages*, 1–51. Cambridge, Mass.: MIT Press.

DIMMENDAAL, G. (1983). *The Turkana Language*. Dordrecht: Foris.

—— (2002). 'Morphology', in B. Heine and D. Nurse (eds.), *African Languages: An Introduction*, 161–93. Cambridge: Cambridge University Press.

DISCIULLO, A. M., and WILLIAMS, E. (1987). *On the Definition of Word*. Cambridge, Mass.: MIT Press.

DIXON, R. M. W. (1977). *A Grammar of Yidiɲ*. Cambridge: Cambridge University Press.

—— (1994). *Ergativity*. Cambridge: Cambridge University Press.

—— and AIKHENVALD, A. Y. (eds.) (2000). *Changing Valency: Case Studies in Transitivity*. Cambridge: Cambridge University Press.

DOWNING, P. (1977). 'On the Creation and Use of English Compound Nouns', *Lg* 53: 810–42.

DOWTY, D. (1991). 'Thematic Proto-Roles and Argument Selection', *Lg* 67: 547–619.

DRESSLER, W. U., and BARBARESI, L. MERLINI (1994). *Morphopragmatics: Diminutives and Intensifiers in Italian, German, and Other Languages*. Berlin and New York: Mouton de Gruyter.

DYK, S. (1988). 'Oer it foarheaksel *witte-* (*withoe-*) en syn syntaktysk komôf', in S. Dyk and G. de Haan (eds.), *Wurdfoarried en Wurdgrammatika*, 21–44. Ljouwert: Fryske Akademy.

—— (1997). *Noun Incorporation in Frisian*. Ljouwert: Fryske Akademy.

EISENBERG, P. (1994). *Grundriss der deutschen Grammatik*. Stuttgart and Weimar: Verlag J. B. Metzler.

ELBERS, L. (1988). 'New Names for Old Words: Related Aspects of Children's Metaphors and Word Compounds', *Journal of Child Language* 5: 591–617.

EVERAERT, M., EVERS, A., HUYBREGTS, R., and TROMMELEN, M. (eds.) (1988). *Morphology and Modularity: In Honour of Henk Schultink*. Dordrecht: Foris.

FABB, N. (1988). 'English Suffixation is Constrained Only by Selectional Restrictions', *NLLT* 6: 527–39.

FLEISCHMANN, S. (1977). *Cultural and Linguistic Factors in Word Formation: An Integrated Approach to the Development of the Suffix-age*. Berkeley, Calif.: University of California Press.

FORTESCUE, M. (1984). *West-Greenlandic*. Beckenham: Croom Helm.

FRAUENFELDER, U. H., and SCHREUDER, R. (1992). 'Constraining Psycholinguistic Models of Morphological Processing and Representation: The Role of Productivity', *YoM 1991*, 165–84.

FROMKIN, V. (ed.) (1973). *Speech Errors as Linguistic Evidence*. The Hague and Paris: Mouton.

GOLDBERG, A., and ACKERMAN, F. (2001). 'The Pragmatics of Obligatory Adjuncts', *Lg* 77: 798–814.

GONZÁLEZ, P. (2003). *Aspects on Aspect: Theory and Applications of Grammatical Aspect in Spanish*. Utrecht: LOT.

GREENBERG J. (1963). 'Some Universals of Grammar with Particular Reference to the Order of Meaningful Elements', in id. (ed.), *Universals of Language*, 73–113. Cambridge Mass.: MIT Press. [1966²].

GRIMES, B. (ed.) (2003). *Ethnologue: Languages of the World*. Dallas, Tex.: SIL [14th edn, also on the internet: www.ethnologue.com].

GRIMSHAW, J. (1990). *Argument Structure*. Cambridge, Mass.: MIT Press.

GÜREL, A. (1999). 'Decomposition: To What Extent? The Case of Turkish', *Brain and Language* 68: 218–24.

HAGEMEIJER, T. (2001). 'Underspecification in Serial Verb Constructions', in N. Corver and H. van Riemsdijk (eds.), *Semi-Lexical Categories*, 415–51. Berlin and New York: Mouton de Gruyter.

HALL, C. J. (1988). 'Integrating Diachronic and Processing Principles in Explaining the Suffix Preference', in Hawkins 1988: 321–59.

—— (1991). *Morphology and Mind: A Unified Approach to Explanation in Linguistics*. London and New York: Routledge.

HALLE, M. (1992). 'The Latvian Declension', *YoM 2001*, 33–47.

—— and MARANTZ, A. (1993). 'Distributed Morphology', in K. Hale and S. J. Keyser (eds.), *The View from Building 20: Essays in Linguistics in Honor of Sylvain Bromberger*, 111–76. Cambridge Mass.: MIT Press.

HAMMOND, M., and NOONAN, M. (eds.) (1988). *Theoretical Morphology: Approaches in Modern Linguistics*. San Diego: Academic Press.

HARADA, S. I. (1976). 'Honorofics', in M. Shibatani (ed.), *Japanese Generative Grammar*, 499–561. New York: Academic Press.

HARLEY, H., and NOYER, R. (2003). 'Distributed Morphology', in L. Cheng and R. Sybesma (eds.), *The Second GLOT International State-of-the-Article Book*, 463–96. Berlin: Mouton de Gruyter.

HASPELMATH, M. (1996). 'Wordclass-Changing Inflection and Morphological Theory', *YoM 1995*, 43–66.

HAWKINS, J. A. (ed.) (1988). *Explaining Language Universals*. Oxford: Blackwell.

—— and CUTLER, A. (1988). 'Psycholinguistic Factors in Morphological Asymmetry', in Hawkins 1988: 280–317.

HAY, J. (2001). 'Lexical Frequency in Morphology. Is Everything Relative?', *Linguistics* 39: 1041–70.

—— (2002). 'From Speech Perception to Morphology: Affix Ordering Revisited', *Lg* 78: 527–55.

—— and BAAYEN, R. H. (2002). 'Parsing and Productivity', *YoM 2001*, 203–36.

HEINE, B. (2003). 'Grammaticalization', in Joseph and Janda 2003: 575–601.

—— and KUTEVA, T. (2002). *World Lexicon of Grammaticalization*. Cambridge: Cambridge University Press.

—— CLAUDI, U., and HÜNNEMEYER, F. (1991). *Grammaticalization: A Conceptual Framework*. Chicago and London: University of Chicago Press.

HOEKSEMA, J. (1985). *Categorial Morphology*. New York: Garland Press.

HOEKSTRA, T. (1986). 'Deverbalization and Inheritance', *Linguistics* 24: 549–84.

—— and VAN DER PUTTEN, F. (1988). 'Inheritance Phenomena', in Everaert *et al.* 1988: 163–86.

HOPPER, P. J., and CLOSS TRAUGOTT, E. (1993). *Grammaticalization*. Cambridge: Cambridge University Press.

HYMAN, L. (2003). 'Suffix Ordering in Bantu: A Morphocentric Approach', *YoM 2003*, 245–83.

INKELAS, S. (1993). 'Nimboran Position Class Morphology', *NLLT* 11: 559–624.

JACKENDOFF, R. S. (1975). 'Semantic and Morphological Regularities in the Lexicon', *Lg* 51: 639–71.

—— (1983). *Semantics and Cognition*. Cambridge, Mass.: MIT Press.

—— (1997). *The Architecture of the Language Faculty*. Cambridge, Mass.: MIT Press.

—— (2002). *Foundations of Language*. Oxford: Oxford University Press.

JAEGER, J. J., LOCKWOOD, A. H., KEMMERER, D. L., VAN VALIN, R. D., MURPHY, B. W., and KHALAK, H. G. (1996). 'A Positron Emission Tomographic Study of Regular and Irregular Verb Morphology in English', *Lg* 72: 451–97.

JAKOBSON, R. (1936). 'Beitrag zur allgemeinen Kasuslehre', reprinted in *Roman Jakobson: Selected Writings*, ii. *Word and Language*, 23–71. The Hague and Paris: Mouton.

JANSSEN, D., ROELOFS, A., and LEVELT, W. J. M. (2002). 'Inflectional Frames in Language Production', *Language and Cognitive Processes* 17: 209–36.

JONG, N. H. DE, SCHREUDER, R., and BAAYEN, R. H. (2000). 'The Morphological Family Size Effect and Morphology', *Language and Cognitive Processes* 15: 329–65.

JOSEPH, B. D., and JANDA, R. D. (eds.) (2003). *The Handbook of Historical Linguistics*. Oxford: Blackwell.

JURAFSKY, D. (1996). 'Universal Tendencies in the Semantics of the Diminutive', *Lg* 72: 533–78.

KAGER, R. (1999). *Optimality Theory*. Cambridge: Cambridge University Press.

KASTOVSKY, D. (1986). 'The Problem of Productivity in Word Formation', *Linguistics* 24: 585–600.

KATAMBA, F. (ed.) (2003). *Morphology. Critical Concepts in Linguistics*, 6 vols. London: Routledge.

KEENAN, E. (1976). 'Towards a Universal Definition of Subject', in C. Li (ed.), *Subject and Topic*, 303–34. New York: Academic Press.

—— and POLINSKY, M. (1998). 'Malagasy (Austronesian)', in Spencer and Zwicky 1998: 563–623.

KELLER, R. (1994). *On Language Change: The Invisible Hand in Language*. London: Routledge.

KEMENADE, A. VAN, and LOS, B. (2003). 'Particles and Prefixes in Dutch and English', *YoM 2003*, 79–118.

KERKE, S. C. VAN DE (1996). 'Affix Order and Interpretation in Bolivian Quechua', Ph.D. diss. Univ. of Amsterdam.

KIEFER, F. (1992). 'Compounding in Hungarian', *Rivista di Linguistica* 4: 61–78.

KIPARSKY. P. (1994). 'Allomorphy or Morphophonology?', in R. Singh (ed.), *Trubetzkoy's Orphan: Proceedings of the Montréal Round-Table 'Morphonology: Contemporary Responses'*, 13–62. Amsterdam and Philadelphia: Benjamins.

KLAIMAN, M. H. (1991). *Grammatical Voice*. Cambridge: Cambridge University Press.

KLAMER, M. (1998). *A Grammar of Kambera*. Berlin: Mouton de Gruyter.

KÖNIG, E., and VAN DER AUWERA, J. (eds.) (1994). *The Germanic Languages*. New York: Routledge.

KOPTJEVSKAJA-TAMM, M. (1993). *Nominalizations*. London and New York: Routledge.

KORNFILT, J. (1997). *Turkish*. London and New York: Routledge.

KROTT, A. (2001). 'Analogy in Morphology: The Selection of Linking Elements in Dutch Compounds', Ph.D. diss. University of Nijmegen.

—— SCHREUDER, R., and BAAYEN, R. H. (2001). 'Analogy in Morphology: Modeling the Choice of Linking Morphemes in Dutch', *Linguistics* 39: 51–93.

KULA, C. N. (2002). *The Phonology of Verbal Derivation in Bemba*. Utrecht: LOT.

KUTSCH LOJENGA, C. (1994). *Ngiti: A Central-Sudanic Language of Zaire*. Cologne: Rüdiger Köppe Verlag.

LAPPE, S. (2003). 'Monosyllabicity in Prosodic Morphology: the Case of Truncated Personal Names in English', *YoM 2002*, 35–86.

LASS, R. (1990). 'How to Do Things with Junk: Exaptation in Language Evolution', *JL* 26: 79–102.

LEFEBVRE, C. (2003). 'The Emergence of Productive Morphology in Creole Languages: The Case of Haitian Creole', *YoM 2002*, 35–80.

LEHMANN, C. (1982). 'Directions for Interlinear Morphemic Translations', *Folia Linguistica* 16: 199–224.

—— (2004). 'Interlinear Morphemic Glossing', *BLM* ii, art. 169.

LEVELT, W. J. M. (1989). *Speaking: From Intention to Articulation*. Cambridge, Mass.: MIT Press.

LEVI, J. N. (1978). *The Syntax and Semantics of Complex Nominals*. New York: Academic Press.

LEWIS, G. L. (1967). *Turkish Grammar*. Oxford: Oxford University Press.

LIEBER, R. (1980). *On the Organization of the Lexicon*. Ph.D. diss. MIT, published by Garland Press, New York, 1994.

—— (1987). *An Integrated Theory of Autosegmental Processes*. Albany, NY: SUNY Press.

—— (1989). 'On Percolation', *YoM 1989*, 95–138.

—— (1992). *Deconstructing Morphology*. Chicago: University of Chicago Press.

—— (2000). 'Substitution of Segments and Features', *BLM* i. 567–76.

MCCARTHY, J. J. (1981). 'A Prosodic Theory of Non-Concatenative Morphology', *Linguistic Inquiry* 12: 373–418.

—— (1998). 'Prosodic Morphology', in Spencer and Zwicky 1998: 283–305.

—— and PRINCE, A. (1994). 'Generalized Alignment', *YoM 1993*, 79–154.

MCWHORTER, J. (1998). 'Identifying the Creole Prototype: Vindicating a Typological Class', *Lg* 74: 788–818.

MAIDEN, M. (1992). 'Irregularity as a Determinant of Morphological Change', *JL* 28: 285–312.

MALOUF, R. P. (2000). *Mixed Categories in the Hierarchical Lexicon*. Stanford Calif.: CSLI.

MARANTZ, A. (1982). 'Re Reduplication' *Linguistic Inquiry* 13: 83–545.

MARCHAND, H. (1969). *The Categories and Types of Present-Day English Word Formation*, 2nd edn. Munich: Beck.

MARCUS, G. (2001). *The Algebraic Mind: Integrating Connectionism and Cognitive Science*. Cambridge, Mass.: MIT Press.

MARLE, J. VAN (1978). 'Veranderingen in woordstructuur', in G. A. T. Koefoed and J. van Marle (eds.), *Aspecten van taalverandering*, 127–76. Groningen: Wolters-Noordhoff.

—— (1985). *On the Paradigmatic Dimension of Morphological Creativity*. Dordrecht: Foris.

MARTIN, W., and TOPS, G. A. J. (1984). *Van Dale Groot Woordenboek Engels–Nederlands*. Utrecht: Van Dale Lexicografie.

MATTHEWS, P. H. (1972). *Inflectional Morphology: A Theoretical Study Based on Aspects of Latin Verb Conjugation*. Cambridge: Cambridge University Press.

MELČUK, I. (2000). 'Morphological Processes', *BLM* i. 523–34.

MITHUN, M. (1984). 'The Evolution of Noun Incorporation', *Lg* 60: 847–94.

—— (1999). *The Languages of Native North America*. Cambridge: Cambridge University Press.

—— (2000). 'Incorporation', *BLM* i. 916–28.

MUYSKEN, P. C. (1988). 'Affix Order and Interpretation: Quechua', in Everaert *et al.* 1988: 259–79.

NAU N. (2001). 'Introduction', in id. (ed.), *Typological Approaches to Latvian*. Berlin: Akademieverlag (*Sprachtypologie und Universalienforschung* 54/3).

NEWMEYER, F. J. (1998). *Language Form and Language Function*. Cambridge, Mass.: MIT Press.

NICHOLS, J. (1986). 'Head-Marking and Dependent-Marking Grammar', *Lg* 62: 56–119.

NOOTEBOOM, S. G., WEERMAN, F., and WIJNEN, F. (eds.) (2002). *Storage and Computation in the Language Faculty*. Dordrecht: Kluwer.

NORDE, M. (1997). 'The History of the Genitive in Swedish: A Case Study in Degrammaticalization', Ph.D. diss. University of Amsterdam.

—— (2001). 'Deflexion as a Counterdirectional Factor in Grammatical Change', *Language Sciences* 23: 231–64.

OLSEN, S. (2000). 'Composition', *BLM* i. 898–916.

—— (2001). 'Copulative Compounds: A Closer Look at the Interface between Syntax and Morphology', *YoM 2000*, 279–320.

ONIGA, R. (1992). 'Compounding in Latin', *Rivista di Linguistica* 4: 97–116.

PAYNE, T. E. (1997). *Describing Morpho-Syntax: A Guide for Field Linguists.* Cambridge: Cambridge University Press.

PINKER, S. (1999). *Words and Rules.* New York: Basic Books.

PLAG, I. (1996). 'Selectional Restrictions in English Suffixation Revisited', *Linguistics* 34: 769–98.

—— (1999). *Morphological Productivity: Structural Constraints in English Derivation.* Berlin and New York: Mouton de Gruyter.

—— (ed.) (2003a). 'The Morphology of Creole Languages', *YoM 2002*, 1–134.

—— (2003b). *Word-Formation in English.* Cambridge: Cambridge University Press.

PLANK, F. (1981). *Morphologische (Ir-) Regularitäten.* Tübingen: Narr.

RAINER, F. (2000). 'Produktivitätsbeschränkungen', *BLM* i. 877–85.

—— and VARELA, S. (1992). 'Compounding in Spanish', *Rivista di Linguistica* 4: 117–42.

RALLI, A. (1992). 'Compounding in Modern Greek', *Rivista di Linguistica* 4: 143–74.

RAPPAPORT, M., LEVIN, B., and LAUGHREN, M. (1993). 'Levels of Lexical Representation', in J. Pustejovsky (ed.), *Semantics and the Lexicon*, 37–54. Dordrecht: Kluwer.

RICE, K. (1989). *A Grammar of Slave.* Berlin and New York: Mouton de Gruyter.

—— (2000). *Morpheme Order and Semantic Scope: Word Formation in the Athapaskan Verb.* Cambridge: Cambridge University Press.

RIEHEMANN, S. Z. (1998). 'Type-Based Derivational Morphology', *Journal of Comparative Germanic Linguistics* 2: 49–77.

RIEMSDIJK, H. VAN (ed.) (1998). *Clitics in the Languages of Europe.* Berlin and New York: Mouton de Gruyter.

ROBINS, R. H. (1959). 'In Defense of WP', *Transactions of the Royal Philological Society*, 116–44.

RONNEBERGER-SIBOLD, E. (2000). 'On Useful Darkness: Loss and Destruction of Transparency by Linguistic Change, Borrowing and Word-Creation', *YoM 1999*, 97–120.

ROSEN, S. T. (1989). 'Two Types of Noun Incorporation: A Lexical Analysis', *Lg* 65: 294–317.

RUBACH, J., and BOOIJ, G. (2001). 'Allomorphy in Optimality Theory: Polish Iotation', *Lg* 77: 26–60.

RUMELHART, D., and McCLELLAND, J. (1986). 'On Learning the Past Tenses of English Verbs: Implicit Rules or Parallel Distributed Processing?', in J. McClelland, D. Rumelhart, and the PDP Research Group (eds.), *Parallel Distributed Processing. Explorations in the Microstructure of Cognition*, 216–71. Cambridge: Cambridge University Press.

RYDER, M. E. (2001). 'Complex -*er* Nominals: Where Grammaticalization and

Lexicalization Meet', in E. Contini-Morava and Y. Tobin (eds.), *Between Grammar and Lexicon*, 291–331. Amsterdam and Philadelphia: Benjamins.

SADLER, L., and SPENCER, A. (2001). 'Syntax as an Exponent of Morphological Features', *YoM 2000*, 71–96.

SALMON, V. (2000). 'The Term "Morphology" ', *BLM* i. 15–21.

SAUSSURE, F. DE (1916). *Cours de linguistique générale*. Paris: Payot.

SCALISE, S. (1984). *Generative Morphology*. Dordrecht: Foris.

—— (1988). 'The Notion of "Head" in Morphology', *YoM 1988*, 229–46.

—— (1992*a*). 'Compounding in Italian', *Rivista di Linguistica* 4: 175–99.

—— (ed.) (1992*b*). 'The Morphology of Compounding', *Rivista di Linguistica* 4 (1).

SCHREUDER, R., and BAAYEN, R. H. (1997). 'How Complex Simplex Words Can Be', *Journal of Memory and Language* 37: 118–39.

SELKIRK, E. O. (1982). *The Syntax of Words*. Cambridge, Mass.: MIT Press.

SHOPEN, T. (ed.) (1985). *Language Typology and Syntactic Description*, iii. *Grammatical Categories and the Lexicon*. Cambridge: Cambridge University Press.

SIPTÁR, P., and TÖRKENCZY, M. (2000). *The Phonology of Hungarian*. Oxford: Oxford University Press.

SONG, J. J. (1996). *Causativity and Causation: A Universal-Typological Perspective*. London and New York: Longman.

—— (2001). *Linguistic Typology: Morphology and Syntax*. Harlow: Longman.

SPENCER, A. (1988). 'Bracketing Paradoxes and the English Lexicon', *Lg* 64: 663–82.

—— (1991). *Morphological Theory*. Oxford: Blackwell.

—— and ZARETSKAYA, M. (1998). 'Stative Middles in Russian', *Essex Reports in Linguistics*, 22. Colchester: Dept of Language and Linguistics, University of Essex.

—— and ZWICKY, A. (eds.) (1998). *A Handbook of Morphology*. Oxford: Blackwell.

STROOMER, H. (1987). '*A Comparative Study of Three Southern Oromo Dialects in Kenya*', Ph.D. diss. Univ. of Leiden.

STRUIJKE, C. (2002). *Existential Faithfulness: A Study of Reduplicative TETU, Feature Movement, and Dissimilation*. New York and London: Routledge.

STUMP, G. (1993). 'On Rules of Referral', *Lg* 69: 447–79.

—— (2001). *Inflectional Morphology: A Theory of Paradigm Structure*. Cambridge: Cambridge University Press.

SULKALA, H., and KARJALAINEN, M. (1992). *Finnish*. London and New York: Routledge.

SZYMANEK, B. (1989). *Introduction to Morphological Analysis*. Warsaw: Państwowe Wydawnictwo Naukowe.

TALMY, L. (1985). 'Lexicalization Patterns', in Shopen 1985: 57–149.

TAYLOR, J. R. (2002). *Cognitive Grammar*. Oxford: Oxford University Press.

TEKORIENE, D. (1990). *Lithuanian: Basic Grammar and Conversation*. Kaunas: Spindulys.

THRÁINSSON, H. (1994). 'Icelandic', in König and van der Auwera 1994: 142–89.

TIERSMA, P. (1982). 'Local and General Markedness', *Lg* 58: 832–49.

UHLENBECK, E. M. (1978). *Studies in Javanese Morphology*. The Hague: Martinus Nijhoff.

UNTERBECK, B., RISSANEN, M., NEVALAINEN, T., and SAARI, M. (eds.) (2000). *Gender in Grammar and Cognition*, 2 vols. Berlin and New York: Mouton De Gruyter.

VERHEIJ, A. C. J. (2000). *Bits, Bytes, and Binyanim: A Quantitative Study of Verbal Lexeme Formations in the Hebrew Bible*. Leuven: Uitgeverij Peeters and Departement Oosterse Studies.

VOGEL, I. (1994). 'Verbs in Italian Morphology', *YoM 1993*, 219–54.

VOORHOEVE, J. (1979). 'Multifunctionaliteit als derivationeel probleem', in T. Hoekstra and H. van der Hulst (eds.), *Morfologie in Nederland*, special issue of *GLOT* (Leiden: Univ. of Leiden), 41–9.

VRIES, L. DE (1989). 'Studies in Wambon and Kombai', Ph.D. diss. University of Amsterdam.

WEGGELAAR, C. (1986). 'Noun Incorporation in Dutch', *International Journal of American Linguistics*, 52: 301–5.

WELMERS, W. E. (1973). *African Language Structures*. Berkeley, Calif.: University of California Press.

WIERZBICKA, A. (1991). *Cross-Cultural Pragmatics: The Semantics of Human Interaction*. Berlin: Mouton de Gruyter.

WIESE, R. (1996). *The Phonology of German*. Oxford: Clarendon Press.

WILLIAMS, E. (1981). 'On the Notions "Lexically Related" and "Head of a Word" ', *Linguistic Inquiry* 12: 245–74.

WILTSHIRE, C., and MARANTZ, A. (2000). 'Reduplication', *BLM* i. 557–67.

WURZEL, W. U. (1980). 'Ways of Morphologizing Phonological Rules', in J. Fisiak (ed.), *Historical Morphology*, 443–62. The Hague: Mouton.

ZWICKY, A., and PULLUM, G. (1983). 'Cliticization vs Inflection: English *n't*', *Lg* 59: 502–13.

Language index

Index of terms